STRANGER SHORES

J.M. Coetzee is a professor of general literature at the
University of Cape Town. The winner of numerous literary prizes, he is one of only two authors ever to have won
the Booker Prize twice.

ALSO BY J.M. COETZEE

J.M. Coetzee

STRANGER SHORES

Essays 1986–1999

VINTAGE

Published by Vintage 2002

2 4 6 8 10 9 7 5 3 1

Copyright © J.M. Coetzee 2001

J.M. Coetzee has asserted his right under the Copyright,
Designs and Patents Act 1988 to be identified as the
author of this work

First published in Great Britain in 2001 by
Secker & Warburg

Vintage
Random House, 20 Vauxhall Bridge Road,
London SW1V 2SA

Random House Australia (Pty) Limited
20 Alfred Street, Milsons Point, Sydney
New South Wales 2061, Australia

Random House New Zealand Limited
18 Poland Road, Glenfield,
Auckland 10, New Zealand

Random House (Pty) Limited
Endulini, 5A Jubilee Road, Parktown 2193,
South Africa

The Random House Group Limited Reg. No. 954009
www.randomhouse.co.uk

A CIP catalogue record for this book
is available from the British Library

ISBN 0 099 42262 X

Papers used by Random House are natural, recyclable
products made from wood grown in sustainable forests.
The manufacturing processes conform to the environ-
mental regulations of the country of origin

Printed and bound in Great Britain by
Bookmarque Ltd, Croydon, Surrey

Contents

Acknowledgments

'What Is a Classic?' was given as a lecture in Graz, Austria, in 1991, and published in *Current Writing* (1993).

The essay on Defoe first appeared as the introduction to the 1999 World's Classics edition of *Robinson Crusoe* and is reprinted by kind permission of Oxford University Press.

The essay on Rooke first appeared as an afterword to the 1991 Penguin edition of *Mittee* and is republished by kind permission of Penguin U.K.

The essay on Emants first appeared as the introduction to my translation of *A Posthumous Confession* (London: Quartet Books, 1986).

The essay on Paton first appeared in *New Republic* in 1990, that on Pringle in *Research in African Literatures* in 1990, and that on Gordimer and Turgenev in *South African Literary History: Totality and/or Fragment*, ed. Erhard Reckwitz, Karin Reitner, Lucia Vennarini (Essen: Die Blaue Eule, 1997).

The essay on Richardson was first given as a lecture at the University of Chicago in 1995.

All other essays first appeared in the *New York Review of Books* and are reprinted by kind permission of the publishers. Dates are as follows: Mostert, Suzman in 1993; Breytenbach in 1993 and 1999; Mahfouz, Lessing in 1994; Frank in 1995; Brodsky, Rushdie, Byatt, Skvorecky in 1996; Mulisch, Nooteboom, Phillips in 1997; Appelfeld, Oz, Kafka, Borges in 1998; Musil, Gass in 1999.

I   What Is a Classic? A Lecture

I

IN OCTOBER 1944, as Allied forces were battling on the European mainland and German rockets were falling on London, Thomas Stearns Eliot, aged fifty-six, gave his presidential address to the Virgil Society in London. In his lecture Eliot does not mention wartime circumstances, save for a single reference – oblique, understated, in his best British manner – to 'accidents of the present time' that had made it difficult to get access to the books he needed to prepare the lecture. It is a way of reminding his auditors that there is a perspective in which the war is only a hiccup, however massive, in the life of Europe.

The title of the lecture was 'What Is a Classic?' and its aim was to consolidate and re-argue a case Eliot had long been advancing: that the civilisation of Western Europe is a single civilisation, that its descent is from Rome via the Church of Rome and the Holy Roman Empire, and that its originary classic must therefore be the epic of Rome, Virgil's *Aeneid*.[1] Each time this case was re-argued, it was re-argued by a man of greater public authority, a man who by 1944, as poet, dramatist, critic, publisher and cultural commentator, could be said to dominate English letters. This man had targeted London as the metropolis of the English-speaking world, and with a diffidence concealing ruthless singleness of purpose had made himself into the deliberately magisterial voice of that metropolis. Now he was arguing for Virgil as the dominant voice of metropolitan, imperial Rome and Rome, furthermore, imperial in transcendent ways that Virgil could not have been expected to understand.

'What Is a Classic?' is not one of Eliot's best pieces of criticism. The address *de haut en bas*, which in the 1920s he had used to such great effect to impose his personal predilections on the London world of letters, has become mannered. There is a tiredness to the prose, too. Nevertheless, the piece is never less than intelligent, and – once one begins to explore its background – more coherent than might appear at first reading. Furthermore, behind it is a clear awareness that the ending of the Second World War must bring with it a new cultural order, with new opportunities and new threats. What struck me when I reread Eliot's lecture in preparation for the present lecture, however, was the fact that nowhere does Eliot reflect on the fact of his own Americanness, or at least his American origins, and therefore on the somewhat odd angle at which he comes, honouring a European poet to a European audience.

I say 'European', but of course even the Europeanness of Eliot's British audience is an issue, as is the line of descent of English literature from the literature of Rome. For one of the writers Eliot claims not to have been able to re-read in preparation for his lecture is Sainte-Beuve, who in *his* lectures on Virgil claimed Virgil as 'the poet of all Latinity', of France and Spain and Italy but *not* of all Europe.[2] So Eliot's project of claiming a line of descent from Virgil has to start with claiming a fully European identity for Virgil; and also with asserting for England a European identity that has sometimes been begrudged it and that it has not always been eager to embrace.[3]

Rather than follow in detail the moves Eliot makes to link

Virgil's Rome to the England of the 1940s, let me ask how and why Eliot himself became English enough for the issue to matter to him.[4]

Why did Eliot 'become' English at all? My sense is that at first the motives were complex: partly anglophilia, partly solidarity with the English middle-class intelligentsia, partly as a protective disguise in which a certain embarrassment about American barbarousness may have figured, partly as a parody, from a man who enjoyed acting (passing as English is surely one of the most difficult acts to bring off). I would suspect that the inner logic was, first, residence in London (rather than England), then the assumption of a London social identity, then the specific chain of reflections on cultural identity that would eventually lead him to claim a European and *Roman* identity, under which London identity, English identity, and Anglo-American identity were subsumed and transcended.[5]

By 1944 the investment in this identity was total. Eliot *was* an Englishman, though, in his own mind at least, a Roman Englishman. He had just completed a cycle of poems in which he named his forebears and reclaimed as his own East Coker in Somersetshire, home of the Elyots. 'Home is where one starts from,' he writes. 'In my beginning is my end.' 'What you own is what you do not own' – or, to put it another way, what you do not own is what you own.[6] Not only did he now assert that rootedness which is so important to his understanding of culture, but he had equipped himself with a theory of history in which England and America were defined as provinces of an eternal metropolis, Rome.

So one can see how it is that in 1944 Eliot feels no need to present himself to the Virgil Society as an outsider, an American talking to Englishmen. How then does he present himself?

For a poet who had such success, in his heyday, in importing the yardstick of impersonality into criticism, Eliot's poetry is astonishingly personal, not to say autobiographical.[7] So it is not surprising to discover, as we read the Virgil lecture, that it has a subtext and that subtext concerns Eliot himself. The figure of Eliot in the lecture is not, as we might expect, Virgil, but Aeneas, understood or even transformed in a particularly Eliotic way into a rather weary middle-aged man, who 'would have preferred to stop in Troy, but becomes an exile . . . exiled for a purpose greater than he can know, but which he recognises'. 'Not, in a human sense, a happy or successful man,' whose 'reward [is] hardly more than a narrow beachhead and a political marriage in a weary middle age: his youth interred.' (*WIC*, pp. 28, 28, 32)

From the major romantic episode of Aeneas's life, the affair with Queen Dido that ends with Dido's suicide, Eliot singles out for mention neither the high passion of the lovers nor Dido's *Liebestod* but what he calls the 'civilised manners' of the couple when they meet later in the Underworld, and the fact that 'Aeneas does not forgive himself . . . in spite of the fact that all that he has done has been in compliance with destiny' (*WIC*, p. 21). It is hard not to see a parallel between the story of the lovers as related by Eliot and the story of Eliot's own unhappy first marriage.[8]

The element of what I would call compulsiveness – just the opposite of impersonality – which makes Eliot articulate the story of Aeneas, in this lecture and before this audience, as an allegory of his own life is not my concern here. What I want to stress instead is that, in reading the *Aeneid* in this way, Eliot is not only using its fable of exile followed by home-founding – 'In my end is my beginning' – as the pattern of his own intercontinental migration – a migration that I do not call an odyssey precisely because Eliot is concerned to validate the destiny-inspired trajectory of Aeneas over the idle and ultimately circular wanderings of Odysseus – but is also appropriating the cultural weight of the epic to back himself.

Thus in the palimpsest Eliot sets before us, he, Eliot, is not only Virgil's dutiful (*pius*) Aeneas, who leaves the continent of his birth to set up a beachhead in Europe (*beachhead* is a word one could not have used in October 1944 without evoking the landings in Normandy just a few months earlier, as well as the 1943 landings in Italy) but Aeneas's Virgil. If Aeneas is recharacterised as an Eliotic hero, Virgil is characterised as a rather Eliot-like 'learned author', whose task, as seen by Eliot, was that of 're-writing Latin poetry' (the phrase Eliot preferred for himself was 'purifying the dialect of the tribe') (*WIC*, p. 21).

Of course I would be traducing Eliot if I left the impression that in 1944 he was in any simple-minded way setting himself up as the reincarnation of Virgil. His theory of history, and his conception of the classic, are much too sophisticated for that. To Eliot, there can be only one Virgil because there is only one Christ, one Church, one Rome, one Western Christian civilisation, and one originary classic of that Roman-Christian civilisation. Nevertheless, while he does not go so far as to identify himself with the so-called adventist interpretation of the *Aeneid* – namely that Virgil prophesies a new Christian era – he does leave the door open to the suggestion that Virgil was being used by an agency greater than himself for a purpose of which he could not have been aware – that is, that in the greater pattern of European history he may have fulfilled a role that might be called prophetic.[9]

Read from the inside, Eliot's lecture is an attempt to reaffirm the *Aeneid* as a classic not just in Horatian terms – as a book that has lasted a long time (*est vetus atque probus, centum qui perfecit annos*) – but in allegorical terms: as a book that will bear the weight of having read into it a meaning for Eliot's own age. The meaning for Eliot's age includes not only the allegory of Aeneas the sad, long-suffering, middle-aged widower hero but the Virgil who appears in the *Four Quartets* as one element of the composite 'dead master' who speaks to fire-warden Eliot in the ruins of London, the poet without whom, even more than Dante, Eliot would not have become himself. Read from the outside, and read unsympathetic-ally, it is an attempt to give a certain historical backing to a radically conservative political programme for Europe, a programme opened up by the imminent end of hostilities and the challenge of reconstruction. Broadly stated, this would be a programme for a Europe of nation-states in which every effort would be made to keep people on the land, in which national cultures would be encouraged and an overall Christian character maintained – a Europe, in fact, in which the Catholic Church would be left as the principal supra-national organisation.

Continuing this reading from the outside, at a personal but still unsympathetic level, the Virgil lecture can be fitted into a decades-long programme on Eliot's part to redefine and resituate nationality in such a way that he, Eliot, could not be sidelined as an eager American cultural *arriviste* lecturing the English and/or the Europeans about their heritage and trying to persuade them to live up to it – a stereotype into which Eliot's one-time collaborator Ezra Pound all too easily fell. At a more general level, the lecture is an attempt to claim a cultural-historical unity for Western European Christendom, including its provinces, within which the cultures of its constituent nations would belong only as parts of a greater whole.

This is not quite the programme that would be followed by the new North Atlantic order that was to emerge after the war – the urgency for that programme came from events Eliot could not have foreseen in 1944 – but is nevertheless highly compatible with it. Where Eliot went wrong was in failing to foresee that the new order would be directed from Washington, not London and certainly not Rome. Looking further ahead, Eliot would of course have been disappointed by the form towards which Western Europe in fact evolved – towards economic community but even more toward cultural homogeneity.[10]

The process I have been describing, extrapolating from Eliot's 1944 lecture, is one of the most spectacular that occur to me of a writer attempting to *make* a new identity, claiming that identity not on the basis of immigration, settlement, residence, domestication, acculturation, as other people do, or not only by such means – since Eliot with characteristic tenacity did all of the above – but by defining nationality to suit himself and then using all his accumulated cultural power to impose that definition on educated opinion, and by resituating nationality within a specific – in this case Catholic – brand of internationalism or cosmopolitanism, in terms of which he would emerge not as a Johnny-come-lately but as a pioneer and indeed a kind of prophet; a claiming of identity, furthermore, in which a new and hitherto unsuspected paternity is asserted – a line of descent less from the Eliots of New England and/or Somerset than from Virgil and Dante, or at least a line in which the Eliots are an eccentric offshoot of the great Virgil-Dante line.

'Born in a half-savage country, out of date,' Pound called his Hugh Selwyn Mauberley. The feeling of being out of date, of having been born into too late an epoch, or of surviving unnaturally beyond one's term, is all over Eliot's early poetry, from 'Prufrock' to 'Gerontion'. The attempt to understand this feeling or this fate, and indeed to give it meaning, is part of the enterprise of his poetry and criticism. This is a not uncommon sense of the self among colonials – whom Eliot subsumes under what he calls provincials – particularly young colonials struggling to match their inherited culture to their daily experience.

To such young people, the high culture of the metropolis may arrive in the form of powerful experiences which cannot, however, be embedded in their lives in any obvious way, and which seem therefore to have their existence in some transcendent realm. In extreme cases, they are led to blame their environment for not living up to art and to take up residence in an art world. This is a provincial fate – Gustave Flaubert diagnosed it in Emma Bovary, subtitling his case study *Mœurs de province* – but particularly a colonial fate, for those colonials brought up in the culture of what is usually called the mother country but in this context deserves to be called the father country.

Eliot as a man and particularly as a young man was open to experience, both aesthetic and real life, to the point of being suggestible and even vulnerable. His poetry is in many ways a meditation on, and a struggling with, such experiences; in the process of making them into poetry, he makes himself over into a new person. The experiences are perhaps not of the order of religious experience, but they are of the same genre.

There are many ways of understanding a life's enterprise like Eliot's, among which I will isolate two. One, broadly sympathetic, is to treat these transcendental experiences as the subject's point of origin and read the entirety of the rest of the enterprise in their light. This is an approach which would take seriously the call from Virgil that seems to come to Eliot from across the centuries. It would trace the self-fashioning that takes place in the wake of that call as part of a lived poetic vocation. That is, it would read Eliot very much in his own framework, the framework he elected for himself when he defined tradition as an order you cannot escape, in which you may try to locate yourself, but in which your place gets to be defined, and continually redefined, by succeeding generations – an entirely transpersonal order, in fact.

The other (and broadly unsympathetic) way of understanding Eliot is the socio-cultural one I outlined a moment ago: of treating his efforts as the essentially magical enterprise of a man trying to redefine the world around himself – America, Europe – rather than confronting the reality of his not-so-grand position as a man whose narrowly academic, Eurocentric education had prepared him for little else but life as a mandarin in one of the New England ivory towers.

II

I would like to interrogate these alternative readings – the transcendental-poetic and the socio-cultural – further, and bring them closer to our own times, following an autobiographical path that may be methodologically reckless but has the virtue of dramatising the issue.

One Sunday afternoon in the summer of 1955, when I was fifteen years old, I was mooning around our back garden in the suburbs of Cape Town, wondering what to do, boredom being the main problem of existence in those days, when from the house next door I heard music. As long as the music lasted, I was frozen, I dared not breathe. I was being spoken to by the music as music had never spoken to me before.

What I was listening to was a recording of Bach's *Well-Tempered Clavier*, played on the harpsichord. I learned this title only some time later, when I had become more familiar with what, at the age of fifteen, I knew only – in a somewhat suspicious and even hostile teenage manner – as 'classical music'. The house next door had a transient student population; the student who was playing the Bach record must have moved out soon afterwards, or lost his/her taste for Bach, for I heard no more, though I listened intently.

I do not come from a musical family. There was no musical instruction offered at the schools I went to, nor would I have taken it if it had been offered: in the colonies classical music was sissy. I could identify Khatchaturian's 'Sabre Dance', the overture to Rossini's *William Tell*, Rimsky-Korsakov's 'Flight of the Bumble-Bee' – that was the level of my knowledge. At home we had no musical instrument, no record player. There was plenty of the blander American popular music on the radio (George Melachrino and his Silver Strings), but it made no great impact on me.

What I am describing is middle-class musical culture of the age of Eisenhower, as it was to be found in the ex-British colonies, colonies that were rapidly becoming cultural provinces of the United States. The so-called classical component of that musical culture may have been European in origin, but it was Europe mediated and in a sense orchestrated by the Boston Pops.

And then the afternoon in the garden, and the music of Bach, after which everything changed. A moment of revelation which I will not call Eliotic – that would insult the moments of revelation celebrated in Eliot's poetry – but of the greatest significance in my life nevertheless: for the first time I was undergoing the impact of *the classic.*

In Bach nothing is obscure, no single step is so miraculous as to surpass imitation. Yet when the chain of sounds is realised in time, the building process ceases at a certain moment to be the mere linking of units; the units cohere as a higher-order object in a way that I can only describe by analogy as the incarnation of ideas of exposition, complication and resolution that are more general than music. Bach thinks in music. Music thinks itself in Bach.

The revelation in the garden was a key event in my formation. Now I wish to interrogate that moment again, using as a framework both what I have been saying about Eliot – specifically, using Eliot the provincial as a pattern and figure of myself – and, in a more sceptical way, invoking the kinds of question that are asked about culture and cultural ideals by contemporary cultural analysis.

The question I put to myself, somewhat crudely, is this: is there some non-vacuous sense in which I can say that the spirit of Bach was speaking to me across the ages, across the seas, putting before me certain ideals; or was what was really going on at that moment that I was symbolically electing high European culture, and command of the codes of that culture, as a route that would take me out of my class position in white South African society and ultimately out of what I must have felt, in terms however obscure or mystified, as an historical dead end – a road that would culminate (again symbolically) with me on a platform in Europe addressing a cosmopolitan audience on Bach, T. S. Eliot and the question of the classic? In other words, was the experience what I understood it to be – a disinterested and in a sense impersonal aesthetic experience – or was it really the masked expression of a material interest?

This is a question of a kind which one would be deluded to think one could answer about oneself. But that does not mean it should not be asked; and asking it means asking it properly, in terms that are as clear and as full as possible. As part of the enterprise of asking the question clearly, let me therefore ask what I might mean when I talk of being spoken to by the classic across the ages.

In two of the three senses, Bach is a classic of music. Sense one: the classic is that which is not time-bound, which retains meaning for succeeding ages, which 'lives'. Sense two: a proportion of Bach's music belongs to what are loosely called 'the classics', the part of the European musical canon that is still widely played, if not particularly often or before particularly large audiences. The third sense, the sense that Bach does not satisfy, is that he does not belong to the revival of so-called classical values in European art starting in the second quarter of the eighteenth century.

Bach was not only too old, too old-fashioned, for the neo-classical movement: his intellectual affiliations and his whole musical orientation were towards a world that was in the process of passing from sight. In the popular and somewhat romanticised account, Bach, obscure enough in his own day and particularly in his later years, dropped entirely out of public consciousness after his death, and was resurrected only some eighty years later, mainly through the enthusiasm of Felix Mendelssohn. For several generations, in this popular account, Bach was hardly a classic at all: not only was he not neoclassical, but he spoke to no one across those generations. His music was not published, it was rarely played. He was part of music history, he was a name in a footnote in a book, that was all.[11]

It is this unclassical history of misunderstanding, obscurity and silence, which if not exactly history as truth is history as one of the overlays of the historical record, that I wish to emphasise, since it calls into doubt facile notions of the classic as the timeless, as that which unproblematically speaks across all boundaries. Bach the classic was historically constituted, as I will remind you, constituted by identifiable historical forces and within a specific historical context. Only once we have acknowledged this point are we in a position to ask the more difficult questions: what, if any, are the limits to that historical relativisation of the classic? What, if anything, is left of the classic after the classic has been historicised, which may still claim to speak across the ages?

In 1737, in the middle of the third and last phase of his professional life, Bach was the subject of an article in a leading musical journal. The article was by a one-time student of Bach's named Johann Adolf Scheibe. In it, Scheibe attacked Bach's music as 'turgid and sophisticated' rather than 'simple and natural', as merely 'sombre' when it meant to be 'lofty', and generally as marred by signs of 'labour and . . . effort'.[12]

As much as it was an attack by youth upon age, Scheibe's article was a manifesto for a new kind of music based on Enlightenment values of feeling and reason, dismissive of the intellectual heritage (scholastic) and the musical heritage (polyphonic) behind Bach's music. In valuing melody above counterpoint, unity, simplicity, clarity and decorum above architectonic complexity, and feeling above intellect, Scheibe speaks for the blossoming modern age, and in effect makes Bach, and with Bach the whole polyphonic tradition, into the last gasp of the dead Middle Ages.

Scheibe's stance may be polemical, but when we remember that Haydn was only a child of five in 1737 and Mozart not yet born, we must recognise that his sense of where history was going was accurate.[13] Scheibe's verdict was the verdict of the age. By his last years Bach was a man of yesterday. What reputation he had was based on what he had written before he was forty.

All in all, then, it is not so much the case that Bach's music was forgotten after his death as that it did not find a place in public awareness during his lifetime. So if Bach before the Bach revival was a classic, he was not only an invisible classic but a dumb classic. He was marks on paper; he had no presence in society. He was not only not canonical, he was not public.

How, then, did Bach come into his own?

Not, it must be said, via the quality of the music pure and simple, or at least not via the quality of that music until it was appropriately packaged and presented. The name and the music of Bach had first to become part of a cause, the cause of German nationalism rising in reaction to Napoleon, and of the concomitant Protestant revival. The figure of Bach became one of the instruments through which German nationalism and Protestantism were promoted; reciprocally, in the name of Germany and Protestantism Bach was promoted as a classic; the whole enterprise being aided by the Romantic swing against rationalism, and by enthusiasm for music as the one art privileged to speak directly from soul to soul.

The first book on Bach, published in 1802, tells much of the story. It was entitled *The Life, Art and Works of J. S. Bach: For Patriotic Admirers of Genuine Musical Art*. In his introduction the author writes, 'This great man . . . was a German. Be proud of him, German fatherland . . . His works are an invaluable national patrimony with which no other nation has anything to be compared.'[14] We find the same emphasis on the Germanness and even the Nordicness of Bach in later tributes. The figure and the music of Bach became part of the construction of Germany and even of the so-called Germanic race.

The turning-point from obscurity to fame came with the oft-described performances of the *St Matthew Passion* in Berlin in 1829, directed by Mendelssohn. But it would be naive to say that in these performances Bach returned to history on his own terms. Mendelssohn arranged Bach's score not only in the light of the larger orchestral and choral forces at his command, but also in the light of what had been going down well recently with Berlin audiences, audiences that had responded rapturously to the romantic nationalism of Weber's *Der Freischütz*. It was Berlin that called for repeat performances of the *St Matthew Passion*. In Königsberg, Kant's city and still a centre of rationalism, by contrast, the *St Matthew Passion* flopped and the music was criticised as 'out-of-date rubbish'.[15]

I am not criticising Mendelssohn's performances for not being 'the real Bach'. The point I make is a simple and limited one: the Berlin performances, and indeed the whole Bach revival, were powerfully historical in ways that were largely invisible to the moving spirits behind them. Furthermore, one thing we can be certain of about our own understanding and performance of Bach, even – and perhaps even particularly – when our intentions are of the purest, the most puristic, is that they are historically conditioned in ways invisible to us. And the same holds for the opinions about history and historical conditioning that I am expressing at this moment.

By saying this I do not mean to fall back into a helpless kind of relativism. The Romantic Bach was partly the product of men and women responding to unfamiliar music with a stunned overwhelmedness analogous to what I myself experienced in South Africa in 1955, and partly the product of a tide of communal feeling that found in Bach a vehicle for its own expression. Many strands of that feeling – its aesthetic emotionalism, its nationalistic fervour – are gone with the wind, and we no longer weave them into our performances of Bach. Scholarship since Mendelssohn's day has given us a different Bach, enabling us to see features of Bach invisible to the revivalist generation, for instance, the sophisticated Lutheran scholasticism within whose ambit he worked.

Such recognitions constitute a real advance in historical understanding. Historical understanding is understanding of the past as a shaping force upon the present. Insofar as that shaping force is tangibly felt upon our lives, historical understanding is part of the present. Our historical being is part of our present. It is that part of our present – namely the part that belongs to history – that we cannot fully understand, since it requires us to understand ourselves not only as objects of historical forces but as subjects of our own historical self-understanding.

It is in the context of paradox and impossibility I have been outlining that I ask myself the question: am I far away enough from 1955, in time and in identity, to begin to understand my first relation to the classic – which is a relation to Bach – in an historical way? And what does it mean to say that I was being spoken to by a classic in 1955 when the self which is asking the questions acknowledges that the classic – to say nothing of the self – is historically constituted? As Bach for Mendelssohn's 1829 Berlin audience was an occasion to embody and, in memory and reperformance, to express aspirations, feelings, self-validations which we can identify, diagnose, give names to, place, even foresee the consequences of, what was Bach in South Africa in 1955, and in particular what was the nomination of Bach as the classic, the occasion for? If the notion of the classic as the timeless is undermined by a fully historical account of Bach-reception, then is the moment in the garden – the kind of moment that Eliot experienced, no doubt more mystically and more intensely, and turned into some of his greatest poetry – undermined as well? Is being spoken to across the ages a notion that we can entertain today only in bad faith?

To answer this question, to which I aspire to give the answer No, and therefore to see what can be rescued of the idea of the classic, let me return to the story of Bach, to the half of the story not yet told.

III

A simple question. If Bach was so obscure a composer, how did Mendelssohn know his music?

If we follow closely the fortunes of Bach's music after his death, attending not to the reputation of the composer but to actual performance, it begins to emerge that, though obscure, Bach was not quite as forgotten as the revivalist history would lead us to believe. Twenty years after his death, there was a circle of musicians in Berlin regularly performing his instrumental music in private, as a kind of esoteric recreation. The Austrian ambassador to Prussia was for years a member of this circle and on his departure took Bach scores back to Vienna, where he held performances of Bach in his home. Mozart was part of his circle; Mozart made his own copies and studied the *Art of Fugue* closely. Haydn was also in the circle.

Thus a certain limited Bach tradition, which was not a Bach revival simply because continuity with Bach's own time was never broken, existed in Berlin and branched to Vienna, among professional musicians and serious amateurs, though it did not express itself in public performance.

As for the choral music, a fair amount of it was known to professionals like C.F. Zelter, director of the Berlin Singakademie. Zelter was a friend of Mendelssohn's father. It was at the Singakademie that the young Felix Mendelssohn first came across the choral music, and, against the general unco-operativeness of Zelter, who regarded the *Passions* as unperformable and of specialist interest only, had his own copy of the *St Matthew Passion* made and plunged into the business of adapting it for performance.

I say *of specialist (or professional) interest only*. This is the point where parallels between literature and music, the literary classics and the musical classics, begin to break down, and where the institutions and practice of music emerge as perhaps healthier than the institutions and practice of literature. For the musical profession has ways of keeping what it values alive that are qualitatively different from the ways in which the institutions of literature keep submerged but valued writers alive.

Because becoming a musician, whether executant or creative, not only in the Western tradition but in other major traditions of the world, entails long training and apprenticeship, because the nature of the training entails repeated performance for the ears of others and minute listening and practical criticism, together with memorisation, because a range of kinds of performance has become institutionalised, from playing for one's teacher to playing for one's class to varieties of public performance – for all these reasons, it is possible to keep music alive and indeed vital within professional circles while it is not part of public awareness, even among educated people.

If there is anything that gives one confidence in the classic status of Bach, it is the testing process he has been through within the profession. Not only did this provincial religious mystic outlast the Enlightenment turn toward rationality and the metropolis, but he also survived what turned out to have been a kiss of death, namely, being promoted during the nineteenth-century revival as a great son of the German soil. And today, every time a beginner stumbles through the first prelude of the 'Forty-Eight', Bach is being tested again, within the profession. Dare I suggest that the classic in music is what emerges intact from this process of day-by-day testing?

The criterion of testing and survival is not just a minimal, pragmatic, Horatian standard (Horace says, in effect, that if a work is still around a hundred years after it was written, it must be a classic). It is a criterion that expresses a certain confidence in the tradition of testing, and a confidence that professionals will not devote labour and attention, generation after generation, to sustaining pieces of music whose life-functions have terminated.

It is this confidence that enables me to return to the auto-biographical moment at the centre of this lecture, and to the alternative analyses I proposed of it, with a little more optimism. About my response to Bach in 1955, I asked whether it was truly a response to some inherent quality in the music rather than a symbolic election on my part of European high culture as a way out of a social and historical dead end. It is of the essence of this sceptical questioning that the term *Bach* should stand simply as a counter for European high culture, that Bach or *Bach* should have no value in himself or itself – that the notion of 'value in itself' should in fact be the object of sceptical interrogation.

By not invoking any idealist justification of 'value in itself' or trying to isolate some quality, some essence of the classic, held in common by works that survive the process of testing, I hope I have allowed the terms *Bach, the classic* to emerge with a value of their own, even if that value is only in the first place professional and in the second place social. Whether at the age of fifteen I understood what I was getting into is beside the point: Bach is some kind of touchstone because he has passed the scrutiny of hundreds of thousands of intelligences before me, by hundreds of thousands of fellow human beings.

What does it mean in living terms to say that the classic is what survives? How does such a conception of the classic manifest itself in people's lives?

For the most serious answer to this question, we cannot do better than turn to the great poet of the classic of our own times, the Pole Zbigniew Herbert. To Herbert the opposite of the classic is not the Romantic but the barbarian; furthermore, classic versus barbarian is not so much an opposition as a confrontation. Herbert writes from the historical perspective of Poland, a country with an embattled Western culture caught between intermittently barbarous neighbours. It is not the possession of some essential quality that, in Herbert's eyes, makes it possible for the classic to withstand the assault of barbarism. Rather, what survives the worst of barbarism, surviving because generations of people cannot afford to let go of it and therefore hold on to it at all costs – that is the classic.

So we arrive at a certain paradox. The classic defines itself by surviving. Therefore the interrogation of the classic, no matter how hostile, is part of the history of the classic, inevitable and even to be welcomed. For as long as the classic needs to be protected from attack, it can never prove itself classic.

One might even venture further along this road to say that the function of criticism is defined by the classic: criticism is that which is duty-bound to interrogate the classic. Thus the fear that the classic will not survive the de-centring acts of criticism may be turned on its head: rather than being the foe of the classic, criticism, and indeed criticism of the most sceptical kind, may be what the classic uses to define itself and ensure its survival. Criticism may in that sense be one of the instruments of the cunning of history.

2   Daniel Defoe, *Robinson Crusoe*

LIKE ODYSSEUS EMBARKED for Ithaca, like Quixote mounted on Rocinante, Robinson Crusoe with his parrot and umbrella has become a figure in the collective consciousness of the West, transcending the book which – in its multitude of editions, translations, imitations and adaptations ('Robinsonades') – celebrates his adventures. Having pretended once to belong to history, he finds himself in the sphere of myth.

His pretended history – *The Life and Strange Surprising Adventures of Robinson Crusoe, of York, Mariner: Written by Himself* – appeared on the market in 1719 and sold well. Four months later it was followed by a second instalment, *The Farther Adventures of Robinson Crusoe*, and a year later by *Serious Reflections During the Life and Surprising Adventures of Robinson Crusoe: with His Vision of the Angelic World*. Though the second volume managed to travel some distance on the coattails of the first, it is nowadays the *Strange Surprising Adventures* to which we refer when we speak of *Robinson Crusoe*.

In his *Serious Reflections*, the author of the earlier volumes finds it necessary to defend himself against charges that his life-story is made up, that it is simply a romance, that he is not even a real person. 'I Robinson Crusoe', he writes in his preface, 'do affirm that the story, though allegorical, is also historical . . . Further, that there is a man alive, and well known too, the actions of whose life are the just subject of these three volumes, and to whom all or most part of the story most directly alludes . . . and to this I set my name.' And with a bravado worthy of Cervantes he signs his name: Robinson Crusoe.

When the writer of these words says that 'Robinson Crusoe' is a living person, what, beyond maintaining the by now tired auto-biographical charade, might he mean? The most obvious inter-pretation, at least among sympathetically inclined contemporaries, particularly those brought up in the nonconformist religious tradition, would be that Crusoe is Everyman, that every man is an island, and every life, seen in an allegorical light, a life of isolation under the scrutiny of God.

But the preface seems to hint as well at a personal and even confessional level of meaning. 'I can affirm that I enjoy much more solitude in the middle of the greatest collection of mankind in the world, I mean, at London, while I am writing this, than ever I could say I enjoyed in eight and twenty years confinement to a desolate island.' The castaway returned in late life to the country of his birth seems at this moment to merge with the sixty-year-old Londoner, Daniel Defoe, from whose head he was born.

'Not one person in ten,' wrote Edgar Allan Poe, 'nay, not one person in five hundred, has, during the perusal of "Robinson Crusoe", the most remote conception that any particle of genius, or even of common talent, has been employed in its creation! Men do not look upon it in the light of a literary performance. Defoe has none of their thoughts – Robinson all.'[1] It is a tribute to an author, one supposes, though of a rather backhanded kind, that he should be eclipsed by one of his creations. Literary realism, at least of a certain kind, likes to hide its literary nature and Defoe is often advanced as a pioneer realist – as, along with Fielding and Richardson, the inventor of the realist novel in England. But if Defoe is a realist, it is hard to see what his realism has to do with that of Fielding, which is a matter of bringing together high and low genres, high and low speech, high and low manners and social types; or with that of Richardson, which is a matter of asserting bourgeois habits and standards, of appropriating in prose narrative the enthralments of romance without the supernatural machinery, the intensities of high drama without the verse.

Defoe is even less like those great European novelists of the next century, the novelists of the realist *school*, to whom the term realism would have some doctrinal meaning. *Madame Bovary* does not pretend to be the utterances or the handiwork of Emma Bovary, housewife of Tostes. The nineteenth-century realist novel flourished on the basis of a web of tacit contracts between writer and reader about how 'the real' might be represented. For Defoe no such contracts exist – not only because in the milieu in which he worked the idea of representing everyday life with no didactic intent would have seemed strange and suspect, but because he himself was too much a loner at heart (and here the contrast with Fielding could not be more marked) to put faith in tacit contracts.

Properly speaking, Defoe is a realist only in that he is an empiricist, and empiricism is one of the tenets of the realist novel. Defoe is in fact something simpler: an impersonator, a ventri-loquist, even a forger (his *Journal of the Plague Year* is as close to a forgery of an historical document as one can get without beginning to play with ink and old paper). The kind of 'novel' he is writing (he did not, of course, use the term) is a more or less literal imitation of the kind of recital his hero or heroine would have given had he or she really existed. It is fake autobiography heavily influenced by the genres of the deathbed confession and the spiritual autobiography.

In the case of *Robinson Crusoe* one can see Defoe trying – with incomplete success – to bend the story of his adventurer hero to fit a scriptural pattern of disobedience, punishment, repentance and deliverance. In the first pages Crusoe is counselled by his father to devote himself to the family business, to be content with 'sliding gently through the world' in a state of modest prosperity. Instead he goes to sea, is enslaved, escapes, becomes a planter in Brazil, ventures into slave-trading himself, suffers shipwreck and spends half a lifetime as a castaway, overcomes cannibals and pirates, and ends up as not only the founder of a colony but a plantation owner far wealthier (to say nothing of more famous) than he would have been had he listened to his father and stayed at home.

The same might be said, *mutatis mutandis*, of other heroes and heroines of Defoe's fake autobiographies: Moll Flanders, Colonel Jack, Roxana. None, choosing to slide gently through the world, would have had a life-story worth telling. The disobedience that Crusoe claims as his original sin is in fact a precondition of the interest of his story. No one wants to read about docile sons.

Robinson Crusoe was Defoe's first attempt at a long prose fiction. It is not his best book: *Moll Flanders* is more consistent in its execution; *Roxana*, though uneven, rises to greater heights. *Robinson Crusoe* suffers as a result of hasty composition and lack of revision. Its moral is confused. The last quarter of the book, as well as Crusoe's early adventures, could have been carried off by any capable writer.

Furthermore, though the treatment of the emotions shows flashes of power – for instance when waves of depression or loneliness overtake Crusoe – Defoe is still too close to the analysis of the soul and its movements perfected in Christian therapeutics to be properly modern. He does not – at least in this first attempt at book-length fiction – look forward to a later realism that will reveal inner life in unconscious gesture, or in moments of speech or action whose meaning is unguessed at by its subject.

Nevertheless, the core of *Robinson Crusoe* – Crusoe alone on the island – is Defoe at his best. In representing the distress of the castaway, the method of bald empirical description works wonderfully: 'As for my comrades, I never saw them afterwards, nor any sign of them, except three of their hats, one cap, and two shoes that were not fellows.' And when Crusoe has to solve the hundreds of little practical problems involved in getting the contents of the ship ashore, or in making a clay cooking pot, one can feel the writing move into higher gear, a more intense level of engagement. For page after page – for the first time in the history of fiction – we see a minute, ordered description of how things are done. It is a matter of pure writerly attentiveness, pure submission to the exigencies of a world which, through being submitted to in a state so close to spiritual absorption, becomes transfigured, real. Defoe is a great writer, one of the purest writers we have. This, I think, Poe recognised, and Virginia Woolf, and others among Defoe's large and unlikely seeming band of admirers.

Crusoe does not, of course, abandon 'his' island when, along with Friday, he is rescued. He leaves it peopled with mutineers and castaways; though he returns to England, he cannily retains a foothold in the colony he has thus founded. *Robinson Crusoe* is unabashed propaganda for the extension of British mercantile power in the New World and the establishment of new British colonies. As for the native peoples of the Americas and the obstacle they represent, all one need say is that Defoe chooses to represent them as cannibals. The treatment Crusoe metes out to them is accordingly savage.

An exception is, of course, made for Friday, the cannibal Crusoe chooses to save: 'I made him know his name should be *Friday* . . . I likewise taught him to say *Master*, and then let him know, that was to be my name.' Friday becomes inseparable from Crusoe, in more than one sense his shadow. Now and then he is allowed to play Sancho Panza to Crusoe's Quixote, and to express common-sense opinions about, for instance, the more baffling features of the

Christian faith. For the rest, he is seen through Crusoe's eyes alone, and treated with self-congratulatory paternalism.

In his lack of autonomy, Friday is not unique. All secondary characters in Defoe's I-centred fictions tend to be ciphers. But Friday's self-evident goodness of heart does prompt Crusoe to reflect on the relevance of Christian doctrine to the Americas, and hence on the rationale that Western colonialism offered for its activities there: the spreading of the gospel. What, Crusoe muses, if mankind had been twice and separately created – in the Old World and the New – and what if in the New World there were no history of rebellion against God? What if Friday and his countryfolk are unfallen creatures, in no need of redemption?

The same question had, of course, been raised by the more enlightened of the Spanish clergy from the first days of conquest. Making his Amerindians cannibals and thus beyond the pale of humanity allows Defoe to obscure the question rather than answer it.

Yet conceding a double creation, and thus conceding the irrelevance of a gospel of redemption to the New World, would not necessarily be to the advantage of its peoples. In anthropological guise as the theory of polygenesis, we should not forget, separate creations became a basis for ranking humankind into higher and lower races, and thus for scientific racism.

'Defoe is like one of those brave, obscure, and useful soldiers who, with empty belly and burdened shoulders, go through their duties with their feet in the mud, pocket blows, receive the whole day long the fire of the enemy . . . and die sergeants . . . [He] had the kind of mind suitable to such a hard service, solid, exact, entirely destitute of refinement, enthusiasm, agreeableness. His imagination was that of a man of business, not of an artist.'[2] So wrote Hippolyte Taine in his influential *History of English Literature*. One can see what Taine meant, and indeed for each charge there there can be found some justification. Yet as a whole the verdict could not be more wrong. If there is something of the dogged infantryman about Defoe, that is only because he made his living from writing, paid by the page, outside the regime of patronage. He is indeed not an artist, or at least not the kind of artist Taine had in mind, but then he would not have wanted to be thought of as one. He is indeed, as Taine says, a businessman; but a businessman trading in words and ideas, with a businessman's clear sense of what each word or idea weighs, how much it is worth. As a thinker he may not be original, but his mind is acute and curious about life in all its aspects. The careers he followed were various, productive and interesting. Nothing he set down on paper is less than intelligent; the subjects he was led to in the novels of his old age – crime, conquest, ambition, loneliness – are as lively today as they were three centuries ago.

3   Samuel Richardson, *Clarissa*

I Beauty

THERE HAS BEEN a deal of critical debate about Samuel Richardson's novel *Clarissa* in the past decade, much of it fuelled by concern about rape. *Clarissa* is read as a novel about violability and violation, about the rights of the self to self-determination.

I will be approaching *Clarissa* from a different angle. For years I had the rather idle ambition to write an adaptation of *Clarissa* for film, either as a two-hour feature film or, more realistically, as a four- or five-hour television series. An idle ambition in the sense that I did not put pen to paper or even resolve in my mind the general question of how to bring to life an action that consists so much of people sitting and writing letters to one another.

I was therefore vexed when I learned that an adaptation had been screened on the BBC. I made it my business to see this version, and disliked it, principally because it lacked any grandeur of conception. In my view there is still room for an adaptation that will do justice to Richardson's book.

One failing of the BBC film is that it casts in the title role an actress who is decidedly plain, decidedly homely: a pleasant, decent, quiet, middle-class girl who could pass for seventeen, the age Richardson's Clarissa is supposed to be. As she plays the role, this actress never really gets beyond being the suffering, quietly dignified victim of Lovelace's manipulations and eventual outrages.

I have no doubt that the people who made the film thought carefully about this piece of casting, and that the muted way in which the part is played represents a deliberate reading of the book, perhaps a typical late-twentieth-century reading, in which Clarissa is unexceptional because she stands for any and every victim of patriarchal power.

I would prefer a quite different casting of the female lead, to match a quite different interpretation of her fate. I would give the role to an actress who is not merely more attractive but of, as Lovelace puts it, 'soul-harrowing beauty'.[1]

The word *beautiful* is slipping into disuse today in relation to women, replaced mainly by *attractive* and its intensifier *very attractive*. *Beautiful* seems to be more and more reserved for women who have made it into their forties without losing their looks.

Beautiful and *attractive* are not synonyms. Beauty has a range of meanings extending into the realms of aesthetics and even of Platonic metaphysics. Beauty is not specific to living beings; attractiveness is. Applied to human beings, *beautiful* may in psychological contexts carry overtones of a certain narcissism or self-enclosedness which may be attractive, even sexually exciting, but is not generated by the beautiful being's sexual biology.

In casting Clarissa, I would guess that the BBC team made their choice on a range between attractive and mildly attractive. To make Clarissa soul-harrowingly beautiful was not, I suspect, an option they seriously entertained.

Beauty is an absolute, in the sense that it is not relative to the spectatorial subject or the subject's desire. In fact it overwhelms efforts to treat it relatively. Whether or not an absolute beauty can be made to manifest itself in the 1990s, in film, on the streets, or anywhere else, is an open question and an interesting one. About the 1740s, when Richardson was writing, we can be altogether firmer. In the 1740s the idea of beauty was not dead or even dying (whether Richardson would have thought one was fortunate to be born beautiful is another matter).

On the question of Clarissa's looks depends Lovelace's ambition and his master plan with regard to her. There is an influential reading of Lovelace which makes him the representative of the values of a class on the wane, a Restoration aristocrat full of resentment against the rising landowning gentry represented by the Harlowes, with their ambitions to buy their way into the aristocracy. Lovelace's courtship, abduction and, finally, rape of Clarissa, in this reading, are animated by a wish to teach an upstart family a lesson.

This reading coheres closely with a view of Lovelace as a rake, a model of a male stance towards women that was soon to become unfashionable, in no small part due to the endeavours of Richardson. The model of the rake would be eclipsed by the model of the feminised man of feeling.

This reading of Lovelace – which happens not to be mine – finds a great deal of support in the text. In his letters to his rakish male friends Lovelace is much concerned to present himself as a great seducer and abandoner of maidens, particularly of middle-class maidens whose fathers and brothers don't have the training with weapons, or, when matters really get serious, the political connections which would enable them to take their revenge. In this reading Clarissa represents the greatest challenge that Lovelace has yet faced: a girl of irreproachable virtue and great self-possession, a member of a family that, without having any lineage, is nevertheless powerful. Bringing down the girl would bring down the family, teach it a lesson. It would also prove a point about the will to virtue in women in general: that it is not proof against the traitorous sexual desire which a skilful seducer can arouse in them. The soul or spirit in a woman is an undeveloped entity: the seducer drives home the lesson that woman is body.

This is effectively what Lovelace says in his letters to his friends. His courtship of Clarissa is part of a plot against the Harlowes and what they represent, as well as of a general plot against women. Lovelace, in this reading, is an entirely self-aware person. He knows what he is up to.

Knowing what he is up to entails, to his mind, knowing what he is up against. This is, of course, his biggest mistake. In Clarissa he is up against a rock-like virtue. Unable to move it, he is eventually driven to force it. Of course he knows that the resort to force is an admission of failure. But at the beginning he does have a way of justifying the rape, of integrating it into his ideological project. In the folklore of the rake, even unwilling contact with the magic of the phallus will sexualise a girl.

Lovelace is a hunter, a man who speaks of women as his 'sportive prey'. I need hardly remark that Richardson is less than fair to hunting as a sport, as he is less than fair to Lovelace and his code throughout. Whether or not Lovelace is a good exemplar of his class, he invokes the code of that class, which is a code of nobility, archaic, masculine, pre-individualist, based on warfare and the hunt. The demands of the code can be evaded only at the cost of forfeiting one's manhood and becoming a slave or a woman. Richardson dislikes the code and attacks its prized values, denigrating them and asserting counter-values that turn weakness into a strength.

In contrast to Lovelace is Clarissa herself. Clarissa, at least in one influential reading, does not fully know herself. The mistakes she makes in relation to Lovelace – principally the mistake of running away with him – result from an attraction to him that she spends a lot of her time denying, and a hope, against her better judgement, that eventually he can be made to turn into the kind of man she wants him to be, that is to say, a gentle and attentive lover and husband.

Whether it is possible to domesticate a rake and woman-hunter like Lovelace without destroying most of what makes him interesting and even attractive – his wit, his energy, his continual self-invention – is a question that Clarissa does not ask herself and that Richardson, by implication, answers in the negative. (There is a tamed and reformed version of Lovelace in the book – Lovelace's friend Belford – and marriage between Clarissa and Belford is one of the directions that the plot could in theory take. Belford is a nice enough man. But merely to be in Clarissa's proximity he has to desexualise himself and treat her not as a woman but as an angel, that is to say, as a creature marked as of a higher order by its asexuality.)

Without going into textual particulars, let me offer an alternative understanding of Lovelace: as a man who is smitten by the beauty of a woman, who presents to his circle of fellow rakes a face or mask that hides his feelings, and who is animated, with respect to the woman herself, by feelings that he does not understand but which certainly include baffled rage – rage at her impenetrability.

Through Lovelace, impenetrability becomes a key concept to the understanding of Clarissa, or perhaps just to the understanding of the conception Lovelace has of her. What is there to do with beauty, impenetrable and self-enclosed as it is, except to stand outside it and contemplate it? I quote the Florentine Platonist Marsilio Ficino: 'The urgings of a lover are not quenched by beholding or touching any particular body, for it is not this or that body that he desires but the splendour of the celestial majesty shining through bodies, a splendour that fills him with wonder. That is the reason why lovers do not know what they desire, what they seek: because they do not know God.'[2]

II Virginity

If we are going to talk about penetrability, we must talk about virginity and about the cultural and religious meanings of virginity, in particular in and around the novel *Clarissa*.

In the strand of Christianity represented by Paul, the virginal state – what was sometimes called the *vita angelica* – is higher than the married state. The Pauline strand is perpetuated in the ascetic tradition of the first two centuries of the Christian era, which offered women freedom from the inferior status determined by their biology in return for a life of celibacy. I quote St Jerome: when a woman becomes a servant of Christ 'then she will cease to be a woman, and will be called man'.[3] Rape is not the only means that Richardson's Lovelace hopes to use to recall Clarissa from the *vita angelica*. He also has fantasies of fathering children upon her: the sheer physicality of gestation and motherhood will be an ingenious humiliation, a way of reducing her to her body again.

The Harlowe family argue that Clarissa's refusal to marry the candidate of their choice is selfish. Given the lack of appeal of the candidate of their choice, Solmes, this is not a convincing argument. Nevertheless, the accusation of selfishness is one that Clarissa has to wrestle with in private. Her earnest, Puritan way of justifying herself to herself is to respond that there is an inner voice she cannot disobey which tells her she may not prostitute herself, even for her family's sake. But her case is not wholly convincing, or perhaps convincing only to a Protestant Christian. How does she know she is not self-deceived, that her aversion to Solmes is not mere fastidiousness? Why does she think she knows better than her father?

Clarissa obeys her inner voice. But there is or ought to be a competing inner voice speaking a competing imperative, one that we may today think of as Darwinian but which goes back at least to Roman times, namely that the finest representatives of the species owe a higher duty to their kind to mate.

> From fairest creatures we desire increase,
> That thereby beauty's rose might never die.

In Shakespeare's Sonnet I, this argument is addressed to a young man, but we should remember that Shakespeare took it over from Sidney's *Arcadia*, where it is addressed to a girl who has sworn to lead a virgin's life.

Richardson is a Christian but not a religious writer in the way that Bunyan, for example, is. Although Clarissa herself conceives of her destiny more and more in religious terms, her turn to religion occurs only after the rape and within the shadow of death. Up to this point, religion has no more and no less of a presence in the book than it had in the society in which the story is set. Clarissa's religious preoccupations remove her increasingly from everyone else in the novel, and from the reader too. This is clearly Richardson's intention. Clarissa is moving into an exalted area where ordinary folk cannot follow.

Clarissa is not a religious novel but it invokes religious forces. What religious forces? Pervasively, Puritan Protestantism, with its emphasis on personal salvation and on individual self-scrutiny, its stern mistrust of the passions, of display, of social role-playing, all role-playing being, by definition, insincere. But Clarissa also yearns for elements of Catholicism which Protestantism has put behind it, specifically the destiny of martyrdom and the vocation of saint-hood. In other words, some of the energies Richardson calls upon come directly from Catholic hagiography; it is they (together with the incompletely digested example of Shakespeare) that lend a somewhat theatrical and Italianate colouring to this otherwise Puritan and puritanical novel.

Virginity, martyrdom and sainthood have no particular religious meaning within Protestantism. Why are they important to Richardson?

Virgin is a word used often in *Clarissa*, but almost always as an adjective ('virgin cheek', 'virgin fame') and thus in a metonymic sense. (A telling exception: Hickman is jeered at as a 'male virgin'.) Clarissa is a virgin, and we all know it, but Richardson does not say so explicitly. Why not? First, because 'Virgin' as a name, a status, has been captured by Catholicism. Second, because the conception of virginity that Richardson and his audience hold is a narrowly physicalist and therefore mildly indecent one.

Why, once she has escaped the toils of Lovelace, can Clarissa not put the rape behind her and make a new life for herself – if not in the role advocated by her friend Anna and by Lovelace's family, as Mrs Lovelace, then as a woman of independent means, if necessary an old maid, in retirement on the estate left to her by her grandfather? Why must she die? This is the question Richardson asks and answers, even though – to his eternal credit – his answer alienates him from his readers and perhaps from himself too, as he knew himself.

His answer is that Clarissa turns towards death because she cannot put the rape behind her. She cannot put the rape behind her because she adheres to a certain conception of virginity with which her self-conception is closely bound. She cannot recover the old self-conception because she cannot recover her virginity.

There are certain mythic dualisms within which Clarissa is trapped and beyond which she (perhaps Richardson too) cannot think her way, dualisms that are irreversible in the sense that you can move from state A to state B but not from state B to state A: child–adult, presexual–sexual, virgin–woman, unfallen–fallen, perhaps also wife–whore (although Daniel Defoe had no trouble imagining that one could return to being a wife after having been a whore). Faced with Lovelace's desire, Clarissa's intuitive need (this is hardly in Richardson's book, but might have to emerge in performance) is not to have to commit herself, not to have to elect between the alternatives. This need is denied not only by Lovelace but by the Harlowe family too. After the rape, what she needs but cannot conceive of – because here the Christian understanding of virginity fails her – is a way of returning to virginity.

Her crisis is a real one. Nevertheless, it is specific to a Christian understanding of virginity. In Greek mythic thought – to name only one instance – a loss of virginity is not final or irreversible. As Marina Warner points out, goddesses like Aphrodite, Ishtar, Astarte and Anat were titled virgin (*parthenos*) despite taking lovers. Though a *parthenos* in ancient Greece was forbidden to have sex, sexual intercourse did not lose her her *parthenia* as long as it remained concealed; and it could be concealed because the definition of *parthenia* did not turn on the physical state of her genitalia. As Giulia Sissa puts it, genital penetration was not an 'irreparable' act.[4]

The rape of Clarissa, writes Nancy Miller, '[does] violence . . . to her sense of self'. It forces upon her 'a sexual personality' and thereby paralyses her, robs her of flexibility of movement. What has been inflicted on her is a 'hypertrophic reduction of human identity to sexual definition'.[5]

I take it that when Miller refers here to Clarissa's 'personality' and 'identity' she intends her deepest being: Clarissa would not be a worthy heroine if she could be defeated by the mere ascription of a social fate or the mere infliction of a psychological trauma. Through being raped, I take Miller to say, Clarissa has suffered ontological damage. Clarissa herself seems to agree: 'I am no longer what I was in any one thing,' she says a few days after the rape. (p. 890) Yet the damage has to be ontological only in a particular religious tradition and a particular religious ontology, within which

Clarissa, her author and many of her commentators seem to find themselves.

This is not to say that the only perspective on rape in the book is the one they adopt. Lovelace, in a baffled comment which must find an echo in some readers, asks why Clarissa cannot put the rape behind her, since what occurred was 'a mere notional violation' in which her innermost being was not touched. Clarissa's best friend, Anna Howe, though condemning Lovelace, in effect agrees: what damage there is has been done to Clarissa's name alone, she says, not to her self; the situation is recoverable; rehabilitation of her name is possible, and indeed, once the circumstances are known, will be readily forthcoming. (That Anna's recipe is for Clarissa to marry Lovelace is neither here nor there.)

Clarissa's response to Anna is threefold: that she can never reward Lovelace by marrying him; that what Anna proposes is merely a resolution of the crisis at a social level; and (cannily) that the forgiveness of society will never be wholehearted.

In all, there is no realistically convincing argument for suicide or at least for the turning towards death that Clarissa undergoes and chooses to undergo, particularly when, after two months of reflection, she reverses her earlier judgement and announces that Lovelace has indeed not touched her deepest self, that in this sense she is unviolated.[6] Although the death of the heroine is a goal towards which Richardson has clearly been working from the moment he conceived the novel, he is from this point onward unable to present it plausibly, at least at the level of psychology.

Why must Clarissa die? What has happened that is so final, so ineradicable, that even the stern sense of absolute rightness, absolute cleanness of conscience, that Clarissa begins to exhibit after her period of post-traumatic mourning is overridden by the will to die? I return to the matter of virginity. In the narrowest, most physical, but also most Christian sense of the term, she has lost her virginity, and nothing will bring it back. The measure of the distance between the Richardson who penned the last books of *Clarissa* and his modern-age, Protestant audience – even his 1748 audience, who clamoured, as the last instalments of the story approached, for the heroine to be allowed to live – is that, like Lovelace, his audience cannot regard the loss of virginity as enough of a tragedy to justify suicide. To them, what Clarissa has suffered has been an affront to her dignity, in her own eyes and in the eyes of the world. Her dignity can be restored, the damage can be repaired.

In wondering with Lovelace whether there is not something 'merely notional' in the violation, in being reluctant to see Clarissa as indelibly marked by it, I as reader and potential re-representer of Clarissa concede to participating in a certain violence of inter-pretation, a violence against which Clarissa in effect protests on those numerous occasions when she resists the right assumed by others to interpret her (to interpret such involuntary motions of her body as blushing, for instance). The rape is in the first place Clarissa's, not Lovelace's or anyone else's, to interpret, and the second half of the book is given over to her own very powerful interpretation of the event, an interpretation of whose rightness she is convinced to the point of dying for it.

Because of Clarissa's protests, and because of the conviction carried by her self-interpretation, my attempt to frame that self-interpretation, together with the interpretation of rape that Richardson offers by creating a fable in which the raped woman dies, by placing both within a specific historically bounded religious and cultural tradition, must itself carry overtones of violation. But such a countercharge must have its limits. If it is further claimed that for a man – any man – to interpret rape or to interpret a woman's interpretation of rape in itself carries overtones of violation, then we are still under the sway of the sentimental

notion of womanhood that Richardson did so much to establish –
the notion of the woman's body as special, compounded of the
animal and the angelic in ways beyond a man's comprehending.

III Lovelace

There is a crisis going on in Lovelace too, to which Richardson
does less than justice. What is the proper response of a human
being, and specifically a man, to beauty? That is the question which
exercises, or ought to exercise, Lovelace. Rape is only one of the
answers he gives to the question, and the least satisfying, even to
him. The rape is his attempt to break the grip of soul-harrowing
beauty upon him by familiarising himself (overfamiliarising himself) with its earthly embodiment; in a sense, it is an attempt to kill
whatever is other-worldly in beauty. At times the novel *Clarissa*, in
its overheated language, trembles on the edge of the Gothic: if rape
is the last resort of a man in a state of possession, then there are
moments after the rape when Clarissa seems capable of rising up
against Lovelace as an indestructible, murderous demon-bride.

The rape brings down to earth the woman, and specifically the
virgin, who enthrals Lovelace. I quote Simone de Beauvoir: 'The
virgin would seem to represent the most consummate form of the
feminine mystery; she is therefore its most disturbing and at the
same time most fascinating aspect.'[7]

De Beauvoir here echoes a specifically male conception of
woman as embodiment of a mystery or secret that can be unlocked
only via the phallus. In this conception the virgin is the most
closed, the most secret, and therefore the most fascinating avatar of
the feminine.

It is because of the conjunction of Lovelace's desire to know
with the fantasy of Clarissa as the closed female body that the rape
of Clarissa has become such a *locus classicus* in contemporary critical

thought, in its project of uncovering the genealogy of the Western will to know. 'She is absolutely impenetrable, least of all by rape,' writes Terry Eagleton. The 'reality of the woman's body', evinced by Clarissa even after the rape, is that it 'resists all representation and remains stubbornly recalcitrant to [the man's] fictions'.[8]

Lovelace, of course, comes around to Clarissa's way of thinking, though only when it is too late; indeed, he follows her in his own version of *contemptus mundi* and then in death. Through the couple Clarissa–Lovelace Richardson evokes, sometimes consciously, a gallery of types in which the angel-woman redeems or tries to redeem the man from his merely animal state. To Lovelace the Roman persecutor, Clarissa plays the Christian martyr who converts him by her steadfast adherence to her faith, even under torture; or she plays Beatrice to Lovelace's Dante (one of the stories she tells herself is that she is Lovelace's better self, bringing him closer to the light); or Lady Philosophy to Boethius; or the Virgin Mary, bridge and intercessor between matter and spirit, earth and heaven.

The powers of all these angelic intercessors are linked to their sexually closed state. We are back with Ficino: 'It is not this or that body that [the lover] desires but the splendour of the celestial majesty shining through bodies, a splendour that fills him with wonder.'

It is a proper grasp of this variety of masculine love, rooted in the late medieval cult of service of the *donna* and given philosophical depth by Renaissance neoplatonism, that is lost, by 1748, to Richardson. If his Lovelace is a thoroughly debased version of the lover-worshipper, that is not only because Richardson wants to set him within the English social scene as the representative of a hostile class with a hostile ethos, but also because Richardson has never been properly in touch with this Catholic-mystical, neoplatonic tradition and is therefore unable to conceive the scale of the betrayal of love that occurs when the lover takes the beloved by force.

My sketch of what Lovelace might have been makes him a larger figure than Richardson allows him to be. In fairness I must admit that there exists a sub-reading of Lovelace that does some justice to the genealogy I have been outlining, yet preserves Richardson's hostility to him. In this reading the real-life problem created by that male construct, the angel-woman, is that men cannot always maintain their fiction that the woman's chastity is a sign of angelic indifference to desire; the woman's self-containedness is felt as a disturbing autonomy or self-sufficiency. In this reading, Lovelace the rapist-revenger is the dark side of the coin of which Dante the pilgrim-lover is the bright, ideal side.

4 Marcellus Emants, *A Posthumous Confession*

THE NETHERLANDS OF the mid-nineteenth century was one of the cultural backwaters of Europe. The great current of the Romantic movement had barely stirred its complacent materialism. It had produced only a single literary work of stature, Eduard Douwes Dekker's novel *Max Havelaar* (1860), an attack on abuses in the colonial East Indies.

In the last quarter of the century, however, the new waves of Impressionism, Wagnerism and Naturalism began to wash Dutch shores, and by the 1880s a full literary awakening, the Movement of Eighty, was under way. Among the prophetic forerunners claimed for themselves by the young men of the movement was the writer Marcellus Emants. It was a role Emants declined, as he was to decline affiliation to any group or school.

Born in 1848 into a patrician family from The Hague, Emants was intended for a career in the law. But he detested the joyless drinking and promiscuity of Leiden student life and abandoned his studies as soon as his father died. Thereafter he lived as a writer of independent means, travelling abroad to avoid the Dutch winters. He made three marriages, the last of them singularly wretched. After the First World War, fearing Socialist government and high taxes, he removed to Switzerland, where he died in 1923.

Though Emants thought of himself as a playwright first and

foremost, it is his novels and stories that have kept his name alive,
principally *Een nagelaten bekentenis* (*A Posthumous Confession*, 1894),
Inwijding (*Initiation*, 1900), *Waan* (*Delusion*, 1905), *Liefdesleven*
(*Love-life*, 1916), and *Mensen* (*People*, 1920). Their principal subjects
are love and marriage: deluded love, unhappy marriage. Emants is
one of a line of European novelists who, in dissecting the intimate
discords of modern marriage, have also explored the discontents of
modern Western civilisation: Flaubert, Tolstoy, F.M. Ford,
Lawrence.

In the literary handbooks Emants is usually classed among the
Naturalists. He seems to belong there because (like the Goncourt
brothers) he is interested in the sexual underlife of the bourgeoisie
and because (like Zola) he uses the language of the new sciences of
heredity and psychopathology to explain human motivation.

But though Emants was influenced by the patron thinkers of
Naturalism – Taine, Spencer, Charcot – he differs from the
Naturalists in important respects. His pessimism is far removed
from Zola's faith in the power of the novelist to guide man toward
a better future. Nor is there in Emants much of the painstaking and
systematic description of milieu characteristic of Naturalism. His
interest is in psychological processes, his style analytic rather than
descriptive. Where the committed Naturalist gathers a corpus of
data on which to base his *roman expérimental*, Emants comes to his
material in the traditional way, via chance, memory and intro-
spection. His true sympathies lie with the older generation of
European realists, in particular with Flaubert and Turgenev.

In 1880 Emants published an essay on Turgenev which describes
his own philosophy rather better than it does Turgenev's. In youth,
he writes, we create a fantasy ideal of the self we hope to be. The
pattern our life takes, however, is determined not by any ideal but
by unconscious forces within us. These forces impel us to acts; and
in our acts it is revealed to us who we truly are. The transition from

living in terms of fantasy ideals to living in self-knowledge always entails disillusionment and pain. Such pain becomes most acute when we recognise how unbridgeably vast the gap is between the ideal and the true self.

There is a dual emphasis in this account: on the powerlessness of the individual before unconscious inner forces, and on the painful disillusionment of coming to maturity. In Willem Termeer, the narrator of *A Posthumous Confession*, we find both aspects present: a helpless drifting in a sea of passions, fears and envies; and an agonised twisting and turning to escape confrontation with the true self his life-history reveals to him: impotent, cowardly, ridiculous.

Yet in terms of his own view of life, Termeer cannot be blamed for being what he is. The son of a cold, spiteful mother and a sickly, irascible father with a taste for pornography, who ends his life in a mental asylum – a 'degenerate', in the language of the day – Termeer is doomed (or at least feels himself to be doomed) by his birthright to repeat the past: to become a voluptuary and crypto-sado-masochist terrified of women, to choose a cold, dutiful spouse with whom to recreate his parents' loveless marriage, and at last to descend into madness.

As for social relations, the first memory Termeer has is of being taken to school and abandoned there like a rabbit in a cage of wild beasts. All around him he senses antagonism: people know there is something wrong with him, and for the good of the species want to put an end to him. His fellow men are savage beasts, and society itself a gigantic system of cogs and wheels in which ineffectual creatures like himself are doomed to be crushed.

From the beginning of his life-story, Termeer thus presents himself as a victim, a victim of heredity, of the Darwinian jungle of life, of the impersonal social machinery. Quite as much as it is a piece of self-rending analysis and sly exhibitionism, his confession is an agonised plea for pity.

But is Termeer simply a victim? His self-fulfilling conviction that everyone hates him can equally well be read as a projection of his own malevolence. Before he commits his murder, he experiences episodes of blind rage during which he barely deflects himself from assaulting his wife, whom he has already contemplated raping. When he eventually kills her, the act is directed not only against a woman who denies him both love (the mothering love he craves) and – in the name of her duty to the institution of marriage – freedom, but also against the society on whose behalf she stands like a wardress barring his way to what he wants: bliss. (Like Emma Bovary, Willem Termeer has read of bliss and is convinced it exists, somewhere.) Indeed, the agitated leaping and darting of his language is indication enough of the violence within him.

Only when words fail him does Termeer resort to action in his battle with society. The document he bequeaths us, we should remember, is his *second* confession. The first, 'an unadorned revelation of my most secret feelings', has been offered for publication and turned down as 'trivial'. In his failure to become a writer – an occupation for which he feels eminently qualified, being 'sick, highly complex, neurasthenic, in some respects of unsound mind, in other respects perverse' – we detect what is perhaps Termeer's deepest crisis. If there is no symbolic avenue by which he can claim a value for his life, then the only recourse left is a direct act. Since revelation of his inner self, no matter how bizarre and wretched that self, is not enough to win him currency, he must create something outside himself and display that to the world, to give himself substance.

From this point of view we can see Termeer, and perhaps Emants too, as children of Rousseau, who in his *Confessions* inaugurated the literary mode of the exhaustive secular confession. Since Rousseau's time there has grown up the genre of the confessional novel, of which *A Posthumous Confession* is a singularly pure example. Termeer, claiming to be unable to keep his dreadful secret, records his confession and leaves it behind as a monument to himself, thereby turning a worthless life into art.

But what of his author? In the name of investigating the inner life of this superfluous man, this marginal member of the upper bourgeoisie, what exactly is Emants doing?

Some twenty years after *A Posthumous Confession*, in the heyday of Freud, Emants was to defend his interest in psychopathology by claiming scientific goals. The deviant, he suggested, is characterised above all by an inability to censor and repress the forces at work within him. By documenting the self-expression of the deviant psyche, can we not expect to uncover fragments of what is kept so carefully hidden in the 'normal' inner life?

I would not deny the importance of the aims Emants claims here. Artists have told us as much about our inner life as psychologists ever have. But are the artist's motives ever as clear-cut and dispassionate as Emants would have us believe? Marcellus Emants is not disjunct from Willem Termeer: the author is implicated in his creature's devious project to transmute the base metal of his self into gold.

The gabble of Termeer, so frank, so perceptive, yet so mad, is not new. We have heard these accents at least once before, in 1864, from the nameless 'underground man' of Dostoevsky's story. Both he and Termeer tell their woes and pick their sores in the name of the truth; both acknowledge the exhibitionism of their performance, despise themselves for it, yet go on nevertheless. The difference between Dostoevsky and Emants is that, after *Notes from Underground*, Dostoevsky, with deeper insight into the motives behind and inherent demands of the confessional mode, would go on to write *The Idiot* and *The Possessed*, in which he would destroy the pretensions of Rousseau and his heirs to arrive at true self-knowledge, uncovering the worm of ambition at the heart of the feigned disinterestedness of secular confession. Emants, a lesser thinker, a lesser artist, a lesser psychologist (as who is not?), remains bound in Rousseau's toils.

5   Harry Mulisch, *The Discovery of Heaven*

I

LET US IMAGINE, says the Dutch novelist Harry Mulisch, that there exists a clique of celestial beings with an unlimited capacity to intervene in human affairs, gods as the Olympians were, powerful without necessarily being good. Let us imagine further that for nearly four hundred years, since a pawn of the infernal powers named Francis Bacon set in train the inductive-scientific revolution, these celestial beings have been waging a losing battle for the allegiance of humankind. Let us imagine that in 1968, as a last resort, they plant an agent of theirs, an innocent child, on earth. Now, in 1985, that agent is about to be brought into play. His orders will be to sever the last tie between God ('the Chief') and man, after which humankind must fare as best it can. 'From now on Lucifer has a free hand.'[1]

The Discovery of Heaven is the story of 'our man on earth', an emissary who in olden times would have been called an angel. His story is told in a natural way, the way of the realist novel, that is to say, without intervention by the author (until the very end of a long book) to remind us that the personages whose lives we follow are in the hands of puppet-masters. Thus, aside from occasional eerie moments and a few disconcerting coincidences, we might as well be reading a story of our own world, a world that is ruled – or so we presume – not by gods but by blind laws of nature.

The paternal grandparents selected for the agent of the heavenly forces are Wolfgang Delius, born in 1892 in Austro-Hungary, and Eva Weiss, born in 1908 in Belgium of German Jewish parents, both settled in the Netherlands. Their son Max is marked out to father the angel.

Max is still a child when the Second World War breaks out. During the war Wolfgang Delius runs 'a semi-governmental institution' specialising in the plunder of Jewish goods. (p. 32) Though Eva is by now separated from him, her status as his wife ought to save her from arrest. But Delius chooses to repudiate her, and she joins thousands of other Dutch Jews transported to Auschwitz.

With telling modifications, this happens to be the story of Mulisch's own parents. An important figure in banking, Mulisch Senior had a Jewish wife (estranged) and a half-Jewish son. When the Germans took over, he was able to shield them from persecution. Unlike the fictional Delius, he did not cast them off. His wife survived the Occupation and in 1951 emigrated to the United States. After the Liberation he was arrested as a collaborator and spent three years in detention.

Harry Mulisch has written frequently, even obsessively, about his ancestry, and particularly about his father (among the few books in Max Delius's apartment is Franz Kafka's *Letter to My Father*, the cry of another son struggling to escape from under the suffocating weight of a father). In doing so Mulisch has to some extent mythologised his origins. In an autobiographical essay published in 1974, he traces his lineage on the paternal side back to the Turks, who invaded Europe in the sixteenth century, and thence to the Huns of central Asia, and on the maternal side to the Israelites in bondage in Egypt.[2] 'One can hardly imagine a more ethnically "impure" Dutchman than myself,' he writes in *A Ghost Story* (1993). 'I . . . embody, not a struggle, but a continuous dialogue, between Christianity and Judaism, between Germany and the Netherlands, and several other things as well.'[3]

Pursuing this self-mythologisation further in *The Discovery of Heaven* (Max Delius is transparently a fictional version of himself), Mulisch awards to Max's parents the fates that fortune spared his own: death in Auschwitz for his Jewish mother, execution for his collaborationist German-speaking father. This revision allows him to grant Max an intensified awareness of the terrible fissure in European history opened by the Holocaust, as well as of the diagnostic and perhaps even prophetic role that might be filled by a man who, 'Dutch, Austrian, Jewish and Aryan all at once . . . belonged only with those who, like him, belonged with no one'. (*The Discovery of Heaven*, p. 40)

As a grown man, Max visits Auschwitz. There he has an uncanny experience: it is as if he refuses to be fully present, as if his real presence were lagging behind his physical self. Why? What is he resisting?

The reluctance of Europe to face the enormity of Auschwitz, and in general the failure of the imagination in the face of atrocious evil, has been one of Mulisch's recurrent themes since *The Stone Bridal Bed* (1959; English translation 1962), a novel in which he tries to fix a steady, Nietzschean gaze upon the peculiarly male pleasure in violation, a joy in destruction that is to be found as much among Homer's Greeks as among the American airmen who bombed Dresden. What happened in the death camps, reflects Max after his visit, must surely have shaken the foundations of the divine order and of the universe itself. 'Was everything possible and could anything be done?' he asks himself, echoing Ivan Karamazov. Surely, even in heaven, bliss will henceforth be possible only at the price of a criminal loss of memory. 'Should the blessed not be punished with hell for this? Everything had been wrecked for all eternity – not only here, but by thousands of earlier and later occasions, which no one remembered. Heaven was impossible; only hell might perhaps exist. Anyone who believed in God . . . should be executed.' (p. 116)

'If hell had this branch [Auschwitz] on earth, where was heaven's?' (p. 117) Auschwitz belongs to what Mulisch elsewhere calls anti-history, 'the anti-history of . . . Attila, Tamerlane, Genghis Khan, Hitler . . . [where] there is no . . . thought, no purpose, no result – only nothingness . . . The massacres of the Huns and the concentration camps of Hitler . . . lie side by side at the bottom of eternity.'[4] Max sees Auschwitz as Satan's challenge to God, a challenge that resounds even across the spaces of heaven. Nothing in *The Discovery of Heaven* leads one to believe that God knows how to answer that challenge.

Max is trained as a physicist and astronomer. In the 1960s he accepts the position of chief astronomer at an observatory situated at Westerbork in rural Holland. Westerbork is a place with a shameful history. Set up in 1939 by the then Dutch government as a camp for Jewish refugees from Germany, it was taken over by the Nazis and turned into a trans-shipment camp to Birkenau. A hundred thousand Dutch Jews – including, presumably, Max's mother – passed through it. After the war, Dutch fascists were imprisoned in Westerbork. Later the camp was used to house allies of the Dutch colonial regime in Indonesia fleeing reprisals. To Max it is an accursed place, the 'asshole of the Netherlands' (as Auschwitz itself is *anus mundi*). The twelve huge dish aerials of the observatory look to him like 'sacrificial altars [entreating] the blessing of heaven'. Yet there is no other place on earth where he can imagine working. 'He belonged here; here was where he must spend his life.' (pp. 375, 117, 378)

Max's best friend is Onno Quist, scion of a wealthy patrician family. Onno has already made a scholarly name for himself by decoding certain baffling pre-Hellenic inscriptions. Meeting by chance (except that in their lives chance and design are not mutually exclusive), they discover that they are, in a sense, twins, having been conceived on the same day. They become inseparable, '[creating] a kind of infinity, like two mirrors reflecting each other'. (p. 37) Even the entry of Ada Brons into their lives, first as Max's mistress, then as Onno's wife, does not cause a rift. Together they form a threesome; to Ada falls the role of admiring listener as Max and Onno conduct their 'intellectual fencing match[es].' (p. 69) (These fencing matches, of which Mulisch gives extended samples, read uncomfortably like raillery of a rather juvenile kind.)

Ada, a professional musician, is invited to an arts festival in Havana. Max and Onno accompany her (the year is 1967, the Cuban cause is popular among the European Left – Mulisch himself published a starry-eyed report on Cuba in 1968). Because of a bureaucratic slip-up the Cubans take them to be delegates to a concurrent congress of world revolutionary parties. They go along with the charade until the speech-making bores them, then withdraw to the pleasures of sun and surf. Max enjoys the anarchic feel of Cuban life; when he catches a glimpse of Fidel, the cup of his happiness runs over. 'It must be possible to found a just society on earth . . . If Fidel succeeds, if only a little, I'm quite prepared in a manner of speaking to grant him a reflection of something like the divine.' (p. 179)

In this paradisal setting Max and Ada succumb to a moment of passion and make love among the waves. Ada falls pregnant; but since she makes sure she sleeps with her husband the same night, she is never sure of the paternity of her child. 'Was she pregnant by the friendship between the two of them?' she wonders. (p. 218)

As the gods (or fate) have dictated the sexual union of Max and Ada, so they crudely see to it that Ada never learns the answer to her question. Back in Holland, as the trio drive through a storm, their car is hit by a falling tree. Ada suffers irreparable brain damage. Her baby son Quinten is delivered by Caesarean section; Ada herself is kept alive for years in a hospital but never recovers consciousness.

Without a mother, and with a nominal father temperamentally unequipped to look after him, the baby passes into the joint care of Ada's mother Sophia and Max. Soon Sophia is creeping into Max's bed and overpowering his senses with the sweetness of her love-making. Yet in the light of day she seems to bear no memory of their nocturnal congress – indeed, will not have it alluded to. Though she reminds him of the Sphinx, her sexual hold over him is so powerful that he abandons his libertine ways and settles into staid if secret paternity. Thus do the gods constitute this strange family: child, grandmother, secret father masquerading as foster father. (Mulisch does not allow us to forget that Moses and Jesus came from equally strange family set-ups: in his fiction – most directly in *Two Women* [1975; English translation 1980], about the attempts of a woman to give her lesbian lover a child – he has repeatedly explored alternatives to the nuclear family.)

Quinten Quist, agent of the heavenly powers, is a strangely beautiful child with eyes a shade of blue never seen before in a human being. His first word is 'obelisk'. Though his early years are unexceptional, he is haunted by memories of sights he has not seen and experiences he has not had, memories imprinted on him before birth. His duty, programmed into him, is to find their earthly originals. Among these is a certain lofty, temple-like interior, for which his private name is 'the Citadel'. The words 'the centre of the world' also trouble his dreams. (pp. 399, 448, 436)

A casual observation by young Quinten allows Max to take the first step on his own path toward illumination, bringing together his obsession with the Holocaust and his vocation as astronomer. If a star is forty light years away, says Quinten, then watchers on that star must be able to see what happened on earth forty years ago in earth time. Furthermore, the star is bouncing the same visual impulses back to earth, however weakly: once the technical problem of picking them up has been solved, we ourselves will be able to see what happened on earth eighty years ago.

If Quinten is right, thinks Max, the whole of human history is still being propagated in the form of light waves somewhere in the universe. Somewhere his mother is still getting into the cattle truck that will take her to Auschwitz. Nothing is truly past, nothing is ineluctably hidden. Once technology enables us to see the past in all its fullness, the 'whole truth' will be revealed and humanity will finally be 'liberated'. (p. 455) Then he checks himself: will humanity really welcome the whole truth – would he himself, for instance, want Onno to see a replay of his wife's adultery?

As a child Max had had the Promethean ambition of laying bare the secrets of the universe, but his scientific research has never been quite of the highest order. At Westerbork he has a second great moment of illumination, one that balances the dark illumination of Auschwitz. Astronomers all over the world have been puzzled by the pulses emanating from a quasar named MQ 3412. It occurs to Max that it is not MQ 3412 itself that is behaving oddly, but something behind it. MQ 3412 is directly in line with, and hiding, 'the primeval singularity itself,' the origin of the universe. (p. 525) In a creative outburst rivalling Newton's or Einstein's, Max is led to conceive a unified theory of space and time, a theory linking the four fundamental forces of nature and the seventeen natural constants. In essence the theory is Pythagorean: the principle underlying the universe turns out to be musical harmony. But at the moment Max attains this godlike insight he is struck by a meteorite, hurled by the beings whose secrets he is about to unveil, and killed.

II

Max Delius's Pythagoreanism belongs to a neoplatonic cosmology that Harry Mulisch himself has been propagandising, under the name 'octavity', since the 1970s. (He claims that he laid the foundations of his system during a spurt of creative energy as a teenager in the late 1940s.) Octavity embraces an alternative, post-scientific physics based on an anti-Aristotelian, post-logical logic in which contradiction is not excluded: just as a musical note and its octave both are and are not the same sound, so, in post-logic, an entity is both non-identical to itself and (as a boundary condition) identical to itself.

For Mulisch octavity is not a mere metaphor, an *as if* for some other, more truly scientific account of the universe. Instead, it is by its nature a philosophy of metaphor, of homologies or correspondences that may seem to be accidental (like the homology between Westerbork and Auschwitz) but that in fact echo or rhyme significantly with each other – as do coincidences in fiction, including the coincidences in *The Discovery of Heaven*. Octavity is the most basic of all principles, underlying not only the structure of the heavens but the broad sweep of human history. Thus, for instance, the Renaissance was marked by a rediscovery of Pythagorean principles of number and harmony in art and architecture, while in the anti-Renaissance constituted by the grand tyrannies of the twentieth century – principally Nazism – we witness the submergence of these humanistic principles and a return to pre-Pythagorean, Pharaonic gigantism and the cult of death.

In the person of Max Delius, Mulisch is thus able to bring together an intensely felt personal preoccupation with the historical trauma of European fascism with an idiosyncratic, even arcane, vision of the cosmological order. As Max's son, the banished and brainwashed angel, will later remark, 'I have the feeling that the world is very complicated, but that there's something behind it that is very simple and at the same time incomprehensible.' (p. 601) In this respect *The Discovery of Heaven* marks an advance on *The Assault* (1982; English translation 1985), Mulisch's best-known novel to date. *The Assault* is also about forgetting, about the use of oblivion by individuals and societies to protect themselves from the pain of memory. By comparison, *The Discovery of Heaven* explores forgetting in a broader, more metaphysical sweep. (In what amounts to a private joke on Mulisch's part, the central figure of *The Assault* reappears in a walk-on role in *The Discovery of Heaven*.)

Meanwhile Onno has abandoned scholarship for politics. He spends some years as a junior Cabinet Minister (the chapters devoted to the internal squabbles of Dutch politics of the 1970s are largely wasted on the foreign reader), and seems to be a rising star until a malicious rival discloses his participation in the Havana conference and puts an end to his career.

In disgust he quits the country. For several years he lives incognito in Rome, speaking only to a pet raven named Edgar (after Edgar Allan Poe). The raven would seem to be a spy planted by the celestial watchers; Quinten too is dogged by flies, wasps, ants, as well as by tempters and temptresses. Onno's monologues to the raven, mainly diatribes on world history, make for less than gripping reading, and confirm one's suspicion that with the death of Max the novel has lost its moral *raison d'être* and its backbone.

In Rome Onno is miraculously tracked down by Quinten, now aged seventeen, obeying the inner voice that controls him. Slowly the place of Onno in the cosmic plot begins to become clear. He is needed as a palaeographer and antiquarian, to decode the various inscriptions (in Latin, in Hebrew) that will guide Quinten to the Citadel of his dreams and bring to fruition his mission on earth, which turns out to be the theft of the tablets of Moses from where they have been secreted in the crypt of the Lateran Chapel, and the return of the tablets to Jerusalem. For this purpose Quinten has conveniently been provided with a crash course in pre-modern lock technology; the long sequence in which philologist and cracksman unite in a race against time to pick the locks of the Lateran comes straight out of Hollywood and will feed back seamlessly into the film of the book if and when that is made.

Onno has begun to find 'something inhuman' in Quinten, 'a touch of interstellar coldness'. (p. 593) But both are by now in the grip of greater forces. With the sapphire tablets in a suitcase they fly off to Jerusalem, where they catch a glimpse of a mysterious woman with Quinten's blue eyes and a number tattooed on her arm: Eva Weiss, Max's mother and (the cuckolded Onno now realises) Quinten's grandmother, who has either survived Auschwitz or come back from the grave.

Everything is coming to a head: walking like a zombie, guided by Edgar the raven, Quinten carries the tablets to the Temple Mount – the centre of the world – where, in a climax mingling Judaic, Christian and Muslim motifs, the tablets crumble to nothing, signalling the end of God's covenant with mankind; whereupon Quinten is borne back into the heavens.

III

Along with W.F. Hermans (1921–95), Gerhard Reve (b.1923), the Fleming Hugo Claus (b.1929), and Cees Nooteboom (b.1933), Harry Mulisch (b.1927) makes up the first rank of Dutch novelists of his generation. All except Hermans have had a fair quota of their work translated into English; none has hitherto made quite the impact on the English-speaking public as in France, Scandinavia, and (particularly) Germany.

With *The Assault* and *Last Call* (1985; translation 1989), Mulisch has to an extent overcome this fate (it helped that *The Assault* was turned into a successful film). *The Discovery of Heaven* will certainly add to his reputation. Mulisch has always known how to tell a story and here he interweaves three life-stories – Max's, Onno's, and Quinten's – with admirable dexterity. In creating Max his stroke of inspiration has been to situate the malaise of the Dutch intellectual of his own generation, belonging to a peaceful, prosperous, unified Europe, yet haunted by the nightmare past of the Occupation, within a larger question: has humanity truly moved beyond good and evil, and, if so, how did it happen?

In the case of Quinten, Mulisch gives a moving portrayal of the inner life of a baffled other-worldly being struggling to find the reason for his existence (the precocious younger Quinten has his cloying moments, however); while the eerie liaison between Max and Quinten's grandmother is entirely convincing. If the action is rather slow-paced, this is compensated for by the intellectual adventurousness of the whole. Though at times Mulisch seems merely to be showing off, the play of ideas is generally lively.

It is probably best not to let the foundational conceit of *The Discovery of Heaven* – that God is about to give up – bear too much weight, just as we need not take too seriously the idea that since the time of Constantine the popes have been in possession of the tablets of Moses. Mulisch's myth of the abandoning of humankind to the prince of darkness implies an apocalyptic reading of the trajectory of the twentieth century, a reading that is hardly borne out by the picture of contemporary life he gives in his book. Aside from miserable weather, vandalised callboxes, nouveau-riche philistines, and boring politics, Mulisch's Holland does not seem too bad a place, certainly not bad enough to deserve the diatribes it gets from the heavenly beings or to justify Mulisch's lament (sounded elsewhere) that it is simply part of 'an increasingly fascistic-technological world'.[5] Indeed, if anyone comes out badly from the story, it is the gods. Even if humanity has fallen into the trap that Satan, employing Aristotle and Bacon, has prepared, who would want to be saved by beings as petulant, despotic, and amoral as Mulisch's heavenly crew?

IV

The translation of *The Discovery of Heaven* by Paul Vincent is good without being exemplary. More often than is excusable, Vincent quails before the problems posed by the plethora of fussy little modifiers characteristic of Dutch. Complex verb constructions are simplified at the cost of nuance. There are a fair number of outright errors (instead of 'the dilemma of theodicy', for instance, Vincent writes of a 'Theodicean dilemma', as though there had been a person named Theodicea). (p. 281) Further errors have crept in that ought to have been picked up by an editor – for instance, sixty million Jews are said to have perished in the Nazi camps. (p. 558) Vincent also goes in for locutions that make Mulisch's Holland sound like England: 'Stop that nonsense, mate!' (p. 89) He might have taken a lesson from Adrienne Dixon, translator of *The Stone Bridal Bed* and *Last Call*, who creates for Mulisch a discreetly neutral variety of English, neither British nor American.

6   Cees Nooteboom, Novelist and Traveller

TOWARD THE END of Cees Nooteboom's novel *In the Dutch Mountains*, his novelist-narrator – by this point all but indistinguishable from Nooteboom himself – gets into a debate about truth and fiction with the shades of Plato, Milan Kundera and Hans Christian Andersen. Why, asks the Nooteboom figure, do I have this irrepressible desire to fictionalise, to tell lies? 'From unhappiness,' answers Andersen. 'But you are not unhappy enough. That's why you can't bring it off.'[1]

This is the most penetrating stab of self-insight in a novel which – like the rest of Nooteboom's fiction – is as much about its own processes and *raisons-d'être* as it is about the fictitious activities of its personages. For, despite contortions of self-reflexiveness that in another writer (Samuel Beckett, for instance) might give rise to agonies of the spirit, Nooteboom and his narrator-avatars strike one as too much at home in the world genuinely to suffer. This – as the ghost of Andersen suggests – is Nooteboom's peculiar misfortune as writer: he is too intelligent, too sophisticated, too urbane, to be able to commit himself to the grand illusioneering of realism, yet too little anguished by this fate – this expulsion from the world of the heartfelt imagination – to work it up into a tragedy of its own.

59

At one of its reflexive levels, Nooteboom's fiction has therefore had to be about a search for a level of feeling that can be carried over undiminished into literary creativity. In the novel *The Following Story* (1991; English translation 1993), in the love of a bumbling classics teacher for one of his students, he has been able to tap into feeling that is both passionate and creative. In the novella *A Song of Truth and Semblance* (1981; English translation 1984), where the writer-hero and his nineteenth-century characters inhabit the same rooms and even the same emotional space, life, Eros and fiction seem to be on the brink of inter-penetrating. Then Nooteboom falters, terminating what had promised to be the most eerily Jamesian of his tales with a trick ending. And in *In the Dutch Mountains* itself, Andersen's diagnosis turns out to be correct: for all the wit, for all the insight into the self and its fictions, for all the elegance of style, there is finally not enough feeling to drive the story.

II

In the Dutch Mountains began its life as a film text under the title 'The Snow Queen' (the film was never made). Based on Andersen's story of the same name, it plays quite openly on its debt to Andersen.

'The Snow Queen' is one of Andersen's most remarkable tales, a plea for the precious uniqueness of childhood, an appeal against the premature induction of the child into rationality. Little Kai is stolen by the Snow Queen and kept captive in her castle in the far, cold North. His faithful playmate Gerda goes in quest of him. After many adventures and tribulations she arrives, borne on the back of a reindeer, at the Snow Queen's great hall of ice. Here she finds Kai, blue with cold, playing an endless, solitary game, trying to fit shards of ice together like pieces of a broken mirror. Her warm tears melt the ice around Kai's heart and he is freed from the Queen's spell.

In Nooteboom's version, Andersen's children become Kai and Lucia, a perfectly handsome, perfectly happy young couple who make a living as illusionists in the theatre. Their act consists of Kai blindfolding Lucia and holding up an object before her, which she then 'sees'. Their serene perfection (they are of one mind; they are continually compared with the reunited halves of the self which – in the fable of Plato's *Symposium* – has been split in two) arouses the envy of a mysterious *femme fatale*, who has Kai kidnapped and whisked off to her castle. There she keeps him in thrall, obliterating his memories of Lucia, subjecting him to her lust. For his Snow Queen mistress Kai feels both fear and unwilling desire: her eyes are like 'tunnels of glass and ice that led to a world where it was so cold that, if you penetrated too far . . . you would freeze to death'. (p. 99)

But Lucia has not forgotten him. Guided by a fairy-godmother figure who playfully metamorphoses into a reindeer, she tracks him down; with the aid of the police, the wicked Queen is killed and Kai rescued.

This is pretty much the whole of Nooteboom's core story. Kai and Lucia are no more individualised than the hero and heroine of any fairy tale. Lucia has 'blue eyes like a summer sky . . . lips . . . red as cherries . . . teeth white as milk': as her creator candidly admits, she is constructed according to 'the conventions of European literary culture'. (p. 11) Their adventures take place against a vaguely realised Ruritanian background; for the rescue of Kai the clichés of the escapist thriller are unabashedly called upon.

Together with the shadow of Andersen's original, this version of the Snow Queen story constitutes the pre-text of Nooteboom's novel. But the pre-text is surrounded by a substantial frame, namely, the story of how the Snow Queen story gets to be told;

and the frame story – in a move by now common in post-realist fiction – takes over the status of being the primary and 'real' story.

The hero and narrator of the frame story is Alfonso Tiburón de Mendoza, a middle-aged Aragonese with a reverence for Plato and an affection for the Dutch language, a road engineer by profession and an amateur novelist. It is he who conducts Kai and Lucia through the ritualised movements of the European fairy tale, it is he who hopes to feel their story take on a life of its own under his hands, and it is he who, in the end, has to hear the ghost of Hans Christian Andersen tell him he is not a real writer because he is not unhappy enough.

Tiburón's story of Kai and Lucia is set in a land that is fictional but not mythical. He calls it the Southern Netherlands: from the map on the wall of their theatrical agent (reproduced on the back cover of the Dutch edition) it would appear to encompass most of Hungary, Romania, Bulgaria, Albania and the old Yugoslav Federation. The South is joined to the Northern Netherlands (the Netherlands we know) by a corridor snaking through Belgium, Alsace, Bavaria and the Austrian Tyrol.

In this split, bipartite country, migrants from the South congregate in *bidonvilles* around Northern cities. Northerners look down on Southerners as dirty and sly and use them for cheap labour; Southerners, for their part, call Northerners 'the Dour Ones'. Tiburón, a Southerner at heart, dislikes Northerners for 'their complacency and their unbridled greed, and the hypocrisy with which they [try] to conceal both'. For the North Tiburón feels Fear, 'a fear that demands a capital letter, German style'. Whereas the South is mountainous (hence the title of the English translation: Nooteboom's title is simply *In Nederland*, In the Netherlands), the landscape of the North is flat, a landscape of 'absolutism' where one is forced to live in 'total visibility'. (pp. 40, 4, 2)

The South can obviously be taken to stand for north-west

Europe's Second- and Third-World hinterlands. However, Nooteboom is not concerned to develop the political dimension of his fable, or to exploit with much energy the possibilities it offers for polemic against his countrymen. Like Vladimir Nabokov in *Pale Fire*, he has some incidental fun concocting a language (here a Netherlandic dialect) for his Southerners. For the rest, he uses the South as a frankly fictitious backdrop to his action – an action which, as Andersen's ghost implies, never quite comes to life.

The failure on Tiburón's part to *feel* the story he is telling deeply enough to move the reader emerges in two ways: in a certain arbitrariness in the emotional logic of the core story, the story of Kai and Lucia; and in a failure, in the frame story, to raise the intensity of the writer-hero's quest for the meaning of what he is engaged in beyond the levels of quizzical puzzlement, irritation and bombast.

Tiburón chooses to see his version of the fairy tale as being about 'perfect beauty and perfect happiness', about 'the marring of the sublime by the trivial'. (pp. 9, 23) But in making his hero and heroine adults and turning Kai into the Snow Queen's sex slave rather than her little reasoning automaton, Nooteboom not only changes the point of the kernel story or fable – which, of course, he is entitled to do – but also loses touch with what in Andersen's version becomes its moral driving force: outrage and anguish at the corruption of innocence, at the robbing of children of their childhood. The prelapsarian innocence that Tiburón wishes to claim for the grown-up Kai and Lucia is, by comparison, abstract, without emotional resonance. The fate of Andersen's little Kai, the steadfastness of little Gerda, touch the heart; the plight of grown-up Kai in the Snow Queen's bed simply does not.

Tiburón's lucubrations on the differences between myth, fairy tale and realist fiction evade this rather obvious point. Nooteboom's ambition is to write a meditation on the nature of fiction, constructed as a story of the writing of a fiction with authorial digressions that will at the same time reflect on (and reflect) the collapse, in our time, of the illusions that gave energy to the great fiction of the past. As a further complication (to a writer who has never been afraid of complications), the fiction that the storyteller invents will become an allegory of his own life (or vice versa, depending on how much of a philosophical idealist he is). Thus as Tiburón drives around Spain inspecting roads and thinking about the book he is writing, and as the 'real' Spanish landscape and the 'fictitious' Southern Netherlands landscape interpenetrate in his mind, he picks up a hitchhiker, an attractive young woman of brisk, no-nonsense Dutch common sense (she dismisses the story of Jesus as 'a fairy tale') who nearly succeeds in seducing him: she is the Snow Queen in his own life. (p. 93)

'Fairy tales are written by people,' Tiburón reflects – 'that is what is wrong with them,' whereas 'myths are . . . written by no one'. The writing of fairy tales betrays 'a false longing for the writing of myths', a longing to be pre-individual. 'It [is] too late for that.' (pp. 94–5)

This is elegantly put, but, in the context within which Tiburón speaks, off the point. Fairy tales are not always written by people, not *authored*, though Andersen's were; and in any event, what is wrong with the updated fairy tale which Tiburón writes is not that it is authored but that it is unmotivated, lacks a rationale. As the ghost of Andersen hints, one cannot see what, at the deepest level, has driven Tiburón (or Nooteboom) to write it.

III

For the first quarter century of his writing career, until the success of his third novel *Rituals* (1980; English translation 1983), Cees Nooteboom's reputation in the Netherlands was as a travel writer who also dabbled in poetry and fiction. While underestimating his rather cerebral verse, this view is not inaccurate with regard to the two earlier novels, which, though avant-garde by the standards of Dutch fiction of their day, are otherwise unremarkable.[2]

In his first travel books, put together from his regular column in the newspaper *De Volkskrant*, Nooteboom can be seen gradually shifting away from the journalistic travelogue as a genre in which to pass comment, at a necessarily superficial level, on the society and politics of another country, toward travel writing as a matrix within which to reflect on the deeper currents of life of a foreign culture.

With his move to the glossy magazine *Avenue* in 1969 he was freed to write longer pieces, and began to develop travel narrative in the direction of the personal essay, marked by a more ironic distance from his subject, as well as by a new richness of style, by excursions into art criticism, and by a growing preoccupation with the subject of memory, both personal and communal.

Roads to Santiago is the first of Nooteboom's travel books to be translated into English, despite the fact that one of them, *De zucht naar het Westen* (The Longing for the West) (1985), grew out of a series of visits to the United States during the 1970s and 1980s.

De zucht naar het Westen is not a particularly good book. It shows the weaker side of Nooteboom as an observer: his interpretive skills, trained on Old World landscapes rich in cultural associations and on architecture layered with historical meaning, turn out to be of little use in America, where surfaces are often all there is and meanings are anything but hidden. Too much time is spent on the futile task of checking American reality against images of America exported by the U.S. entertainment industry. Toward the end Nooteboom is moved to write despairingly, from a small town in Montana, 'There is no transcendence in these places, as in an Italian mountain village, nothing refers to anything else, nothing evokes a memory or a thought of the future, no reflection is possible.'[3] The book comes to life only when he is able to read small-town Wisconsin against an opportunely discovered collection of turn-of-the-century photographs of the same sites, which bring back the dimension of historical depth; or to smuggle meditations on artworks (including some vivid pages on Edward Hopper) into his travel narrative.

Roads to Santiago originates in travel essays written between 1979 and 1992. Generally speaking, the later pieces are more thoughtful and substantial than the earlier. The text has been lightly edited to mask its Dutch origins and a few pages added. Too lightly edited, perhaps: the foreign reader will hardly be interested by the problems of writing about Spanish churches in a language (Dutch) that lacks technical terms for Romanesque architecture. The decision to omit the dates of the original pieces is also questionable: Nooteboom has much to say about Basque terrorism, but the text does not indicate that the events referred to belong to the mid-1980s.

IV

'One of the few constants in my life', writes Nooteboom, 'is my love – a lesser expression will not do – of Spain . . . The Spanish character and the Spanish landscape correspond to what in essence I am.'[4] As a writer he even claims Spanish paternity: accused of being an epigone of Borges, he has responded that both Borges and he emerge from the hand of Calderón.[5]

The landscape that speaks to Nooteboom most directly is the *meseta*, the high, empty plain of Castile, which evokes in him 'feelings of eternity', and which he contrasts with the 'spiritual bleakness' of the Mediterranean coast, the Mecca of millions of tourists but to him 'the curse of Spain'. For the discerning traveller he recommends instead those provincial towns of the interior – Soria, for instance – that have retained their native poverty. 'Poverty does not shine, poverty is quiet, poverty does not discard the old in favour of the veneer of emblematic junk which, like a botched facelift, has messed up so much of what was old and authentic.' (pp. 52, 313, 44, 22)

More of the medieval past survives in Spain, says Nooteboom, than anywhere else in Europe, aided in no small part by what he calls the Spanish 'mania for preservation'. (p. 35) Much of his attention is devoted to little-known churches and monasteries, to which he is led by scholarly and antiquarian sources rather than by popular guidebooks.

Here the posture he adopts is that of a man of the late twentieth century wandering among survivals of a world that can still, to an extent, be read and understood, while simultaneously projecting himself in his imagination into a not too distant future when Christian traditions of symbolism will have died out entirely – in other words, into a future in which Christianity will have crossed the line separating religion from myth. The gaze he rests on the Spanish scene – on 'stooped, gnarled peasants with broad medieval faces of the kind that will have disappeared from the face of the earth in a hundred years' time' – is thus full of melancholy foreknowledge. (p. 141)

The two most considerable chapters of *Roads to Santiago* are on the painters Velázquez and Zurbarán (the chapter on Cervantes is, by comparison, pedestrian: from a writer as much in the Cervantean line as Nooteboom, this is surprising).

The language in which he discusses Velázquez is unabashedly idealistic. 'From the depths of each portrait', he writes of the paired paintings of Philip IV and his dwarf, 'radiates the spirit, the soul, that which tells you that Velázquez recognized the intrinsic qualities of each, because he knew their truth.' (p. 77)

This is a move worth noting on the part of a writer whose own fiction – witness *In the Dutch Mountains* – revolves so much around the sceptical interrogation of claims to truth, and who in *Roads to Santiago* itself shows himself at home in what he calls 'the church of Borges, Calvino, Barthes', a church that treats the visible world as a labyrinth of signs. (p. 196)

At issue here is the question not only of how we read paintings but of how, and in what terms, we value them. Nooteboom confronts the question in a passage as woolly in the original as in translation: 'Truth, reality, lies, illusion, the thing itself or its name, are all will-o'-the-wisps seeking to relegate the confusing tangos of meaning to the ballroom of postmodernism or of metafiction, just to be rid of them for a while, like a hornet that you chase away either because you are afraid or because you find it annoying.' (p. 75)

What Nooteboom seems to be saying here is that although pictures can be looked at as tricks with paint (just as poems can be looked at as tricks with words), and although much of his own art criticism consists of detecting the trick of the brush behind the illusion of truth, certain artworks seem to compel us to return to the language of the real and the true, a language that may be old and despised but remains the only one adequate to the task.

More original than the chapter on Velázquez is the one on Zurbarán (which has little to do with Nooteboom's travels in Spain, having been occasioned by the big Zurbarán exhibition in Paris in 1988). Here Nooteboom concentrates on Zurbarán's renderings of cloth and fabric, which to him constitute 'an essay on the relation between light, colour and material such as would not be seen again before Cézanne. [Zurbarán] was concerned with something that lay far beyond the borders of human psychology or the anecdotal, a passion of such intensity as to justify calling it mystical.' (p. 85)

V

Religious tourism – which includes not only genuine pilgrimage but visits to religious sites by travellers with no spiritual goal in view – makes up a large part of the tourism industry in Europe. Each year some one hundred million religiously motivated visits take place to the six thousand places of pilgrimage on the Continent.

In Spain the principal destination remains the shrine of the St James the Apostle (Santiago) in Galicia. As Nooteboom points out, it was the traffic of pilgrims heading for Santiago from countries to the north that kept the idea of a Christian Spain alive during the Middle Ages, making Santiago the spiritual source for the reconquest of Iberia. Santiago in the title of Nooteboom's book is the nominal end-point of his travels. However, as both he and road engineer Tiburón are aware, the detour – or, in the Dutch word preferred by Tiburón, the *omweg*, the roundabout way – usually yields more adventures than the high road; being a pilgrim is more important than arriving at the shrine.

Nooteboom's book is more about Spain and its detours than about Spaniards, who appear only as waiters, museum guides, and other background figures. It contains illuminating pages on Visigothic civilisation in Spain, on the Reconquista, on Philip II, but little on contemporary history, and in particular on the economic determinants of that history. Why, for instance, is Castile so empty? 'The young people no longer want to stay,' suggests an informant, and Nooteboom passes this on as a good enough explanation. (p. 314) Yet behind the depopulation of central Spain – depopulation so bad that some observers have called it desertification – lie deliberate policies set in train by Franco's technocratic ministers of the 1960s. These policies brought about a huge transfer of population from the agricultural heartland of Spain to the cities. Millions of people quit the countryside; hundreds of thousands of small farms disappeared; thousands of villages were abandoned by their inhabitants. It is thus that the melancholy spaces were achieved that so move Nooteboom's spirit.

Throughout, Nooteboom stresses the fragility of what we call Spain, the way in which an ethnically diverse nation has throughout its history kept collapsing into its 'singular, idiosyncratic fragments'. (p. 18) Like Gerald Brenan in *The Spanish Labyrinth*, he sees the bonds of nation as less important to ordinary Spaniards than those of town or village. In this respect Spain has kept the social culture of pre-modern Europe alive:

> Sometimes it is as if Spain is out to preserve the past for the rest of Europe; sounds, smells, occupations which have long since vanished elsewhere . . . human voices uttering long-drawn-out cries, exhortations reverberating among the houses, fruit and fish and flowers in carts and donkey baskets, all those things that have been rendered obsolete by social justice, technology and big business, leaving the world both richer and poorer. (p. 298)

To these eloquent words one can only add that – alas! – they are less true today than when they were written in 1985. Old Spain is growing harder and harder to find; and, tragically, the travel writings of Cees Nooteboom are contributing to its disappearance. Throngs of Dutch and German readers, heeding Nooteboom's advice, will already have skipped the Costa Brava in favour of the 'mysterious, secluded, unknown' provincial towns of the interior, where – he promises – 'the food is simple and the wine cheap'. (pp. 204, 45) *Roads to Santiago* will persuade thousands more from the United States and Britain to head for these less and less mysterious, secluded, or unknown destinations. Whether he likes it or not, Nooteboom is part of the tourism industry.

7   William Gass's Rilke

I

IN ONE OF the many polls that marked the year 1999, the Folio
Society, a fairly staid British book club, asked respondents to name
the five Poems of the Century. Four of the titles that came up were
– not surprisingly – by English-language poets: Yeats, Eliot,
Auden, Plath. The fifth was Rainer Maria Rilke's *Duino Elegies*.

The fact that Rilke, a foreigner and a considerable Anglophobe,
could make it on to the Folio Society's list with a poem as difficult
as the *Elegies* suggests that even in England the grand poetic manner
and the trappings of German metaphysics are not fatal drawbacks as
long as the poetry itself speaks with passion and urgency to the
great questions of human existence.

William Gass, whose achievements as fiction writer and
philosopher-aesthetician are already considerable, has now come
forth with *Reading Rilke*, a book that manages to be several things
at once: a Rilke anthology; an essay on the craft of translation; and
an account of Rilke's growth as a poet, into which an outline of
Rilke's life is woven.[1] It includes translations of all ten *Duino Elegies*
and of some forty other poems, among them well-known pieces
like 'The Panther', 'Torso of an Archaic Apollo', and 'Requiem for
a Friend', as well as of ten of the *Sonnets to Orpheus*. It concludes

with a handy bibliography of translations into English of this much-translated poet, from which we learn that Gass's *Duino Elegies* have been preceded by eighteen other full versions. A nineteenth, by Galway Kinnell and Hannah Liebmann, appeared while his book was in preparation, a twentieth, by Edward Snow, soon afterwards.[2]

II

Born in 1875 in Prague, third city of the Austro-Hungarian Empire, Rilke loathed Austria and all it stood for, and escaped as soon as he could. In part this was a reaction to the miserable childhood years he spent in military schools. But there were wider reasons too for his sense of alienation. Like much of the German-speaking minority in the imperial province of Bohemia, the Rilkes – who liked to think they were descended from an ancient noble family, the Rülkes, but were in fact not – lived on hostile terms with the native population; yet they were estranged from their cultural fatherland. Rilke himself was brought up to look down on Czechs.

His feelings toward Germany, where he spent intermittent spells as a young man, were no warmer. After his marriage in 1901 he moved to France and, aside from the war years, when he was trapped in the territories of the Central Powers by the fact of his nationality, never returned.

The attractions of a non-German identity were strong. After visits to Russia in 1899 and 1900 Rilke tried earnestly to learn and even to write in Russian. Back home he acted the Russophile for a while, affecting a Russian peasant blouse and pretending to speak only broken German. Then, after the First World War and his move to Switzerland, he tried to remake himself as a French writer, keeping up to date with developments in Paris, cultivating contacts with French writers, particularly Paul Valéry, courting the French literary press, even switching to French in his speech and correspondence. In his last years, between the completion of the *Duino Elegies* in 1922 and his death from leukemia in 1926, he wrote more in French than in German.

This shift of allegiance did not pass unnoticed in Germany. In the nationalistic German press he was attacked as a cultural renegade. His defence was that he was merely being 'a good European'. In fact Rilke had no developed idea of what it meant to be a European. He did not wish to be an Austrian or a German or, for that matter, a Czech in the postwar state of Czechoslovakia (though for a while he was forced to travel on a Czech passport). As a young man he liked to say he was *heimatlos*, homeless, without a country. He even asserted a right to decide his own origin. 'We are born, so to speak, provisionally, it doesn't matter where; it is only gradually that we compose, within ourselves, our true place of origin, so that we may be born there retrospectively.'[3] There is no reason to think that being a good European meant much more to Rilke than being *heimatlos*, except that it had a more positive spin to it.

In Rilke's Europe, England had no place. One of his affectations was to pretend to have no English. Even hearing the language spoken, he said, got on his nerves. The truth is that at the commercial college he briefly attended at the age of sixteen he took English as a subject (grade: Satisfactory). He even produced, with the aid of a friend, a translation into German of Elizabeth Barrett Browning's 'Sonnets from the Portuguese'. He had a gift for languages: besides his near perfect French, he had a good command of Russian, Danish and Italian, and more than a little Swedish and Spanish.

If England was not part of Europe, America was beyond the pale. America stood for the mechanisation of life and the flood of mass-produced objects that Rilke came to loathe. This emerges most explicitly in a 1925 letter to his Polish translator, one of many letters in which he expounded to correspondents the message of the *Duino Elegies* (Erich Heller called these letters 'the bad prose side of the good poetry').[4]

'We are the bees of the invisible,' writes Rilke. 'Tremulously we gather in the honey of the visible to store up in the great golden hive of the Invisible.' In the old days, the days before mass production,

> hardly a thing was not a vessel in which our grandparents found human sentiment inhering, or in which they did not, in their turn, store up an additional hoard of human senti-ment. But now empty, indifferent things come surging down upon us, across from America, mere semblances of things, mere dummies of life . . . A house in the American sense, an American apple or one of their vines, have nothing whatso-ever in common with the house, the fruit, the grapes, into which the hopes and pensiveness of our forefathers have been transfused . . . We are perhaps the last who have known such things. On us rests the responsibility to preserve not only their memory . . . but also their human and laral value ('laral' in the sense of household deities).[5]

Here Rilke has his seventh and ninth Elegies particularly in mind. I quote, in the Kinnell/Liebmann translation – Gass's version understresses Rilke's historical argument – a key passage.

> Nowhere, Beloved, will there be world but within. Our
> lives pass in transforming. Into less and less,
> the external dwindles. Where once an enduring house was,
> a contrived structure proposes itself, at odds with everything,

completely conceptual, as if it still stood in the brain.
The modern age builds enormous reservoirs of power,
    formless
as the tensing stress it extracts from everything.
It doesn't know temples any more. These heart's
    squanderings
we hoard up more secretly. Yes, where a thing survives,
something once venerated, served, knelt before —,
it bears itself, unchanged, into the unseen. (pp. 119–21)

As a critique of the capitalist-industrial dynamic and the mental habits that go with it, this is, by the time of the 1920s, neither novel nor particularly interesting. It comes out of the reading of Carlyle, Nietzsche, Ruskin, Pater and Jacob Burckhardt that Rilke did when, as a young man, he was most deeply under the influence of Lou Andreas-Salomé; it is of a piece with his youthful enthusiasms for Russia as the home of true spirituality and for *quattrocento* Florence. As a programme for preserving old Europe from the simulacra (the 'dummies of life') that come surging in from America, it offers nothing practical. It is only when the Rilkean project of rescuing the world by the act of absorbing and transforming it (*Verwandlung* or, in Gass's coinage, 'withinwarding') is dramatised in the speaking voice that it begins to come alive. Here is Elegy 9, whose urgency Gass's translation captures well:

Are we, perhaps, here just to utter: house,
bridge, fountain, gate, jug, fruit tree, window –
at most: column, tower . . . but to utter them, remember,
to speak in a way which the named never dreamed
they could be? . . .
These things whose life
Is a constant leaving, they know when you praise them.

Transient, they trust us, the most transient, to come
to their rescue; they wish us to alter them utterly,
within our invisible hearts, into – so endlessly – us!
Whoever we may finally be.

You earthly things – is this not what you want,
to arise invisible in us? Is not your dream
to be one day invisible? Earth! – things! – invisible!
What, if not this deep translation, is your ardent aim?
Earth, my loved one, I will. (Gass, pp. 214–15)

Through a sacred or sacramental form of speech, the elemental
things that share our earthly journey – house, bridge – cease to be
distinguishable from their names, are brought into the heart,
transformed (translated) into ourselves and given a transient
salvation. (The transience of that promised salvation is what turns
even this ecstatic poem into an elegy.)

III

As biographer, Gass treats his subject with a breeziness of style that
aims at the epigrammatic and continually runs the risk of over-
simplification. Gass has a gift for the snappy phrase; his insights into
Rilke are often mordantly accurate; but a side effect is to convey
an attitude toward Rilke that is perhaps unintended: that, compared with William Gass, Rilke was a bit of a fool, a bit of a booby.

'With a romantic naiveté for which we may feel some nostalgia
now,' Gass writes,

Rilke struggled his entire life to be a poet – not a pure poet,
but purely a poet – because he felt, against good advice and
much experience to the contrary, that poetry could only be

written by one who was already a poet: and a poet was above
ordinary life . . .; the true poet dwelt in a realm devoted
entirely to the spirit (yes, Rilke had 'realms' in which he
'dwelt'); the true poet was always 'on the job'; the true poet
never hankered for a flagon of wine or a leg of mutton or a
leg of lady either (women were 'the Muse', to be courted
through the post); nor did the true poet mop floors or dandle
babies or masturbate or follow the horses or use the john; the
true poet was an agent of transfiguration whose sole function
was the almost magical movement of matter into mind. (pp.
23–4)

The rhetorical effect of a paragraph like this is so skilfully
achieved, the barbs so artfully chosen, that to protest against its
unfairness, its exaggerations and half-truths, is futile. Gass has little
respect for Rilke the daimon-driven Poet, whom he finds juvenile,
pretentious and hypocritically self-serving. He is impatient with the
Romantic cult of genius to which Rilke so unquestioningly
subscribed. Rilke's snobbery, his dandyism ('Mr Fastidious,' Gass
calls him), and what one can only call a certain oiliness of manner,
are further black marks against him. (p. 142)

There have been artists before Rilke who neglected their
families, courted wealthy patrons, seduced and abandoned women.
What makes Rilke so vulnerable to attack is that he not only
adhered to a doctrine that excuses all sins except those against Art,
but took this doctrine seriously. If there is one thing above all about
Rilke that invites Gass the satirist's ridicule, it is his humourlessness,
his lack of a saving sense of irony.

Yet even if we share Gass's feelings, uncomfortable questions
remain. How was it possible for such a poseur to write poetry that
still – clearly – touches us and moves us? The *Duino Elegies* were,
for the most part, written in two brief creative bursts, in 1912 and

1922. 'A nameless storm, a hurricane in the spirit,' Rilke called the second spell.[6] Are the *Elegies* – which, if we include the story or myth of their composition, are surely the great poem of our age about being called as a poet – imaginable in the absence of the notion of an artistic destiny? Could the vatic poetry of the *Elegies* have come into existence without the theory and (imperfect) practice of the vatic life that preceded them?

Gass treats Rilke's recurrent pattern of wooing women, arousing their interest, then withdrawing, as evidence of timorousness, a quest for a mother rather than a lover, a failure to grow up. It was a syndrome Rilke was thoroughly aware of. In the years (roughly 1902–10) when he was most deeply under the influence first of Rodin (for whom he worked as secretary-apprentice), then of Cézanne, he justified his refusal of commitments as a renunciation demanded by his art: emptying himself, breaking all ties, even ties of love, was a necessary purification before he could see the world with fresh eyes. Later he would look back with nostalgia on the year of acute isolation, 1907, during which he composed his *New Poems*. 'I expected nothing and nobody and the whole world streamed towards me as an ever greater task which I answered clearly and surely.' He quoted Beethoven: 'I have no friend. I must live by myself alone. But I am aware that in my art God is closer to me than to all others.'[7]

In his poetry he developed a theory of essential gestures, archetypal movements of the body–soul, among which the gesture of withdrawal had a central place and a complex meaning, simultaneously blessing and denying. 'There is nothing I understand better in the life of the gods than the moment when they withdraw themselves,' he wrote in a letter; he described himself as 'a place where giving and taking back have often been almost one and the same thing'.[8]

The withdrawal of the gods from our modern world is one of

the great themes of Hölderlin, whom Rilke began to read seriously in 1915 and whose example made the later *Duino Elegies* possible. Withdrawal in all its aspects is thus close to the heart of Rilke as man and poet. We are well advised not to psychologise it too hastily, treating it as a mere manifestation of some deeper cause.

In a passage important enough to quote in full, Gass effectively responds to the concerns I raise, and to the overriding question of what he actually thinks of Rilke when he is not occupied in making jibes at his expense. Here Gass drops the satirical manner, trying to judge Rilke evenhandedly, according full weight to the mystery of the relation between Rilke the poet and Rilke the man, namely, that out of levels of insecurity and coldness of heart which, in anyone else, might have spelled a stunted emotional life, there could grow a body of work that included, if not great love poetry, great poetry about love.

> He hid inside The Poet he eventually became, both secure there and scared, empty and fulfilled; the inspired author of the *Duino Elegies*, sensitive, insightful, gifted nearly beyond compare; a man with many devoted and distant friends, many extraordinary though frequently fatuous enthusiasms, but still a lonely unloving homeless boy as well . . . enjoying a self-pity there were rarely buckets enough to contain; yet with a persistence in the pursuit of his goals, a courage, which overcame weakness and worry and made them into poems . . . no . . . into lyrics that love, however pure or passionate or sacrificial, could never have achieved by itself . . . lines only frailty, terror, emotional duplicity even, could accomplish – the consequence of an honesty bitter about the weaknesses from which it took its strength. (pp. 31–2)

Aside from the cliché of the lonely boy, this is well and generously said, facing up to the issues that the passage quoted earlier found it convenient to evade, and at the end – 'an honesty bitter about the weaknesses from which it took its strength' – getting very nearly to the heart of the Rilkean labyrinth.

IV

One of the secondary aims of *Reading Rilke* is to rescue some of the women who crossed Rilke's path from going down in history as just that – women in a famous man's life, minor characters. Lou Salomé does not really need Gass's intercession, since her stature as an intellectual in her own right is now widely recognised. But the excursus on the painter Paula Modersohn Becker (1876–1907) with which Gass prefaces his translation of 'Requiem for a Friend', the poem Rilke wrote after Becker's death, is welcome.

Paula Becker, whom Rilke had met at the artists' colony of Worpswede in 1900, died in the aftermath of childbirth. Gass suggests that the 'Requiem' originates in feelings of guilt in Rilke, partly for failing to support Becker in her effort to strike out and make a life for herself as an artist, partly because his own attitudes to women, the family, and marriage (he was married to her one-time close friend Clara Westhoff) would not bear close scrutiny, partly for what women in general have to suffer at the hands of men.

Doubtless Gass is right about Rilke. Doubtless, when put to the test, Rilke and Becker's artist husband Otto Modersohn were not as enlightened, as far ahead of the times, as they pretended to be. But it is a pity that the case for Becker has to be made at the expense of Rilke (who, when all is said and done, played no great part in her life), and has to depend on such wild generalisations as the following:

Most women in Rilke's day, unless they were barren or rich, were married off early and sent into a life of loveless broodmaring that led, after an interval that demonstrated their decency, to the bearing, the nursing, the raising, and the burying of children – six, eight, ten – losing their health and figure in the bargain, as well as any chance of achievement. (p. 118)

At a deeper level, Gass asks why Rilke was so often moved to write by the death of young women (the creative burst in 1922 that brought forth the later *Duino Elegies* was sparked by the reading of the diary of a girl who had died at the age of nineteen). He suggests that Rilke was working out guilt over the death of the sister who died before he was born: 'A girl had to die to make room in the world for him.' (p. 107) This piece of speculation is of less interest than what Rilke himself has to say on the subject of his dead sister: that he had a sense of her alive within him. Reaching the sister within him became part of his maturation, an attempt to face and accept his own narcissism and turn it into a positive force.

V

At the centre of Gass's book is a chapter devoted to close scrutiny of the various English versions of the *Elegies* and the *Sonnets to Orpheus*. Here his aim is less to produce a ranking of Rilke's translators than to explain and illustrate the rationale behind his own versions. His commentary on the rival translations is acute yet fair. However, given that his rivals must be mute while he alone gets to state his case, the outcome is predictable. Gass, 'a jackal who comes along after the kill', (p. 76) as he calls himself, wins every time, though three of his rivals get respectful mention: J.B. Leishman, whose translations, going back to the 1930s, have proved surprisingly durable, André Poulin Jr., and Stephen Mitchell.[9]

Sensibly, Gass treats literary translation as a craft rather than an art, with nothing so grand as a general theory behind it. To translate a poem, says Gass, is to resign oneself to the loss of a certain quantum of meaning. The question, with each poem, is what must be held on to at all costs, what may be allowed to go. Using a short poem by Hölderlin as a specimen, Gass, careful as a watchmaker, takes apart versions by two of the finest translators of German poetry today, Christopher Middleton and Michael Hamburger, approving or questioning each word-choice, weighing the movement of each line. Being no coward, he offers a competing version of his own, which, though very good, is not, to my ear, and for all Gass's persuasiveness, better than Hamburger's.

What the translator of Hölderlin is trying to achieve, Gass suggests, is 'the poem Hölderlin would have written had he been English'. (p. 52) As the formulation of an ideal, this simply will not do. A human language is not a neutral code like a computer language. To 'be English' is to be embedded in the English language and the English language's way of seeing the world. If Hölderlin had 'been English' in any sense, he could not but have written a different poem. What Middleton and Hamburger and Gass himself give us, in their various ways, is something less ambitious than the poem a hypothetical English Hölderlin might have written: three poems in English based on a common source, poems as good as their authors can make them but – to a reader with access to both German and English – not, finally, as rich as Hölderlin's.

To be able to translate a literary text, says Gass, it is not enough just to know the source language, however well; it is not even enough to be able to transpose the text sentence by sentence. You have to understand it. 'Many translators do not bother to understand their texts. That would interfere with their own creativity

and with their perception of what the poet ought to have said . . .
They would rather be original than right.' (p. 69)

Gass's point is less obvious, and more contentious, than might at
first sight appear. *Ein jeder Engel ist schrecklich*, writes Rilke at the
beginning of Elegy 1: every angel is terrible. Am I failing as a
translator if, despite poring over the Elegies, over Rilke's numerous
explanations, over the best that literary criticism has to offer, I am
still not sure what an angel – one of Rilke's angels – looks like? Is
it not good enough for the translator simply to call *ein Engel* an
angel and be done with it?

Yes and no. *Ein Engel* is an angel is *ein Engel*, but until I know
what sort of angel Rilke has in mind I am not sure what *schrecklich*
means: terrible (Leishman) or terrifying (Poulin, Mitchell) or
awesome (Gass).

So again Gass's point needs refining. The translator does not first
need to understand the text before he translates it. Rather, translating the text becomes part of the process of finding – and making
– its meaning; translating turns out to be only a more intense and
more demanding form of what we do whenever we read.

How well does the translator need to know the source language?
One extreme is represented by Ezra Pound. Pound's knowledge of
written Chinese was amateurish. In translating classic Chinese
poetry he used cribs, and for the rest guessed, falling back on the
highly questionable theory that Chinese characters are stylised
pictographs which any trained eye can 'read'. The other extreme is
represented by Vladimir Nabokov, who demanded that the
translator be fully at home in the source language in all its nuances
and ephemeral connotations.

Gass's position is somewhere in the middle. A native command
of the source language, he says, is less important than a 'native-like'
command of the language into which one is translating (in translators' jargon, the target language). (p. 70) He might have added that

a non-native translator who does not have native informants to call on – in the case of poetry, sensitive, well-read informants – is in a parlous position. Gass himself worked closely with Heide Ziegler of the University of Stuttgart, whose help he handsomely acknowledges though he does not list her as co-translator.

Finally, in setting out the rules of his craft, Gass warns against 'construing' the poem, by which he seems to mean stitching into the translation, at difficult points, an explanation of what you think it means. 'Render the poem as the poet wrote it and let the poet's poem explain itself,' he writes. (p. 84)

Once more the common-sensical formulation evades a substantial question: what might 'the poet's poem' be, as distinct from my understanding of the poem? Gass's own practice involves a fair amount of construal, as we see in his rendering of Elegy 8. The eighth Elegy is one of the most compact of the sequence. Its subject is the sundering of man from the natural world; its project, a paradoxical one, is to find words that will take us back to before words and allow us to glimpse the world as seen by creatures who do not have words, or, if that glimpse is barred to us, then to allow us the sad experience of standing at the rim of an unknowable mode of being. Although one of the more abstract of the Elegies, it is accessible on its own terms, not least because such earlier poems of Rilke's as 'The Panther' have prepared us for it.

Gass the professor of philosophy is in his element in this Elegy. He understands what Rilke is up to, understands so well that more than once he succumbs to the temptation to clarify – to us his readers, but in a sense to Rilke as well – thoughts that Rilke is still struggling to articulate.

For instance, Rilke writes (I transpose into English word for word): 'What *is* out there, we know it from the animal's face alone; for even the young child we turn around and compel to look back, seeing form/formation [*Gestaltung*], not the open [*das Offne*], that in animal vision is so deep.'

Rilke's main point – that for an unmediated experience of the world we have to fall back on empathy with animals – is clear enough, but the details are less easy to decode. (In retrospect, Rilke would admit that one reason why the *Elegies* were so difficult to understand was that in places he had, so to speak, written down the total without revealing what was being added up.) Gass translates the lines as follows:

> What *is* outside, we read solely from the animal's gaze,
> for we compel even the young child to turn and look back at
> preconceived things,
> never to know the acceptance so deeply set inside
> the animal's face. (p. 210)

Though the English here is clearer than the German, Gass's decision to interpret or construe the problematic terms *Gestaltung* (as 'preconceived things') and *das Offne* (as 'acceptance'), rather than giving their closest semantic equivalents, even at the risk of producing a version as opaque as the original, is open to question. Gass's English breathes an assurance – the assurance of the speaker who knows his subject – not present in the German, with its general effect of a speaker pushing at the limits of language, striving to find his own meaning. Furthermore, *offen* (open) and *öffnen* (to open) are key words in Rilke, revisited again and again, each time with a different nuance. By hiding Rilke's *das Offne* behind the unrelated word 'acceptance', Gass is false to a characteristic movement of Rilke's poetic thinking.

At a philosophical level, Elegy 8 is concerned with relations between thought and language and with the problem of other minds. If we wanted to find out something about these topics in general, Gass's Elegy 8 would probably be a better guide than Rilke's hesitating effort. What we lose, as Gass tightens up Rilke's terminology and oils the joints of his syntax, is the drama of a poet at the height of his powers striving to find words for intuitions at the limit of his grasp.

VI

Gass justly denies Rilke the status of a philosophical poet: what present themselves as ideas in Rilke, he says, are for the most part emotions, moods, attitudes. The chapter in which he unpicks Rilke's characteristic paradoxes constitutes the best brief exposition of Rilke's thought I know of.

He gets the quality of Rilke's verse exactly right: the typical poem is, as he says, 'obdurate, complex, and compacted . . . made of plucked tough sounds, yet as rapid and light and fragile as fountain water'. (p. 32) On the wide appeal of the *Duino Elegies* he is equally illuminating: 'These poems are the most oral I know . . . They must be spoken – not merely by but for yourself, as if you were the one who wondered whether you had anyone to call to.' (p. 101)

As for his treatment of Rilke the man, the problem here is not that Gass is uncharitably inclined toward his subject but that he is out of sympathy with the milieu that formed him. *Reading Rilke* is an ambitious book, but one of the things it does not attempt is to situate Rilke historically. We could do with more on Rilke and Nietzsche (at whom Gass takes a few disparaging swipes), and on the cult of the lonely genius in late Romantic times. It would also help to learn more about the back-to-nature movement that was so strong in German-speaking countries at the turn of the century, divorced from which Rilke's nude sunbathing, vegetarianism, etc., look like mere personal fads.

Gass's Rilke translations will not satisfy readers who prefer to stay as close to the original as possible, even if at the risk of finding themselves in a no man's land between German and English. Nor, on the other hand, will they please readers who want to be swept away by grand verbal music. What Gass provides are versions which, if not inspired verse-making in their own right, reflect a lucid appreciation of the original based on years of close reading, realised with verbal resourcefulness of the highest order.

8 Translating Kafka

I

IN 1921 THE Scottish poet Edwin Muir and his wife Willa gave up their jobs in London and went to live on the Continent. The dollar was strong; they hoped to make ends meet by reviewing books for the American periodical *The Freeman*.

After a nine-month spell in Prague, the Muirs moved to Dresden and began to learn German. Willa did some school-teaching while Edwin stayed at home reading the latest German-language writers. When hyperinflation struck Germany, they moved to Austria, then to Italy, then back to England. There they put their newly acquired German to use and became professional translators. For the next fifteen years, until the outbreak of war, they were, in Edwin's words, 'a sort of translation factory'. Together they translated over thirty books; Willa did a further half-dozen by herself. 'Too much of our lives was wasted . . . in turning German into English,' wrote Edwin afterwards, ruefully.[1]

With one of their first projects, a translation of Lion Feuchtwanger's *Jud Süss*, they struck it lucky: the book became a bestseller and their London publisher asked what other writers they could recommend. Edwin had been reading Franz Kafka's posthumously published *Das Schloss*. 'It is a purely metaphysical and mystical dramatic novel . . . quite unique,' he wrote in a letter.[2] His and Willa's translation was published in 1930. Despite selling only 500 copies, it was followed by further Kafka translations: *The Great Wall of China* (1933), a collection of shorter pieces; *The Trial* (1937); *America* (1938); and, after the war years, *In the Penal Colony* (1948). These translations, despite their many defects, have dominated the English-language market since then.

Edwin Muir saw his task as not only translating Kafka but also guiding English readers through these new and difficult texts. The Muir translations therefore came armed with forewords in which Edwin, relying heavily on Kafka's friend and editor Max Brod, explained what Kafka was all about. These forewords proved highly influential. They proposed Kafka as 'a religious genius . . . in an age of skepticism', a writer of 'religious allegory' preoccupied with the incommensurability of the human and the divine.[3]

Inevitably the conception of Kafka as a religious writer influenced the choices the Muirs made as they translated his words. The English versions they produced conformed to the interpretation supplied in the forewords. So it is not surprising that Kafka's first English-speaking readers accepted without demurral the Muirs' version of him. Their interpretation, embedded in their translations – particularly of *The Castle* and *The Trial* – has long been a source of concern to Kafka scholars. In the United States, in particular, the Muirs' 1930 translation of *The Castle*, implicitly packaged with the Muirs' 1930 reading and reprinted time and again, has seemed to hold an unfair monopoly. (The situation has not been as bad in Britain, where a new translation of *The Trial* appeared in 1977 and of *The Castle* in 1997.)

There are other reasons as well why the Muir translation and the Muir monopoly have assumed a faintly scandalous air. The 1930 translation was based on the 1926 text given to the world by Brod, and this text was heavily edited. Brod was the one who made decisions about which parts of Kafka's fragmentary manuscript should go into the printed text and which not, and about where the chapter divisions should fall. Brod also augmented Kafka's light, even minimal punctuation. Further errors were introduced by the printers. Thus the Muirs, through no fault of their own, were working from an original that was, by scholarly standards, unacceptable.

II

The main challenge facing a translator of Kafka, in the eyes of the Muirs, was to reconcile fidelity to Kafka's word order – which was, of course, subject to the rules of German grammar – with the ideal of a natural-sounding, idiomatic English. To Edwin Muir, Kafka's word order was 'naked and infallible . . . Only in that order could he have said what he had to say . . . Our main problem was to write an English prose as natural in the English way as [Kafka's] was in his own way.'[4]

Naturalness is a concept not easily pinned down, but to Edwin Muir it appears to have included freshness of phrasing and lexical variousness. Thus, paradoxically, the Muirs are often more vivid than Kafka, whose German tends to be restrained, even neutral, and who is not afraid to repeat key words again and again.

Furthermore, although the Muirs' mastery of German – particularly Willa's – was astonishing, given the fact that they were more or less self-taught, and although Edwin in particular had read widely in contemporary German and Austrian writing, neither had a systematic grounding in German literature, so their ability to pick up literary references was rather haphazard. Finally, there were areas of German or Austrian life, each with its own specialised vocabulary, that they knew only sketchily.

One of these – unfortunately for them as translators of Kafka –

was the law and legal bureaucracy. I give one instance. In *The Trial* Josef K. tells the men arresting him that he wants to telephone *Staatsanwalt Hasterer*. The Muirs translate this as 'advocate Hasterer'.[5] Readers brought up in the Anglo-American legal system will assume that K. is asking to call his lawyer. In fact K. is trying a bluff, threatening to call a friend in the prosecutor's office.

In *The Castle* in particular, the Muir translation embodies scores, perhaps hundreds of errors of detail which, while they may not be important individually, have a cumulative effect, putting readers on an insecure footing, driving them back to check the original at every crux of interpretation.

I cite instances to give an idea of the range of the Muirs' inadequacies.

Reading Kafka, Edwin Muir observes, is much like reading 'a travel book which recounts minutely the customs, dresses and utensils of some newly discovered tribe.'[6] But when it comes to the everyday material culture of Central Europe, the Muirs are uncertain guides. The *Strohsack* on which K. beds down in the village inn, for instance, is not a bag of straw (as they say) but a palliasse, a straw mattress. (Muir translation, pp. 9, 120)

The curious telephone system of the Castle, and the related telephone etiquette, also seem to defeat the Muirs. To them, *telephonieren* (to telephone) is the ringing sound a telephone makes. When the Castle officials disconnect the ringing mechanisms on their receivers, the Muirs say they are 'leav[ing] their receivers off'; and when they reconnect them, the Muirs say they are 'hang[ing] the receivers on'. (Muir, pp. 73–4)

If the legal system of the ex-Austrian Empire is strange to them, the practices of Kafka's fictional Castle officials are even stranger. Without expanding words into phrases or adding footnotes, it is hard to explain to the English-speaking reader what is meant by the claim that the only road to Herr Klamm of the Castle leads through the *Protokolle* of his secretary, or quite what the *Briefschaften* are that Castle messengers ceaselessly carry back and forth. Nevertheless, the Muirs are too often content with indicating only approximately what is meant, for instance by replacing a German word with its English cognate (*Protokolle* by 'protocols') or with a term of vaguely similar denotation (*Briefschaften* by 'commissions') and hoping that enough of the meaning comes across. In this respect the Muirs' standards are simply too rough to qualify them as interpreters of *The Castle*, which is partly, though not wholly, a fantasy of bureaucracy run wild. (Muir, pp. 110, 171)

Sometimes the Muirs' guesses at Kafka's meaning are mere stabs in the dark. Kafka writes, for instance, of officials who revel in their despotic power over petitioners, 'against their own will [loving] the scent of wild game like that'. Though he was the least ideological of writers, Kafka had an acute feel for the obscene intimacies of power. Hinted at in his striking metaphor is a bestial, predatory appetite in the officials, sometimes submerged, sometimes baring itself. The Muirs, missing the point, write that the officials 'in spite of themselves, are attracted by those outlaws'. (Muir, p. 209)

When Kafka is obscure enough to defeat any but an inspired reader (what is a clinging street, *eine festhaltende Strasse?*), the Muirs' tactic is to take a guess at what Kafka might have intended, rather than – the last honourable recourse of the baffled translator – to fall back on word-by-word transposition. Their guesses are not always convincing – here 'the obsession of the street'. (Muir, p. 17)

And sometimes the Muirs simply fail to see what is before them. 'Her blank loveless gaze,' writes Kafka. 'Her cold hard eye,' write the Muirs, missing the ambiguity of 'loveless' [*lieblos*]. (Muir, p. 194)

At a broader level, there are occasions when the Muirs, whether consciously or not, sacrifice fidelity to Kafka's text to a vision – their own vision – of the whole. To the Muirs, taking a hint from

Brod, Surveyor K. is a sympathetic pilgrim figure. So when K. claims at one point to have left a wife and child at home, yet at a later point wants to marry the waitress Frieda, the Muirs save their embarrassment by eliding the wife and child.

Finally, however 'natural' the Muirs' English may have been in its day, it is now dated – as we might expect, given that it is nearly seventy years old. Unless readers make conscious allowance for this, they will not know how to interpret moments when the Muirs' language seems to take a dip into the past: 'stoutly-built' rather than powerful; 'guttersnipe' rather than tramp; 'remiss in industry' rather than lacking diligence. (Muir, pp. 172, 10, 11)

But has Kafka himself used outdated forms, the reader might ask, and might the Muirs be signalling this in their word choice? The answer is, in each case, no. Although there are levels of formality in the language of *The Castle*, there is no historical dimension built into it – no old-fashioned usages or up-to-the-minute idioms that are intended to bear a signifying function.

III

Kafka began writing *The Castle* in early 1922 at a mountain resort where he had been sent for a rest cure (tuberculosis had been diagnosed in 1917). The cure did little good, and he returned to Prague. In July he took early retirement from the insurance company for which he worked. His condition deteriorated further and he abandoned *The Castle*. In all he had spent seven months on it, not completing even a first draft.

After Kafka's death in 1924, Max Brod edited and published the three novel fragments his friend had left behind. Alarmed by what he considered to be crass misinterpretations of the first of the three to appear, *The Trial*, Brod accompanied *The Castle* with what Stephen Dowden, in a survey of the reception of *The Castle*, pithily calls 'a preemptive hermeneutic strike on behalf of his own views' in the form of an afterword.[7] This afterword deeply influenced the Muirs' reading of the novel, and in due course their translation of it.

The 1926 edition was the one from which the Muirs worked. In subsequent editions (1935, 1946, 1951) Brod brought forth from his manuscript stock further episodes and fragments, as well as variants and deleted passages. These additions to the text have for some time been available in English, appended to the Muir translation in faithful versions by Eithne Wilkins and Ernst Kaiser, best known as translators of Robert Musil.

For his project of publishing the Kafka manuscripts posthumously, Brod marshalled a public declaration of support by respected intellectuals like Thomas Mann, Martin Buber and Hermann Hesse, who thereby seemed to lend their weight to the readings of Kafka that accompanied the successive volumes. Thus the reading of *The Castle* set out in Brod's 1926 afterword came to dominate the reception of Kafka in the German-speaking world well into the 1950s; in large part through the agency of Edwin Muir, a version of the same reading held sway in the English-speaking world.

In Brod's reading, K., the new Faust, is driven no longer by a desire for ultimate knowledge but by a need for the most basic prerequisites of life – a secure home and job, acceptance into a community. To the later Kafka, says Brod, these simple goals had come to have a religious meaning. The minimal grace that K. seeks from the Castle is permission to settle down, to cease to be an outsider.

One can see why such a reading should have occurred to Brod, knowing as he did Kafka's sense of himself as a lifelong outsider, knowing of Kafka's repeated attempts to get married, undermined each time by an incapacity to imagine himself in the role of husband and father. One can see too why Brod's reading should have resonated with the public mood in postwar Germany and Austria, where the economy was stagnant, where neither Church nor State could give direction to life, and where widespread hopelessness and a sense that humankind had lost its way prevailed.

Brod's optimistic reading of *The Castle* (influenced no doubt by his own Zionism) makes of Kafka – whom Brod revered, yet utterly failed to understand – a rather simple and conservative thinker who responded to the challenges of modern life with a call for a return to old verities. It is thus no idle undertaking to rescue Kafka from Brod's version of him, or at least to complicate and deepen Brod's version enough to situate his Kafka within the history of his times. If, in the English-speaking world, this means scraping off from the Muirs' version of *The Castle* those accretions that belong only to Brod and Brod's vision, or even translating *The Castle* anew, as Mark Harman has now done, this is a task richly worth while.[8]

Indeed, Edwin Muir himself began to have doubts about a religious-allegorical reading of *The Castle* after he had met and spoken to Dora Dymant, Kafka's last companion.[9] Were it not for the fact that Kafka complicates so thoroughly the boundaries between the clownish and the evil, one might call *The Castle* not a religious but a comic novel. The shadow cast by the Castle may be dreadful, but K., the hero of the tale, caught in a labyrinth of bureaucratic hocus-pocus, has more pressing concerns than coping with dread, as he tries busily, sometimes frantically, to get his papers in order and keep the peace among the many women in his life.

IV

The Brod who delivered *The Castle* to the world was, of course, no ordinary editor. His friendship with Kafka was close and deep, dating back to their student years together. There is no reason to doubt his claim to have been told Kafka's plans, such as they were, for the conclusion of *The Castle*, namely, that on his deathbed K. would receive a judgement from the Castle rejecting his petition to settle in the village, yet permitting him to live and work there.

So thoroughly has Brod been taken to task as the jealous impresario of the Kafka reputation and the founder of the dreary science of Kafkology (the term is Milan Kundera's),[10] that it is as well to remind ourselves that Brod saved Kafka's manuscripts from destruction not once but twice: the first time by disobeying Kafka's instructions that they be burned 'unread and to the last page' after his death, the second time in 1939, when Prague was occupied by Hitler's forces and he fled to Tel Aviv bearing the papers with him.[11] In 1956, when war threatened in the Middle East, Brod had the bulk of his collection conveyed to Switzerland. From there it travelled to the Bodleian Library in Oxford, where the eminent Germanist Malcolm Pasley re-edited *The Castle* from scratch, producing in 1982 the two-volume critical edition on which Harman's new translation is based.

Pasley's description of the manuscript, included as an afterword to Harman's translation, gives us a useful glimpse into the unique problems faced by the translator – or retranslator – of *The Castle*.

Kafka seems to have planned to write the entire novel (which in its present unfinished state runs to some 100,000 words) in the form of a tightly knit, temporally consecutive draft which would require neither substantial additions and deletions nor restructuring. The novel was not written in chapters, though some chapter divisions emerged as the text grew. Nor, after the first third of the book, did Kafka employ much paragraphing. His punctuation overall is extremely light, serving in the main to mark rhythm and cadence. Commas, rather than full stops, separate sentences.

Kafka's language is generally clear, specific and neutral; in the novels – *The Castle* in particular – it can seem monotonous if one is not caught up by the forward drive of the sentences, by their urgent but rather abstract energy, for which Kleist's prose provided Kafka with a model. 'Anyone who had the privilege of hearing [Kafka] read his own prose to a small circle, with a rhythmic sweep, a dramatic fire, a spontaneity such as no actor ever achieves, got an immediate impression of the delight in creation and the passion that informed his work,' recalled Brod.[12]

In its spareness and apparent matter-of-factness, Kafka's language has been claimed to be typical of the German of Prague, and particularly of the German of assimilated middle-class Jews. But whether this makes Kafka a Prague German writer is questionable. It is more likely that his language was influenced by the precision of good legal prose, the medium in which he worked day by day. Nevertheless, the manuscript of *The Castle* exhibits a number of Prague German usages. Though Kafka did not change these to standard German in the course of his revisions, he clearly did not intend them to stand in the text as dialect markers, and (correctly, to my mind) neither the Muirs nor Harman translate them into non-standard English. Nor, after the opening chapters of the book, does Kafka maintain any socially realistic distinction between levels of language: the people of the village, as much as the Castle officials, seem able to produce exegetical monologues on the most trivial of questions at the drop of a hat.

Thus the translator, once a variety of English has been settled on that does justice to Kafka's variety of German, does not often have to change gear. Indeed, the temptation to be resisted is to introduce a linguistic variousness that is absent in the original.

This necessary rigour raises certain problems. In the second half of *The Castle* in particular, Kafka slips on occasion into some very tired-sounding prose. Here is an extract from the reported narration of young Hans Brunswick. I give it in Harman's translation, which reproduces Kafka's syntax and gives an indication of how light Kafka's punctuation is.

> Father . . . had actually wanted to go and see K. in order to punish him . . . only Mother had dissuaded him. But above all Mother herself generally didn't want to speak to anyone and her question about K. was no exception to that rule, on the contrary, in mentioning him she could have said that she wished to see him, but she had not done so, and had thus made her intentions plain. (p. 145)

In producing English sentences as slack as Kafka's own, Harman has in principle made the right decision ('I have tried to keep [it] as murky in English as it is in German,' he observes of a comparable passage). ('Preface', p. xv) Nevertheless, it is only Kafka's classic status that gives grounds for such a decision: translating a more run-of-the-mill writer, one would be eminently justified in lightly and silently fixing up the original.

We find inadequacy of a different kind in passages in *The Castle*, where Kafka, groping to record moments of transcendental insight, visibly reaches the limits of expression. Passages such as these provide the harshest test of the translator, demanding not only an ability to follow the utmost nuances of phrasing but, beyond that, an intuitive sense of what the resistances are against which the language is pressing. A case in point is the description, only a sentence long, of the first love-making of K. and Frieda. It is a sentence to which Milan Kundera has already given microscopic attention, using it to test Kafka's French translators, who by his standards fail badly.[13] How does Harman fare? He writes:

> Hours passed there, hours breathing together with a single heartbeat, hours in which K. constantly felt he was lost or had

wandered farther into foreign lands than any human being before him, so foreign that even the air hadn't a single component of the air in his homeland and where one would inevitably suffocate from the foreignness but where the meaningless enticements were such that one had no alternative but to go on and get even more lost. (p. 41)

In the metaphor at the heart of this passage, the poles are *die Fremde* and *die Heimat*, foreign country and home country. To capture in single English synonyms all the connotations of these rich words is a hopeless task: *fremd* has all the associations of English 'strange', yet Kafka's phrase *in der Fremde* is also a perfectly normal expression meaning 'abroad'. In his syntax, Kafka seems intent on making the strange or foreign experience into which K. is drawn with Frieda seem ever stranger and more threatening as the sentence proceeds: 'K. constantly had the feeling he had got lost or was (had gone) further in(to) *die Fremde* than anyone before him, a *Fremde* in which even the air had no component of the air of home [*Heimatluft*, a neologism], in which (in the air? in the *Fremde*?) one must [inevitably] suffocate of *Fremdheit*, and (yet) in (in the midst of?) whose crazy enticements one could do nothing but go further, get further lost.'

In his rendering, Harman copes well with Kafka's strategy of overlaying K., as a wanderer coming from the comforts of *Heimat* into the unsettlingly *fremd* domain of the Castle, with K. wandering into disturbing spiritual territory in the sudden act of sex with Frieda; but rather less well in conveying the impression of a man straining to get a grasp on *fremd* experience in a sentence faltering in its sense of linear direction and on the point of losing its way.

As for the Muirs, they miss the boat entirely, partly because they overtranslate ('K. constantly had the feeling' becomes 'K. was haunted by the feeling'); partly because they evade difficulties –

Kafka's cryptic *unsinnigen Verlockungen*, which Harman translates rather woodenly as 'meaningless enticements', becomes in their version simply 'enchantments'; but mainly because the English sentence they produce is too musically balanced.

In general, in all the large-scale decisions he has had to make – whether or not to remain faithful to the original in its moments of weakness, whether or not to follow Kafka's punctuation and Pasley's chapter divisions, what variety of English to aim for – Harman has done well. Though his renderings of the most baffling moments in the text rarely strike one as inspired, he can certainly claim to have produced a version of the novel that is semantically accurate to an admirable degree, faithful to Kafka's nuances, responsive to the tempo of his sentences and to the larger music of his paragraph construction. For the general reader as for the student, it will be the translation of preference for some time to come.

If there are lapses, such lapses do not point to any larger deficiency. To give an idea of their proportions, I list a few.

1   If the Muirs' English has become dated, Harman's is, in places, unnecessarily colloquial: 'stomped'; 'what he had gone and done'; 'all that great'. (pp. 25, 284, 294) It also sometimes descends into clumsiness. 'Painful, even unbearable' is better than Harman's 'unbearably excruciating'. (p. 152) Word-choice is occasionally off target: 'the village environs' is better than 'the village surroundings'. (p. 183)

2   There are moments when Harman falls into late twentieth-century jargon: 'Perhaps K. was being mistakenly positive now, just as he had been mistakenly negative with the peasants.' (p. 26) Better might be, 'Perhaps K. erred here on the side of good nature, where with the peasants he had erred on the side of bad nature.'

3   The word *Heimat* (home, homeland) creates problems that Harman does not always solve. Though the castle and village have

a telephone system, it is not used for communication with the outside world, nor do the natives seem to venture abroad. K., in contrast, speaks of himself as a wanderer. Nevertheless, there is no suggestion that he is a foreigner in the usual sense of the word. In the world of *The Castle* there seem to be no national boundaries. So when, in Chapter 2, K.'s thoughts return to his *Heimat*, Harman's translation 'homeland' is too specific, particularly when we go on to read that his *Heimat* has a square and a church. 'Home' or even 'home town' would be safer. (p. 28)

4   Harman is not immune from the temptations of over-translating that so mar the Muir version. To translate *Ihre schmutzige Familienwirtschaft* as 'your dirty family shambles' (p. 133) introduces ideas of blood and death not present in the original. 'Your sordid family set-up' would be better. Similarly, 'freaks' (Wilkins/Kaiser) translates *Ausgeburten* rather more soberly than 'evil spawn'. (p. 306)

5   Sometimes fidelity to Kafka's word order becomes mechanical and yields what sounds like a parody of German: 'a large, heavy, and now open gate'. (p. 101) The German is some-times followed even when there is a close English idiom: 'a crying injustice' is better than 'a screaming injustice'. (p. 197)

6   It is not always clear that Harman recognises Prague usages. For instance, the huge, three-doored item of furniture in the landlady's office in Chapter 25, *ein Kasten*, is probably a wardrobe, as Wilkins/Kaiser have it, rather than a cabinet, as Harman has it. (p. 314)

7   There are odd moments of inattention: 'I entrusted a message to you, not so you would forget it or garble it on your cobbler's bench' should surely read 'not so [that] you would forget it on your cobbler's bench and garble it.' (p. 120)

As these instances indicate, points at which Harman lays himself open to criticism are limited in range and small in scale. More significant cruxes emerge at moments when Kafka's prose is at its worst, or – to say the same thing – when it is hardest to ignore that what Kafka has left us is a draft, not a finished work. 'It would after all have been better to have sent the assistants here, for even they would have been capable of conducting themselves as he had done,' writes Harman, following faithfully in the footsteps of a sentence that reads as though Kafka wrote it in his sleep. (p. 104) The trouble here is not only that the writing is slovenly but that Kafka's meaning is unclear. The Muirs clarify the meaning, but only at the cost of importing a notion (foolishness) of which there is no trace in the original: 'Really he would have done better to have sent his assistants here, they couldn't have behaved more foolishly than he had done.' (Muir translation, p. 103) The problem is finally intractable.

V

Besides Malcolm Pasley's afterword on the manuscript sources of *The Castle*, the new translation comes armed with a useful note by Arthur H. Samuelson on the publication history of Kafka's works, and an eleven-page Translator's Preface, in which Harman discusses Kafka's language and some of the problems it presents, illustrating and justifying his own approach, and quoting instances of the Muirs' failings.

It is, of course, to be expected that Harman should be hostile to his rivals (upon whom he delivered an even more trenchant attack in an article published in *New Literary History* in 1996).[14] Everything he says about the Muirs is true: their religious interpretation of the book did indeed bias their rendering of it; they did indeed introduce transitional links to make Kafka's daring leaps more easily negotiable; they did indeed, in general, 'tone down the modernity' of *The Castle*. ('Preface', p. xiii)

But to say of Edwin Muir that '[his] literary sensibility . . . was molded by nineteenth-century figures such as Thackeray and Dickens' goes too far. Nor were the Muirs merely, as Harman describes them, 'a gifted Scottish couple'. (p. xiii) The Muirs, together with their publisher Martin Secker, introduced a difficult, even arcane German modernist to the English-speaking world years earlier than one might reasonably have expected this to happen. Edwin Muir himself was a considerable poet, not quite of the rank of Yeats or Auden, of whom he sometimes reminds one, but a modern master in his own right, certainly no hankerer after a lost nineteenth-century world. If Dickens left an imprint on the Muirs, he left an imprint on Kafka too; as for Thackeray, one searches in vain for any residue of him in the Muir translation.

Harman characterises the Muirs' translations of Kafka as 'elegant' and 'smoothly [readable]'. The compliment is backhanded, and intended to be so. His own English, Harman says, is 'stranger and denser' than theirs. (pp. xiii, xvii) Harman would do well to recognise that, if a striving toward elegance – fluency is a better term – marks the Muir translation as of its time, then, in its very striving toward strangeness and denseness, his own work – welcome though it is today – may, as history moves on and tastes change, be pointed toward obsolescence too.

9 Robert Musil's *Diaries*

I

BORN IN THE autumn years of the Habsburg Empire, Robert Musil served His Imperial and Royal Majesty in one bloody continental convulsion and died halfway through the even worse convulsion that followed. Looking back, he would call the times in which he lived 'an accursed era'; his best energies were spent on trying to understand what Europe was doing to itself. His report is contained in a huge unfinished novel, *The Man without Qualities*; in a series of essays collected in English under the title *Precision and Soul*; and in a set of notebooks newly translated as *Diaries, 1899–1941*.[1]

Musil's path to authorship was an unusual one. His parents, from the Austrian upper bourgeoisie, sent him for his education not to a classical *Gymnasium* but to military boarding schools, where he learned, if little else, to dress dapperly and take care of his body. At university he studied first engineering (he designed and patented an optical instrument which was still being manufactured commercially in the 1920s), then psychology and philosophy, taking his doctorate in 1908.

By this time he was already the author of a precocious first novel, *The Confusions of Young Törless* (1906), set in a cadet school. Abandoning the academic career for which he had prepared himself, he devoted himself to writing. *Unions*, a pair of cerebrally erotic novellas, appeared in 1911.

When war came, Musil served on the Italian Front, with distinction. After the war, troubled by a sense that the best years of his creative life were being stolen from him, he sketched out no fewer than twenty new works, including a series of satirical novels. A play, *The Visionaries* (1921), and a set of stories, *Three Women* (1924), won awards. He was elected vice-president of the Austrian branch of the Organisation of German Writers. Though not widely read, he was on the literary map.

Before long the satirical novels had been abandoned or absorbed into a master project: a novel in which the upper crust of Viennese society, oblivious of the dark clouds gathering on the horizon, discusses endlessly what form their latest festival of self-congratulation should take. It would be, he said, a 'grotesque' vision of Austria on the eve of war, an Austria which would be 'a particularly clearcut case of the modern world'. (*Diaries*, p. 209) Supported financially by his publisher and by a society of admirers, he gave all his energies to *The Man without Qualities*.

The first volume came out in 1930, to so enthusiastic a reception in both Austria and Germany that Musil – a modest man in other respects – thought he might win the Nobel Prize. The continuation proved more intractable. Cajoled by his publisher, yet full of misgiving, he allowed an extended fragment to appear as the second volume in 1933. 'Volume One closes approximately at the high point of an arch,' he wrote. But 'on the other side it has no support'.[2] He began to fear he would never finish the work.

A move to the livelier intellectual environment of Berlin was cut short by the rise to power of the Nazis. Musil and his wife returned to Vienna, to an ominous political atmosphere; he began to suffer from depression and poor health. Then in 1938 Austria was absorbed into the Third Reich. The couple removed themselves to

Switzerland. Switzerland was meant to be a staging post on the way to the United States, but the entry of the United States into the war put paid to that plan. Along with tens of thousands of other exiles, they found themselves trapped.

'Switzerland is renowned for the freedom you can enjoy there,' observed Bertholt Brecht. 'The catch is, you have to be a tourist.' The myth of Switzerland as a land of asylum was badly damaged by its treatment of refugees. The overriding priority of the Swiss government during the years 1933–44 was not to antagonise Germany. Supervision of resident aliens fell under a *Fremdenpolizei* whose chief disparaged philanthropic agencies for their 'sentimental meddling' and made no secret of his dislike of Jews. Ugly scenes took place at border posts as refugees without entry visas were turned back. (To the credit of ordinary Swiss people, it must be said there was a public outcry.)[3]

The Man without Qualities had been banned in Germany and Austria in 1938 (the ban would later extend to all of Musil's writings). In applying to the Swiss government for asylum, Musil was thus able to claim that he could not earn a living as a writer elsewhere in the German-speaking world. Yet nowhere in Switzerland did the Musils feel welcome. The Swiss patronage network disdained them; friends abroad exerted themselves only lackadaisically on their behalf (or so it seemed to Musil); they survived on handouts. 'Today they ignore us. But once we are dead they will boast that they gave us asylum,' said Musil to Ignazio Silone.[4] Depressed, he could make no progress with the novel. 'I don't know why I cannot manage to write. I seem to be under a spell.' (*Diaries*, p. 498) In 1942, at the age of sixty-one, he had a stroke and died.

'He thought he had a long life before him,' said his widow. 'The worst is, an unbelievable body of material – sketches, notes, aphorisms, novel chapters, diaries – is left behind, of which only he could have made sense. I have no idea what to do.'[5] Turned away by commercial publishers, she published privately a third and final volume of the novel, consisting of chapters and drafts in no hard and fast order. After the war she tried to interest American publishers in a translation of the whole, without success. She died in 1949.

II

The diaries to which Martha Musil refers are notebooks which Musil had kept from the age of eighteen. Meant at first to record his inner life, they soon began to serve other purposes as well. By the time of his death he had filled over forty of them, some of which were lost or stolen or destroyed in the postwar years.

Although Musil calls these books *Hefte*, notebooks, his German editor prefers the term *Tagebücher*, diaries, and the English translation follows suit, though what we would think of as diary entries are in fact outweighed by summaries of and extracts from books, sketches for fiction, drafts of essays, lecture notes and so forth. Even the German edition excludes some of this material. The text of the English *Diaries* is less than half as long as the German and gives only a slim selection of drafts. Readers who expect to follow in the *Diaries* the progress of *The Man without Qualities* will be disappointed: they should turn, rather, to the drafts reprinted in the translation of the novel published by Knopf in 1995. On the other hand, the *Diaries* allow a picture to emerge of Musil responding to the history of his times. This is particularly true of his last years, when entries become more expansive, perhaps because by this time his energies were not being poured so fully into *The Man without Qualities*.

In his study *Robert Musil and the Crisis of European Culture*, David S. Luft identifies two key moments in Musil's political evolution, both connected with the First World War. The first was his experience of the wave of patriotic passion that accompanied the outbreak of war, a passion that, to his surprise, he found himself sharing ('the ecstasy of altruism – this feeling of having, for the first time, something in common with one's fellow Germans'). (*Diaries*, p. 271) The second was the Versailles Treaty of 1919, and what this punitive settlement meant for those who had hoped the exhausting war would at least give birth to a new political order.

The account Musil gives, in the *Diaries*, of how the humiliations of Versailles led to the rise of Nazism, will not easily be bettered. Fascism, in Musil's analysis, was a reaction against challenges of modern life – principally industrialisation and urbanisation – for which the German people were unprepared, a reaction which then grew into a revolt against civilisation itself. From the moment the Reichstag burned in 1933, Musil foresaw how badly Germany was about to betray itself. 'All the liberal fundamental rights have now been set aside', he writes from Berlin, 'without one single person feeling utterly outraged . . . It is seen as a spell of bad weather . . . One might feel most profoundly disappointed over this but it is more correct to draw the conclusion that all the things that have been abolished here are no longer of great concern to people.' (p. 379)

Of Hitler he writes, 'We Germans brought forth the greatest moralist of the second half of the preceding century [viz. Nietzsche] and are today bringing forth the greatest aberration in morality that there has been since Christendom. Are we monstrous in every respect?' (p. 388)

Musil was affected at every level of his life by the rise of Nazism and the rejection of the best of the German heritage that Nazism represented. '[Hitler says] you must believe either in the future of N[ational] S[ocialism] or the downfall of [Germany] . . . How is it possible still to work when one is in this position?' (Setting down these words in Vienna in 1938, Musil prudently does not name

Hitler, using instead a private code-name 'Carlyle'.) National Socialism made Musil invisible by driving him into exile and banning his books; it is hard not to suspect that his growing hopelessness before the task of finishing *The Man without Qualities* came, at least in part, from a sense that his project, conceived in a spirit of what he thought of as 'gentle irony', had been overtaken by the chariots of history. (pp. 389, 466)

III

From early on, Musil used people around him, including family and friends, as models for his fiction. The first notebook (1899–1904) includes a fictionalised treatment of his own childhood and adolescence, with a cast of characters who will resurface decades later in *The Man without Qualities*.

His most striking use of personal material is in the story 'Tonka' (in *Three Women*), whose central character is based closely on Herma Dietz, a young working-class woman with whom he had a serious and lengthy liaison despite the intense disapproval of his mother. In the *Diaries* we see Herma fulfilling a double function. At one level, she is closely observed by Musil the writer as a model for the fictional Tonka. At another, she is the source of troubled feelings to Musil the man. Despite her denials, Musil had reason to believe Herma had been unfaithful to him. To his circle of friends he preached the transcendence of jealousy, but privately he felt 'a steady drip of poison'. (p. 60) What should he do?

The move he makes is deeply Musilian. Neither giving in to jealousy, nor, by an act of will, conquering it, instead he turns himself into a character in the story of Herma/Tonka, and tries, through the distancing power which fiction allows, to become the person that, at an ethical level, he wants to be.

To judge from the clarity and intensity of Musil's writing, in both the diary entries relating to Herma and, later, the achieved story 'Tonka', the ethical-aesthetic experiment works. Robert (or his created fictional self R) visibly grows before our eyes, becoming less youthfully brash, less cynical, more tolerant, more loving. 'Her [i.e., Herma/Tonka's] fateful liaison with R', he writes to himself, 'gives symbolical form to the fact that . . . one cannot place faith in the understanding.' (p. 61) If he loves Herma he must believe in her innocence. Fiction has thus become an arena for working out his relations with others, a laboratory for the refinement of the soul. The young Musil is learning to love; and, in a strange way, the more he loves, the more clearsighted and intelligent he becomes.

Herma Dietz died in 1907. By then Musil had already met Martha Marcovaldi, who had left her Italian husband to study art in Berlin. Soon he was living with Martha and her children; in due course they were married. '[Martha] is something that I have become and that has become "I",' he writes in the *Diaries*. (p. 122) The perfecting of their love – a love that would include a perverse readiness to betray each other – became a new ethical project in his life.

IV

To Musil, the most stubborn and retrogressive feature of German culture (of which Austrian culture was a part – at no time did he take seriously the idea of an autonomous Austrian culture) was its tendency to compartmentalise intellect from feeling, to favour an unreflective stupidity of the emotions. He saw this split most clearly among the scientists with whom he worked: men of intellect living coarse emotional lives.

From the earliest notebooks, Musil evinces a concern with erotic feeling and the relations between the erotic and the ethical.

The education of the senses through a refining of erotic life seems to him to hold the best promise of bringing humankind to a higher ethical plane. He deplores the rigid sexual roles that bourgeois society has laid down for women and men. 'Whole countries of the soul have been lost and submerged as a consequence,' he writes.[6]

In asserting the sexual relation as the fundamental cultural relation, and in advocating a sexual revolution as the gateway to a new millennium, Musil is curiously reminiscent of his contemporary, D. H. Lawrence. Where he differs from Lawrence is in not wishing to exclude the intellect from erotic life – indeed, in seeking to eroticise the intellect. As a writer, he is also capable of an unmoralising brutality of observation that is simply not in Lawrence's repertoire. He watches a young woman watching her mother kiss a younger man. 'Up till now she has only known a woman's kiss as a tentative gesture; but this is like a dog sinking its teeth into another.' (*Diaries*, p. 398)

Despite his interest in the metamorphoses of desire, explored with unparalleled subtlety in *Unions*, Musil was unsympathetic to the psychoanalytic movement. He disliked its cultishness, disapproved of its sweeping claims and its unscientific standards of proof. Psychoanalysis, he remarks disparagingly, deploys a mere handful of explanatory concepts; whatever these concepts do not cover is 'left completely barren [with] . . . not a single path . . . [leading] on further from there'. In psychoanalysis, 'insights of great importance [intermingle] with things that are impossible, one-sided, even dilettante'. He prefers psychology of what he ironically calls the 'shallow' – that is, experimental – variety. (pp. 481, 391, 465)

For the widespread view that Musil was indebted to Freud, and more deeply than he cared to acknowledge, the *Diaries* offer little support. The fact is that Musil and Freud were part of a larger movement in European thought. Both were sceptical of the power of reason to guide human conduct; both were critics of Central European civilisation and its discontents; and both assumed the dark continent of the feminine psyche as theirs to explore. To Musil, Freud was a rival rather than a source. Nietzsche remained his true guide in the realm of the unconscious.

Musil is particularly resistant to claims for the universality of Oedipal desire. Looking back on his own adolescence, he can recollect no desire for his mother, only distaste for her ageing body. 'Is that not the truth – the sad and healthy and non-invented truth? It is the opposite of psychoanalysis. The mother is not an object of desire but a mood-barrier, a stripping away of the mood of every desire, should chance present the young man with any sexual opportunity.' (p. 397)

Would Musil have been so sure of himself if, before writing these words in the late 1930s, he had reread his notebook of 1905–6? Here, in breathlessly novelettish prose, the young Musil drafts a scene of erotically charged reconciliation between his fictional hero and the hero's mother. Decades later, the energies at work in this scene will be drawn upon in the incestuous love between Ulrich, the man without qualities, and his sister Agathe.

V

Musil uses his notebooks less to explore memories from the past than to capture useful data in the present. Among the most vivid entries are extended memoranda: pages of close observation of flies caught in flypaper (later to be used in an essay), and of cats mating in the garden of his Geneva home. Some of his notes are marvels of deft precision: birdsong 'like the touch of soft, busy hands'. (p. 88)

Notes on a visit to an insane asylum in Rome in 1913 (*Diaries*, pp. 158–61) form the basis of the chapter entitled 'The Lunatics

Greet Clarisse' in Part 3 of *The Man without Qualities*, via a series of drafts included in the Knopf translation. (vol. 2, pp. 1600–3, 1630–43) Working on the episode, Musil makes it richer and more disturbing by giving it through the eyes of Clarisse, Ulrich's unstable, Nietzsche-worshipping childhood friend and later (in one possible continuation of the story) mistress. (The most striking feature of these and many other drafts is how fully conceived and realised they are, and how finished the writing is. All that is unsettled about them is where they will fit into the whole.)

Among the writers who mattered to Musil and on whom he reflects in the *Diaries*, from Mallarmé in his youth to Tolstoy late in life, the dominating figure remains Nietzsche. He is oddly indifferent to James Joyce, but feels an affinity to G. K. Chesterton. (For a while Musil and Joyce lived a few houses apart in Zürich. They never spoke to each other.)

Musil recognised Nietzsche's influence on him as 'decisive'. (*Diaries*, p. 433) From Nietzsche he took a form of philosophising that is essayistic rather than systematic; a recognition of art as a form of intellectual exploration; the affirmation that man makes his own history; and a way of treating moral questions that goes beyond the polarities of good and evil. 'Master of the floating life within,' he called him. (*MwQ*, vol. 2, p. 62)

Some of the *obiter dicta* in the *Diaries* are memorable. On Emily Brontë: 'A tiny portion of irony and this housekeeper with her righteous misdeeds would be a figure of global dimensions'. On Hermann Hesse: 'He has the weaknesses appropriate to a greater man than he actually is.' (pp. 188, 486)

On culture and politics he can be mordantly aphoristic: 'The German doesn't know which he likes better, Heaven or Hell. But he is definitely thrilled with the task of bringing order to one or the other – and probably he slightly prefers the task of setting Hell in order.' After Goebbels has launched a decree forbidding 'destructive criticism', Musil writes, 'Since criticism is forbidden I have to indulge in self-criticism. No one will take exception to this since it is unknown in Germany.' (pp. 490, 445)

At a humbler level, the *Diaries* include lists of books he has read, coded notations on his sex life with Martha and worries about his health. Musil was a heavy smoker. Smoking was inconvenient (it made it impossible for him to work in public libraries), but he could not give it up. 'I treat life as something unpleasant that one can get through by smoking!' (p. 441)

An unattractive side of Musil's character surfaces in resentment of the success of writers he considers his inferiors, among them Franz Werfel, Stefan George and Stefan Zweig, and in fits of huffiness when he is not paid the respect he believes he is due.

The sculptor Fritz Wotruba, one of the few friends of Musil's last years, remarked on the gap between Musil's polite relations with certain people in public and the sharp attacks he would launch on them in private. The fame of Thomas Mann rankled particularly. Mann has lowered his sights to suit the capacities of his audience, Musil comments scornfully in his *Diaries*, whereas he, Musil, writes for future generations.

Mann's path briefly crossed Musil's in Switzerland, where Mann was fêted as a great writer, Musil ignored. From Switzerland Mann went on to the United States, where, Musil complained, he did little to aid his beleaguered European fellow writers. The truth is that Mann sent a handsome letter to the British PEN proposing that the club sponsor the emigration of 'our great colleague Robert Musil'. Another contemporary whom Musil disparaged in the privacy of his diary, Hermann Broch, added his voice, 'Robert Musil belongs among the absolute epic writers of world stature.' Hearing later what Mann had written on his behalf, Musil was brought up short: he had been unjust, he acknowledged to himself.[7]

Musil is, of course, inconsistent in sneering at Mann for accommodating himself to the taste of his readers while blaming the same readers for neglecting him, Musil. Sometimes Musil recognises this inconsistency and tries to persuade himself that the obscurity of his own 'double exile' – from his home and from public attention – is to his advantage. 'The feeling that I never quite fully belong either here or anywhere else is not weakness anymore but strength. Now I have found myself again and also my way of facing the world.' The stance towards the world to which he refers is, of course, an ironic one. 'Irony has to contain an element of suffering in it. (Otherwise it is the attitude of a know-it-all).' (*Diaries*, p. 485)

VI

Musil had an astute sense of his own capacities. '[I have] an intellectual imagination.' (*Diaries*, p. 327) 'I am alert to processes in me and in others which elude most people.' (Quoted in Luft, p. 72) Equally acute are his insights into weaknesses in his work. The novellas constituting *Unions*, he sees in retrospect, lack narrative tension. 'Grigia', the story in *Three Women* based on his wartime experiences, he dismisses as 'a disaster'. *The Man without Qualities* itself is 'overburdened with essayistic material that is too fluid and does not stick'. (*Diaries*, pp. 458, 411)

There are long periods when he is stalled, unable to write. He wakes in the morning in a state of 'intellectual despair', of 'powerlessness mingled with a dreadful loathing . . . at the thought of having to go back to the thing [i.e., *The Man without Qualities*]'. His books 'do not have any urgent appeal', and he is unable to discover within himself the 'gesture' that would be needed to bring about such appeal. He feels like giving up. Nevertheless, he plods on, with a dim sense that what he is doing may be important. His self-explorations, because they take place within 'an existential crisis' –

a crisis, personal and historical, of failure – might serve to 'shed . . . light on to the surrounding epoch'. (pp. 341, 449, 463)

Now and again he looks forward hopefully to a day when his labours on the novel will have ceased and he can make a living more easily, writing essays. He plays with essay titles, makes notes, drafts passages. But the drafts do not read well: it is as if his mind is elsewhere.

There is much bleakness in the entries from the late years. Libido is waning, and he interprets this as 'the absence of a will to live'. 'Scales fall from one's eyes. You see those you love in a merciless light.' He does not like what he is writing yet does not want to change it. 'I am a total stranger to myself and could be either a critic or a commentator of my own work.' (pp. 442, 393, 490)

VII

As the prospect of completing *The Man without Qualities* began to seem more and more remote, Musil played with the idea of using the notebooks as the basis of a new project. 'I must rather write on the subject of these notebooks,' he tells himself, and even makes up a title: *The Forty Notebooks*. (p. 462)

As he imagines it, the new work will have two aims: to address the future of Germany, including its historical guilt; and to chart the growth of his own œuvre, presenting it 'in the right way' (*richtig*: Musil does not elaborate on what this means). Tracing the rise of 'the present set of problems grouped around [*The Man without Qualities*]', he tells himself, will surely not be difficult. But when he starts exploring the plan in greater depth, he loses heart. Does he have the energy to embark on a 'reconstruction of the almost incomprehensible path' of his own evolution? (p. 467)

Yet the autobiographical project attracts him. 'This epoch

deserves to be handed down just as it is . . . not in the distanced mode of [*The Man without Qualities*] but . . . seen in close-up, as a private life,'· he writes in 1937. 'If I describe my life as being exemplary, as a life in this age that I want to hand down to later ages, this can be toned down with irony and the objections raised [namely that one takes oneself too seriously] will then fall away. My probing of conscience, contemplation of shortcomings and the like, will also find their place here as a reproduction of the times.' (p. 430)

Musil's plans to transform his notebooks into something else were never carried out. Yet in a strange way, it is *as* a body of writing which, intermittently and somewhat wistfully, gives rise to the stillborn hope of becoming a literary work in its own right that the *Diaries* take on a life of their own. In their latter stages they are in effect an admission by a great writer in dark times that he has come to a dead end and that he does not have it in him to rescue himself through a heroic new project, yet half hoping, nevertheless, that the record of his travails, in all its integrity and all the evidence it will present of a true and full engagement with the accursed era into which he was born, can be brought to weigh in his favour. This gives the *Diaries* an emotional dimension, even a dimension of pathos, that Musil could not have planned, and that turns them into a moving document.

VIII

The *Diaries* cannot have been easy to translate. Since Musil is writing for his own eyes only, observations arrive out of the blue, contextless, sometimes in condensed or cryptic form. Philip Payne, their translator, copes admirably. Even when the general drift is dark, he seems able to intuit where Musil is going. His version is, by and large, of the highest order. The few lapses occur in careless moments. Some instances: when Musil remarks in 1941 that the Catholic Church has lost its *Religiosität*, he means that it is without the spirit of religion, not without religiosity, as Payne has it. Musil writes of his admiration for a work of Dostoevsky's called *The Player*; in English the novella is better known as *The Gambler*. Musil imagines Stendhal and Balzac trading insults, Balzac calling Stendhal a scribbler, Stendhal calling Balzac a *Fex*. Payne translates this colloquial Austrian word as 'gusher', but Musil is being more pungent than that: a clown, an eccentric enthusiast. (pp. 491, 469, 491)

Though the notebooks were never reworked for publication, Musil's writing is so disciplined, his word choice so exact, that sentence follows sentence with a pointedness that seems to come naturally. Here and there, even while remaining true to Musil's sense, Payne fails to capture that pointedness; or – a related failing – translates the words without translating their meaning. For instance, Musil observes that by birth he belonged, however peripherally, among the 'class dictators'. (p. 439) What does he mean? The context does not help. Was *Klassendiktator* a jargon term in the 1930s? At moments like this one expects a translator to be an interpreter too.

Certain of the editorial decisions are also open to question. The English *Diaries* consist of a selection from the *Tagebücher* edited by Adolf Frisé. Quite justifiably, Payne relies heavily on Frisé's notes, augmenting them here and there, but more generally cutting them down. This pruning is not always wisely done. In 1939, for instance, Musil read three articles – one on Freud, one on mathematics, one on Polish philosophy – which made such an impact on him that he stapled them to his notebook. What were these articles? Frisé gives not only the bibliographic particulars but, in two cases, brief synopses. Payne gives nothing.

Between April 1908 and August 1910, and again for the period

1926–8, there are no entries. We know that two of Musil's note-books were stolen in 1970. Do the gaps mark the lost notebooks? A few words of explanation would have helped.

The volume ends with a fifteen-page list of the passages in Frisé that Payne has omitted. Valuable though it may be in itself, this list is unlikely to be consulted by anyone who cannot already read German. An index would have been more useful, but there is no index. Four photographs are reproduced, showing Musil at the ages of seven, twenty, and twenty-two, and his wife a year before he met her; there is nothing of later date. In addition to Payne's own concise, informative and critically acute Preface, there is a rambling Introduction by Mark Mirsky which duplicates much of what Payne has already said. All in all, an oddly put together compilation.

IX

Musil's climb to eminence and even to greatness from the obscurity of the war years began in the 1950s. In the English-speaking world his most effective promoters were the scholar-translators Ernst Kaiser and Eithne Wilkins, who in the *Times Literary Supplement* praised him as 'the most important novelist writing in German this half century' and followed up their claim with a translation of *The Man without Qualities* (three parts, 1953–60). The book was well received in Britain but not, at first, in the United States: 'a . . . bumbling mass of Teutonic metaphysics', wrote the *New Republic* reviewer.[8]

The materials left in Martha Musil's hands amounted to some 10,000 manuscript pages. (This *Nachlass* is now available on CD-ROM. Thus, ironically, the merest graduate student can find a way through the Musilian labyrinth with an ease that Musil himself, despite his elaborate cross-referencing system, never possessed.)

Scholarly explorations began in 1951; the first fruits in German were an edition of *The Man without Qualities* by Frisé consisting of the portions of the text more or less finalised by Musil with some supplementary drafts. A war of words then broke out over the question of whether Frisé was entitled to prefer one of Musil's possible endings (carnal union between Ulrich and his sister Agathe) to another (mystical union between the two). The four-volume *Gesammelte Werke* of 1978 presents Frisé's compromise. The draft continuation is no longer given in unambiguous form. Instead, we have first the chapters finished and approved by Musil; then those chapters still being worked on at the time of his death (often with variants); and, finally, a selection from the remaining material.

In the new translation of *The Man without Qualities* (Knopf, 1995), the second volume is bulked out with with some 600 small-print pages of Frisé's supplementary material in a helpful new arrangement by Burton Pike, editor of the Knopf project and perhaps the best translator Musil has had thus far. The main body of the work, consisting of the author-approved chapters, is translated by Sophie Wilkins, previously the translator of Thomas Bernhard, and not to be confused with Eithne Wilkins. Ms Wilkins had gone on record in advance criticising the older Kaiser/Wilkins version for its 'errors and misunderstandings' and for the Britishness of its language.[9] Her translation corrects the old errors but introduces some new ones; it updates the language at the cost of a certain flatness of style. Perhaps the most often quoted sentence in the book – 'If mankind could dream collectively, it would dream Moosbrugger' (Kaiser/Wilkins) – comes out leadenly, in the new version, as 'If mankind could dream as a whole, that dream would be Moosbrugger.' (*MwQ*, vol. 1, p. 77)

Musil did not end and probably could not have ended his huge novel. Even in terms of its internal logic, it is far from complete.

Plot elements are in place for which no outcome is in sight, even in the drafts (one thinks of the consequences for Agathe of forging her father's will); major decisions still loom which Musil seems to be postponing (whether Ulrich is to have an affair with Clarisse, for instance). More seriously, one must doubt whether the framework Musil has built can support the ever-increasing weight of history it is being called upon to bear.

Musil's notes indicate that, even in the 1920s, he was sensitive to the question of why he should have embarked on so determinedly 'pre-war' a novel. (*MwQ*, vol. 2, p. 1723) He seems to have been confident, however, that its conception was flexible enough to allow it to foreshadow, at least at the level of presentiment, the realities of postwar Europe as well. (Here Musil would seem to have been relying heavily on the figure of Moosbrugger, the psychopathic sex murderer, to embody the violently self-liberatory impulses of peoples bewildered by the conditions of modern life – impulses that would in due course be exploited by the fascist movements. Moosbrugger is a minor character in the text as we have it, but he bulks large in the drafts.)

More and more, Musil's last-minute decision, in 1938, to withdraw the last twenty chapters of Part 3 when they were already in the hands of the printers seems the correct one. These chapters consist substantially of an exposition of Ulrich's theory of the emotions; they are the last chapters to have borne, or nearly to have borne, their author's imprimatur. They have been praised for their lyricism, but that lyricism now seems rather too airy, and the whole sequence bereft of the sharpness of observation that characterises Musil's prose at its best.

The problem is not just with the writing but with Ulrich as well. The broad scheme of the novel is to push forward two counter-pointed story lines: while a spiritually bankrupt Austria is allowed to play out its last days, Ulrich, with and through his sister, will negotiate a mystical-erotic withdrawal from society. 'For the sake of a world which could still come, one must hold oneself pure', he says in self-justification. (*MwQ*, vol. 2, p. 1038) But in the context of a fictional Europe of 1914 which was increasingly being asked to take on, at a symbolic level, the burden of the Europe of 1938–9 as well, Ulrich's retreat must have seemed – and here, one must concede, the *Diaries* yield no supporting admission on Musil's part – a less and less adequate or even appropriate gesture. The ethical and the political sides of the novel were drifting apart.

Reading *The Man without Qualities* will always be an unsatisfying experience. In the kind of edition offered by Frisé or by Pike, we reach the last of the 1,700-odd pages in a state of confusion, even of disappointment. But, given the richness of Musil's drafts, given too the scale of the crisis in European culture that he was trying to map, not only in *The Man without Qualities* but in the parallel action of the *Diaries*, too much is preferable to too little.

10 Josef Skvorecky

I

JOSEF SKVORECKY SHOT into notoriety when, at the 1959 congress of the Czech Writers' Union, his novel *The Cowards* (written 1948–9, published 1958, English translation 1970) was denounced by Party spokesmen as 'profoundly alien [in spirit] to our beautiful democratic and humanistic literature'. It is not clear why, at that moment in history, Skvorecky in particular was singled out as whipping-boy. But *The Cowards*, a satirical look at Czech society in 1945, when the German occupiers were moving out and the Soviet liberators moving in, hardly fitted the socialist-realist mould; while its author's middle-class, Catholic background and doctorate from Charles University for a thesis on Thomas Paine clearly made him fair game. The effect of the banning that ensued was predictable: *The Cowards* circulated illegally and was widely read; its author became a cult figure among the young.

News of the 1968 invasion of Czechoslovakia reached Skvorecky while he was on a visit to France. The question was: should he return? In 1948, when the Communists first took power, he was in his twenties and full of energy. Now, in his mid-forties, the resilience and optimism of youth were gone. He and his wife chose exile: a teaching stint in Toronto prolonged itself into residence, and eventually the Skvoreckys became Canadian citizens.

In three decades since quitting his native land Skvorecky has not been prolific as a novelist. As his Czech experience has become more remote, and as Communist Czechoslovakia – indeed, Czechoslovakia itself as a political entity – has receded into the past, the material and the passions out of which the earlier novels grew have – naturally – run dry. At the same time Skvorecky seems to have found it hard to transplant himself imaginatively to a new North American environment. He continues to publish his books in Czech first (until recently via the publishing house Sixty-Eight, run by his wife Zdena Salivarova and himself, an enterprise whose contribution to keeping Czech literature alive during the 1970s and 1980s was incalculable) and only subsequently in English translation.

The Engineer of Human Souls (Czech 1977; English translation 1985) was the last novel to rely heavily on Skvorecky's Czech experience. *Dvořák in Love* (Czech 1983; English translation 1986) follows Anton Dvořák during the four years he spent as director of the National Conservatory in New York, a period that included the composition of his Symphony no. 5 ('From the New World') of 1893. The novel is held together by Skvorecky's love of music – not only Dvořák's but the music of African Americans, of which Dvořák himself was, of course, a passionate advocate ('The future music of this country must be founded upon what are called the Negro melodies . . . These are the folk songs of America,' he wrote).[1] This gentle and affectionate book may be read as Skvorecky's first attempt to locate a Czech American tradition in which there would be space to set loose his imagination, and thus to refashion himself positively as a Czech North American rather than negatively as a Czech exile. *The Bride of Texas* (1992; English translation 1996) is the second.

II

The bride of Texas is not from Texas at all. Born in the 1830s into a family of tenant farmers in Moravia, Lida Toupelikova ought by rights to marry one of the neighbours' sons and spend the rest of her life raising children and doing drudge-work. But besides having a pretty face and striking blue eyes, she burns with ambition to climb the social ladder. Her climb begins when she seduces, gets pregnant by, and comes within an ace of marrying, the son of their landlord. Then, when the Toupelik family is packed off to Texas to get her out of the way, she uses her wiles to ensnare Etienne de Ribordeaux, heir to a cotton plantation. Disinherited by his angry father and discarded by Lida as useless to her further plans, Etienne commits suicide. Lida promptly devirginates and marries a vapid young army officer named Baxter Warren II, prospective head of the Warren Bank in San Francisco.

The philosophy of Lida, bride of Texas, is simple: 'In this world it's the strong ones that win out. And love? Well, go for love – but if you can't get love, then go for anything you can get.'[2] In the course of going for whatever she can get, the eyes of this hard, calculating young immigrant lose their cornflower innocence and acquire a chilling, reptilian glaze.

Lida – or Linda Towpelick as she renames herself on the far side of the Great Waters – and her brother Cyril are among a handful of properly fictional characters in a novel which otherwise takes its stand on the rock of history. In fact the Toupeliks are doubly fictitious: their author has lifted them – as he disarmingly admits – from a story that appeared in a Czech-language magazine in Chicago in 1898. Etienne de Ribordeaux and Warren Baxter II are inventions. Otherwise the stage is thronged with 'real' characters from a far greater drama: the latter years of the American Civil War, the restoration of the Union, the ending of slavery.

The Bride of Texas is only secondarily a romance of ambition and acquisitiveness. It is first of all a war novel, concerned with the progress of the war, battle by battle, and with the fate of some of the humbler soldiers who took part in it. Lida may give the novel its name, but its central character is a man, drawn by Skvorecky from the records of the Twenty-Sixth Wisconsin Volunteers: Jan Kapsa, like Lida an immigrant from the subject lands of Austro-Hungary.

Kapsa has served in two armies: that of the Habsburg Empire, in which he had been used to suppress the nationalist uprisings of 1848; and now that of the Union, where he has risen through the ranks to become a sergeant on the staff of General Sherman. He has come to America in search of freedom. Having seen imperial Austro-Hungary and imperial Russia at work, he is familiar with one version of what freedom is not. 'We're fighting this war [the Civil War] to rid America of everything that's like Russia,' he declares. (p. 95)

Another version of freedom scrutinised and rejected by Kapsa is that put forward by states' rights secessionists. Kapsa knows at first hand what old-fashioned serfdom entails. In fighting to end slavery in America, he is fighting for the liberation of Bohemia too. When the war is over, he is able to look back with satisfaction on a job well done; in old age he is still ruminating on the ugly shape the twentieth century might have taken had the Union lost.

Kapsa is thus no good soldier Schweik. On the contrary, he is a sturdy, thoughtful man, a career soldier who reveres his commanding general. Sherman, for his part, emerges as a modern-style strategist, wary of pitched battles, indifferent to glory.

There is, however, a version of Schweik in the novel, whom Skvorecky has injected into it in order to leaven the life-story of his worthy but otherwise rather plodding hero. Jan Amos Shake is a fellow private, a coward, a 'gnome with the clever, guileless eyes of a con man'. (p. 193) Broadly funny things keep happening to Shake: a Confederate standard bearer trips over him as he cowers on the battlefield, impaling himself on a bayonet; he falls out of a tree and knocks a Confederate major off his horse. For his exploits he receives a battlefield promotion.

Whereas Lida has fled the Old World to escape a life of hardship, Kapsa, by dint of some complicated, Balzacian plotting on his author's part involving a high-born mistress, a *crime passionel*, a diamond necklace, and flight by night, is endowed with a romantic Old World past and enough money, once the Wisconsin Volunteers are disbanded, to woo the widow of a Czech comrade-at-arms and enjoy the well-earned pleasures of marriage and fatherhood. Two versions, then – Lida's, Kapsa's – of successful transplantation.

III

Czech settlement in the United States – principally in Texas and the Midwest – dates back to the 1820s, but the great spur to emigration from the Czech homelands was the failed uprising of 1848 and the repressions that followed. Through Kapsa and his comrades, Skvorecky is concerned to pay tribute to the first generation of Czechs in the New World, and in particular to those Czechs who, though they could have avoided conscription (they were, after all, not citizens), chose to enlist and fight as Americans. An odd change of direction, perhaps, for a novelist who made his name as a satirist; yet from an immigrant of a later generation, it can be seen as a way of asserting continuity with North American traditions of democracy and love of freedom.

During the early 1950s, when Skvorecky began seriously writing novels, he evolved a narrative method that worked well for him and that he has seen no reason to discard. It involves dividing the story into narrative strands and following these strands in parallel, sometimes bringing them together and interweaving them, sometimes intercutting between them. As he has grown more assured in his craft, he has multiplied the number of strands and accelerated the pace of the intercutting, until with *The Bride of Texas* readers may find themselves flashing between Bohemia and the Carolinas, between 1848 and 1864, between the de Ribordeaux plantation and the battlefield of Bentonville, for no more than a paragraph or two at a time.

It is a method that owes much to William Faulkner. In his early years in Prague Skvorecky was known as an Americanist, a translator of Faulkner, Hemingway and Fitzgerald, knowledgeable about American literature and American jazz. There is even a Snopes smuggled in among the minor characters of *The Bride of Texas* as a homage to Faulkner, just as Shake/Schweik pays tribute to Skvorecky's great comic forebear Jaroslav Hašek.

Skvorecky's battle scenes cannot be said to be grippingly written. There is an air of dutifulness about them, as though the example of Stephen Crane were continually before him, intimidating and discouraging him. For the battles around Bentonville he girds his loins almost palpably and throws in his full resources. Here for the first time he manages to create a degree of suspense and an air of impending disaster. But finally his heart is not in it. For an episode of despairing Southern bravery, he falls back into Faulknerian pastiche; his treatment of the carnage is perfunctory, as though the horror repelled yet did not fascinate him.

Similarly, the Texas in which the Toupeliks settle is a rather abstract, unrealised place. Skvorecky conveys no sense of the heat and space of the Southwest; there is no Spanish presence. Skvorecky has confessed to having no interest in landscape; his nineteenth-century America is much more convincing when he gets to the big city and can write about how the politics and rivalries of the Habsburg Empire play themselves out among Chicago's immigrant communities.

The main strands of Skvorecky's narrative concern the doings of Lida and Kapsa in their European and American manifestations, and the fortunes of Lida's likeable younger brother Cyril, who falls hopelessly in love with a slave concubine of Etienne's only to see her sold from under his nose by Lida. The other main presence in the novel is one of Margaret Fuller's more cautious disciples, a woman named Lorraine Henderson Tracy, who as 'Laura Lee' has made a reputation as the author of novels for young girls.

Lorraine breaks into the narrative in a series of four interchapters ('intermezzos') in which she comments on the progress of the war and in particular on the efforts of Clement Laird Vallandigham, leader of the anti-war Copperhead movement, to bring about the defeat of President Lincoln in the 1864 election. Pitted against Vallandigham is General Ambrose Everett Burnside, a 'real' character whose handsome side-whiskers gave rise to the word 'sideburns'.

Burnside, as military commander of Illinois, has the unenviable task of upholding the Constitution and Bill of Rights – to preserve which the war is, after all, being fought – while at the same time ensuring that Vallandigham does not get away with sedition. Lorraine's function as commentator is to set out the legal and ethical issues at stake, and to chart the manoeuvres of the adversaries as each tries to wrongfoot the other (here Skvorecky draws heavily on Shelby Foote's history of the Civil War).

One can see why, at an abstract level, Vallandigham's campaign should interest Skvorecky – it raises questions about the limits of dissent in a democracy – just as one can see why he has created Lorraine – to provide a perspective on the war which extends beyond events on the battlefield. But the issues are inadequately dramatised; Lorraine's intermezzos are not a fictional vehicle adequate to the weight of political history they must bear. The material remains arid and the lengthy passages in which Lorraine does her desperate best to bring it to life are best skipped.

Skvorecky has obviously read widely on the Civil War (his novel comes shored up with a two-page list of sources as well as a four-page historical foreword). He drops interesting asides on the arms used by foot soldiers and on developments in armaments technology. He reminds us that this was a war in which the combatants were for the most part literate and enjoyed writing home; the letters of ordinary soldiers are in some respects more trustworthy than the reports of journalists. It was also a war in which farmers got to argue with generals over whether battles would be fought on their land or their neighbours'.

In particular, Skvorecky is at pains to foreground the role of black Americans in the war, whether as noncombatants actively following the progress of hostilities and aiding the Union forces where they can, or as enlisted men in black regiments. Cyril Toupelik's inamorata, the slave Dinah, is given a substantial speaking part as a storyteller *à la* Sheherazade (though her stories, it must be said, have their longueurs), while by the end of the war Lorraine is at work on a novel of her own, to be called *The Carolina Bride*, about a slave couple who escape to the north on the Underground Railroad.

IV

Josef Skvorecky is not a great stylist. Compared with his contemporary Milan Kundera, whose prose is masterly in its elegance and lucidity, Skvorecky is a only an honest journeyman. His strengths lie elsewhere. Kundera himself has singled out Skvorecky for 'his special way of viewing history from underneath', as well as for the 'anti-revolutionary spirit' of his novels, their 'critique of the spirit of revolution, with its myths, its eschatology, and its all-or-nothing attitude'.[3] 'I can't imagine that a spoken certainty can exist without an unspoken uncertainty behind it,' writes Skvorecky himself.[4]

Nonetheless the linguistic texture of Skvorecky's fiction is anything but simple. Czech readers have reportedly found his post-1968 work heavy going because much of the dialogue is written in a Czech heavily influenced by American or Canadian English. The comic effects that result are by their nature difficult to translate back into English; it is the good fortune of Skvorecky's English translators – first Paul Wilson, more recently Kacá Poláčková Henley – that the author has involved himself in their labours.

V

In the same year as *The Bride of Texas* Skvorecky published a transparently autobiographical fiction in which he appears under the name Danny Smiricky, the hero of several of his novels. *Headed for the Blues* takes us from the early 1940s to the 1980s, though not as far as the end of the Communist era.

Skvorecky calls the Czechoslovakia of late Communism a 'world of exhausted investigators . . . overworked *fizls*' (*fizl* is Czech slang for a security-police operative). The 1950s, in contrast, are epitomised as 'the time of exhausted executioners'. In neither phase of its existence could the regime inspire loyalty in its subjects or, in its servants, anything but the most cynically self-interested fidelity. (pp. 15,10)

Although Skvorecky himself was involved in minor episodes of sabotage against the Nazis (episodes on which he draws in his novels), and although *Headed for the Blues* opens in 1948 with his Danny persona sending illegal messages to the West and authoring political pamphlets, these activities did not grow out of burning political conviction. Skvorecky's awakening to the real intentions of his Communist rulers came only in 1950, when to his astonishment a group of idealistic young Boy Scout leaders had sentences of ten to twenty years passed on them for – so the indictment read – furthering the interests of a foreign power (in this case the Vatican). In the aftermath Skvorecky felt the guilt of the survivor: the only reason why he too was not in the dock was that he 'didn't believe, didn't know, wasn't certain, abstained from belief not out of cowardice . . . but because he just didn't know'. (p. 63)

Headed for the Blues presents totalitarianism, and in particular the culture of spying, as a creeping malaise of the soul. A long anecdote traces the complexities of relations with known or suspected *fizls* in the Czech immigrant community of Toronto. The story reminds Skvorecky – who never falls into self-righteousness – that as a young man he himself almost gave in to pressure from the secret police to write reports on colleagues at the school where he was teaching. Thus he is able to put his finger on what is worst about a society riddled with spying. What spies report is only of secondary importance. By its very nature, institutionalised spying, with the mutual suspiciousness it engenders, corrodes the openness of citizens toward each other. 'Nobody . . . knows who is who . . . You can't trust old friends, sweethearts or maybe even husbands.' (p. 115)

To the Czech bourgeoisie Skvorecky sings a wholly unironic paean: during its dark years under Communism, he suggests, it shed its worst qualities (smugness, philistinism, moral indifference), these qualities being passed on, by the sleight of hand of history, to its persecutors. 'How persistently they rose again . . . not for the love of profit, but because they were the bourgeoisie, the under-pinnings of the world. Diligent, capable, creative, stubborn, opinionated, incorrigible . . . The only genuine creators of successful economic systems.' (pp. 12, 45)

He sets down a profoundly anti-political credo that echoes in spirit not only Confucius but his own eminent contemporary, the Polish poet Zbigniew Herbert: 'Treason, betraying one's homeland, or, in my case, betraying a political conviction . . . is always a lesser sin than betrayal of a friend.' (p. 44) Jazz is important to him because of 'the indomitable defiance contained in that beautiful rhythmic music'. (p. 81)

Looking back over his career, Skvorecky produces a humorously modest obituary: 'After years of socialist realism . . . he was the first to bring to Czech prose a firsthand, deliberately subjective perception of life, an unfettered treatment of motifs that until then had remained taboo (eroticism, jazz), and a colloquial narrative with slang in the dialogue.' He believes that each human being should, in the course of a lifetime, create at least one thing that will outlast him. 'I think . . . *The Cowards* will outlive me the way my father's orthopedic shoes outlived master cobbler Zahálka of Kostelec.' (pp. 86, 87)

Not a bad attempt, one feels, at the treacherous task of self-evaluation. *The Cowards* may well outlive its author, though *The Miracle Game* (Czech 1972; English translation 1990), with its great setpiece scenes (the anguished exchanges between the citizens of Prague in 1968 and the Russian tank troops, the latter no less bewildered by their role than the people they have been sent to liberate; an evening with a famous Russian novelist and his KGB minder in a fashionable Viennese restaurant), is probably a better novel. Yet despite the admirable candour and engaging wryness of Skvorecky's summing up, it is sad to see so considerable a writer admit, however obliquely, that he reached his peak long ago.

11   Dostoevsky: The Miraculous Years

I

SINCE THE 1950s Joseph Frank has been labouring steadily at one of the great biographical projects of our times, a five-volume life of Fyodor Dostoevsky. The volumes can be read independently; each one makes absorbing reading. The fourth, which appeared in 1997, is of particular interest, covering the 'miraculous years' of 1865–71, the years of Dostoevsky's greatest sustained achievement, when he wrote *Crime and Punishment* (1866), *The Idiot* (1868), and *The Devils* (1871–2).[1]

In 1864 both Dostoevsky's first wife and his beloved elder brother Mikhail died. Dostoevsky was a dutiful family man. Without hesitation (but also without guessing what he was letting himself in for) he assumed responsibility for Mikhail's wife and children and for the huge debts Mikhail had left behind, as well as for his deceased wife's son by an earlier marriage. These dependents exploited his dutifulness without mercy: the next seven years of his life would be dominated by efforts to earn by his pen enough to maintain them in the comfort to which they were accustomed.

Writing for his daily bread, Dostoevsky was always under pressure of deadlines. One such deadline led to his second marriage. Contracted to produce a complete novel at short notice, he hired a stenographer, a young woman named Anna Grigoryevna Snitkina. He gave her a dictation test, then offered her a cigarette. She declined, thus unwittingly passing a second test: she had proved she was not a liberated woman and thus probably not a Nihilist. Within a month, with her stenographic aid, Dostoevsky had dictated and revised *The Gambler* and could return to the project he had interrupted, *Crime and Punishment*. Three months later they were married. He was forty-five, she twenty-one.

Dostoevsky disliked living alone. Though Anna was not to know it, he had recently, in quest of the companionship and domesticity he longed for, paid court to several young women, without success. Nor was he cured of his infatuation with Apollinaria Suslova, the young radical with whom he had had a stormy affair in 1863.

As a spouse, Dostoevsky was not an attractive proposition: a widower with few social graces and a string of hungry relatives in tow, a convicted subversive with a ten-year spell in Siberia behind him, a writer who, in the popular eye, had never really lived up to the promise of his first novel, *Poor Folk*, published over twenty years ago. Anna, however, accepted his offer and proved herself an excellent helpmate, standing by him through ill health and poverty, and after his death guarding his memory jealously.

The marriage does not seem to have been a passionate one, at least in the beginning. For one thing, Dostoevsky had a daily routine that ran entirely athwart that of a young wife and mother: he sat at his desk from ten p.m. to six a.m., slept all morning, and took a stroll in the afternoon, dropping by a coffee shop to read the newspapers. When literary friends came visiting, he would closet himself with them, leaving Anna to bear the burden of his family, who for their part resented her as an interloper.

Mikhail's creditors became more pressing. Dostoevsky proposed to Anna that they quit St Petersburg and live abroad. She agreed, if only to get away from his family. For four years (1867–71) the Dostoevskys lived in Germany, Switzerland, Italy and then Germany again, in hotels or rented apartments. It was a period of unrelieved gloom. They survived from hand to mouth, depending on advances from Dostoevsky's ever-tolerant publisher M. N. Katkov. Time and again Anna had to pawn clothes and jewellery to pay their bills.

Living abroad only confirmed a strain of what Frank, in an unusually judgemental moment, calls Dostoevsky's 'rabid xeno-phobia'. (*The Miraculous Years*, p. 191) Dostoevsky had a particular prejudice against Germans: 'There is no limit at all to how much I hate them!' (p. 298) He objected to Florence because the Florentines sang in the streets when he wanted to sleep; in Geneva he grumbled because Swiss houses did not have double glazing. Even Russian émigré society gave him no pleasure. He had nothing in common with reactionary aristocrats who had left Russia in disgust after the abolition of serfdom; toward the most famous of literary émigrés, Ivan Turgenev, he cherished an undying grudge after Turgenev told him that, having settled in Germany, he considered himself a German, not a Russian.

At the risk of exaggeration, Frank calls Dostoevsky 'a literary proletarian forced to write for wages'. (p. 343) About the circumstances that kept him on the literary treadmill Dostoevsky felt considerable bitterness. Even with *Crime and Punishment* – an enormous popular success – and *The Idiot* behind him, he felt a painful sense of inferiority to Turgenev and Tolstoy, both held in higher critical esteem (and paid more per page) than he. He envied these rivals their time and leisure and inherited fortunes; he looked forward to a day when he would be able to tackle a truly major theme and prove himself their equal. He sketched in some detail an ambitious work, called first *Atheism*, then *The Life of a Great Sinner*, intended to bring him recognition as a serious writer. But these sketches had to be cannibalised for *The Devils*, and the major opus was again postponed.

Dostoevsky had recognised the pivotal importance of Turgenev's *Fathers and Sons* when it appeared in 1861, but his judgements on Turgenev's later writings were coloured by personal and political antagonism (Turgenev is satirised in *The Devils* as the vain and affected *littérateur* Karmazinov). As for Tolstoy, he and Dostoevsky kept a respectful distance from each other all their lives, never meeting. Privately, Dostoevsky lumped Tolstoy's writings with Turgenev's as 'gentry-landowner literature' belonging to an era now past. (p. 424)

Anna bore two children during their years abroad. The first died at three months. The parents were shattered; out of shared grief came greater closeness. Anna's unflinching support also began to make an impression on Dostoevsky. His first wife had reacted to his epilepsy with shock and dismay; Anna, despite her youth, nursed him through his attacks and bore their aftermath – days of irritability and quarrelsomeness – with good cheer. Gradually he developed respect for her judgement and began to take her into his confidence about his writing.

Her heaviest burden was not his epilepsy, however, but his gambling. Dostoevsky was an obsessive gambler. His gambling brought down on Anna not only poverty but varieties of moral degradation: having to mistrust someone she loved; being lied to and deceived, and then having to listen afterwards to remorseful breast-beating and self-recriminations which were, finally, not sincerely meant, or not sincerely enough.

Anna used to set aside a proportion of the housekeeping money for her husband's gambling. When he had lost that, he would come back saying (she records in her diary) that 'he was not worthy of me, he was a swine and I an angel', but that he must have more.

Usually she would give in, fearing that if she objected he would get excited and fall into one of his fits. Her mildness got her nowhere, Dostoevsky complaining that he would be better off with a scold for a wife: 'It was positively painful to him the way I was so sweet.' (Frank notes that the inhuman sweetness of Prince Myshkin in *The Idiot*, which Dostoevsky was writing at this time, produces the same exasperating effect on the people around him.) (pp. 205, 206)

Though Dostoevsky did not excuse his gambling, he was prepared to condemn it only on his own terms: as a manifestation of his tendency to go 'everywhere and in everything . . . to the last limit'. (p. 225) In the man who had already created Marmeladov and would shortly create Stavrogin, one need barely point out that this is as much boasting as it is self-castigation. Anna, however, refused to judge her husband. Just as she preferred to read his mistreatment of her as the voice of epilepsy speaking through him ('When he screams at me it is from illness, not from bad temper'), she seems to have succeeded – like Dostoevsky himself, as Frank observes – 'in divorcing his gambling mania from his moral personality, in regarding it as something extraneous to his true character'. (pp. 207, 206) Frank refrains from asking the properly Dostoevskian question: if the devil in Dostoevsky was not his own, if he was not responsible for it, who was?

II

In his youth Dostoevsky had been attracted to utopian Socialism of the Fourierist variety. But four years in a prison camp in Siberia shook his faith in Socialism. There is no reason to doubt the account of his change of mind he himself gave: removed from the hothouse of the dissident urban intelligentsia and forced to live cheek by jowl with ordinary Russians, most of them peasants, he began to see that well-meant ideas imported from Europe simply did not apply to them. The people for whose sake he and his co-conspirators had striven regarded them with suspicion and even hostility: they would forever be 'gentry', and between gentry and peasantry there was a great gulf fixed. On the other hand, no matter how appalling the crimes might be that they had committed, these peasants were not doubters, rebels, nihilists: they might be sinners, but they were believing sinners, 'Godbearing', in the old Russian term. Thus Dostoevsky arrived, in Frank's words, at 'insight into the deeply rooted moral world of the peasantry, who lived inside their native Christianity as they did in their skins'. (p. 5) This insight made atheistic social creeds imported from the West seem irrelevant.

Hence Dostoevsky's enthusiasm, when he returned from Siberia, for the doctrine of *pochvennichestvo*, return to the soil, to native roots. To this doctrine he added, in the late 1860s, a tinge of Russian Messianism: 'The Russian mission . . . consists in the revelation to the world of the Russian Christ.' Under the sway of a false gospel, the gospel of Rome, the West was falling into decay; the time was approaching for Russia to offer the world 'a new message'. 'Russian thought is preparing a grandiose renovation for the entire world . . . and this will occur in about a century – that's my passionate belief.' (pp. 354, 359, 253)

When to a belief in a special world-historical destiny for Russia are added calls for Russian hegemony to be extended over other Slavic nationalities, commitment to great-Russian imperialism, and even justification of war as a purifying fire, we have a picture of an extremist of the Right – a picture of Dostoevsky later to be confirmed in the widely read column 'A Writer's Diary', which he contributed to the newspaper *The Citizen* and afterwards continued independently. In this column – Frank says in a preview of the final volume of the biography – Dostoevsky would emerge as 'the most important public voice in his country, whose every word was eagerly anticipated, commented on, and argued about'. (p. 499)

But the picture of Dostoevsky as a rabid extremist is less than fair. His chauvinism stopped short of glorification of Russia's past, while on social issues, Frank argues, he emerges as 'somewhere in the middle', a supporter of the liberal reforms with which Alexander II initiated his reign, including – crucially – the abolition of serfdom. (p. 250) His letters voice dismay at the reversal of these policies which followed on the attempt on Alexander's life in 1866. Though he had no doubt that the doctrines of the radical intelligentsia spelled disaster for Russia, he accepted that they were animated by genuine 'enthusiasm for the good . . . and purity of heart'. (p. 53) Even the shrill xenophobia of his years abroad belongs more to his letters than to his novels. *The Idiot*, the major novel of the late 1860s, is concerned to portray a man acting in imitation of Christ – a specifically Russian vision of Christ – not to assert the superiority of Eastern over Western theology. To Frank – who untangles the political from the religious/moral skeins of Dostoevsky's thinking particularly lucidly – the novels advance the 'ethical-universalistic' side of Dostoevsky's messianism, but not to a notable extent its 'egoistic-imperialistic' side. (p. 254)

Dostoevsky's contribution to the debate on Russia's future is a huge one. In the major works of the years 1864–80 – *Notes from Underground*, *Crime and Punishment*, *The Idiot*, *The Devils*, and *The Brothers Karamazov* – he conducts a searching interrogation of Reason – the Reason of the Enlightenment – as the basis for a good society, and in particular of the good faith of Reason (does Reason not have its own covert agenda, as much to do with an itch for power as with a disinterested quest after truth and justice?). This interrogation is carried out at white heat not just because that is Dostoevsky's manner but because the books emerge from, and speak to, an historical crisis, Russia's crisis of modernisation. This crisis would culminate in the Bolshevik takeover of 1917, which promised to liberate the country into true modernity but in fact only petrified it.

The symbolic beginning of the crisis can be set in 1862, with the publication of *Fathers and Sons*, in which Turgenev put his finger on a new and ominous social actor, Bazarov the Nihilist.

> 'We act by virtue of what we recognize as useful,' observed Bazarov. 'At the present time, negation is the most useful of all – and we deny—'
>
> 'Everything?'
>
> 'Everything!'
>
> 'What, not only art and poetry . . . but even . . . horrible to say . . .'
>
> 'Everything,' repeated Bazarov, with indescribable composure.[2]

There was something puerile in Nihilism, as both Turgenev and Dostoevsky recognised. Cobbled together out of scraps of scientism and utilitarianism, it barely deserved the name of a philosophical doctrine. Its adherents may have been animated by the same pity and anger as had been Dostoevsky and his conspiratorial *confrères* in their day, but in its intellectual complacency (the 'indescribable composure' of Bazarov), its mindless destructiveness, its hubris, and, after the failure of the peasantry to rise in revolt in 1863, its ill-disguised contempt for those in whose name it claimed to speak, it seemed to Dostoevsky not just a heretical divergence from the utopian communitarianism of the 1840s but a malignant mutation of it – or, to use the master metaphor of *The Devils*, an evil spirit – taking over the minds of a rising generation of half-educated Russian youth.

Dostoevsky admired *Fathers and Sons*, which he read as (in

Frank's words) a 'poignantly lyrical indictment' of nascent Nihilism. (p. 71) There is every reason to believe that Turgenev shared Dostoevsky's reading of Bazarov. The Left, however, preferred not to recognise the critical dimension of the portrait; and Turgenev furthered this slanted reading by declaring mysteriously that Bazarov was himself. Dostoevsky was outraged by this move on Turgenev's part, which he saw as sycophancy toward the youth of the Left.

In his ongoing critique of Nihilism, we can imagine Dostoevsky as projecting the career of Turgenev's hero into the 1860s. Frank traces the metamorphoses of Bazarov at Dostoevsky's hands, from Raskolnikov in *Crime and Punishment* to the younger Verkhovensky in *The Devils* ('Bazarov . . . stiffened into a ruthless fanatic'). (p. 453) This critique is not conducted simply at a political level. In Dostoevsky's eschatological imagination, Nihilism, with its amoral egoism and proto-Nietzschean self-deification, represented a growing spiritual illness: Russia in the hands of Nihilists would be neither more nor less than Russia under the Antichrist.

III

Dostoevsky was a great devourer of newspapers. Several of his novels had their genesis in reports of crimes, which he regarded as telltale symptoms of the maladies of the age. He was elated when, after *Crime and Punishment*, life imitated art and the newspapers reported Raskolnikov-type murders, for this proved to him that what he called the 'fantastic realism' of his novels brought him closer to the deep currents of Russian life than did the verisimilitude of programmatic realists. (pp. 45–6, 308)

His method of composition, to the extent that his *modus operandi* can be called a method, was to assemble and develop a swarm of plots and narratives while waiting for the transformative flash of inspiration that would tell him which of them would be worth following up and which could be combined with which. He called the moment when a viable character emerged from the welter of possibilities, crystallising an action around himself, an 'incarnation'. (p. 269) Once the major character and the story outline were settled on, he would swiftly and confidently create details of scene, character and action as he went along.

Frank elucidates this process well, building upon the labours not only of the Russian editors of Dostoevsky's notebooks but of such American scholars as Edward Wasiolek and Robin Feuer Miller.[3] The early drafts of *The Idiot* and *The Devils* were unfortunately destroyed by Dostoevsky himself, over his wife's protests, before their return to Russia. (As a one-time subversive he had felt he was bound to be searched at the border; he was reluctant to carry suitcases full of papers, fearing they would be held up for days while the frontier police read through them. In the event, the Dostoevskys' baby cried so loudly at the railway station that the police hustled them through.) Frank's analysis of the surviving notebooks and drafts is particularly illuminating. It allows him to explain the disjointedness of *The Idiot* – where Part One articulates weakly with Part Two – and to show how Dostoevsky's narrative tactics in *Crime and Punishment* became more and more daring as composition of the book proceeded. His account of the complex genesis of *The Devils* is a model of clarity.

The Devils presents particularly intransigent problems for the reader. From the time of Nicholas I until recently, censorship has been a constant factor in Russian intellectual life. Like most entrenched censorship systems, the Russian system succeeded in inducing writers, editors and publishers to do its work by policing themselves. In the manuscript presented by Dostoevsky to the *Russian Messenger*, the journal in which *The Devils* was being serialised, there is a chapter in which Stavrogin tells a priest how he seduced a young girl, then refrained from intervening while she killed herself. This chapter was rejected by Katkov, editor of the journal, on moral grounds. Despite numerous rewrites, in which Dostoevsky toned down the chapter as far as he conscientiously could, Katkov, in other respects a tolerant and sympathetic man, refused to relent.

Dostoevsky was in an impossible position. Unless Stavrogin's crime could be recounted, his character would remain too enigmatic, his spiritual despair excessive, and his suicide at the end of the book unmotivated. In the absence of the censored chapter, Dostoevsky did his hurried best to minimise the damage by reworking the rest of *The Devils*; later he revised the text a second time for book publication. Frank traces these revisions as closely as the fragmentary sources allow, showing that the book we have – great though it may be – is not the one Dostoevsky wanted to write; furthermore, that although we possess the text of the suppressed chapter, it cannot simply be reinserted into the book because of the amount of secondary revision Dostoevsky had to perform on its context.

IV

The main trend in Dostoevsky studies today was set by Mikhail Bakhtin, author of *Problems of Dostoevsky's Poetics* (published in 1929, republished in revised form in 1963). From Bakhtin the concept of dialogism has entered critical currency. A fully dialogical novel is one in which there is no dominating, central authorial consciousness, and therefore no claim to truth or authority, only competing voices and discourses. In Bakhtin's account, Dostoevsky was the inventor (or re-inventor) and greatest practitioner of the dialogical novel, which he synthesised from other mixed and for the most part low-status genres: the detective story, the picaresque tale, the saint's life, the eve-of-execution confession.

In the orthodoxy of academic criticism, 'dialogical' has become a term of approval, 'monological' a term of censure. Bakhtin cannot be blamed for vulgarisations of his thought, and in particular for the treatment of monologism and dialogism (or its Bakhtinian near-synonym 'polyphony') as alternatives (alternatives with telling ideological implications) between which a writer is free to choose. Frank refers to Bakhtin only a few times, mainly to correct him on points of detail.[4] In the process Frank loses an opportunity to supply what is missing in Bakhtin, namely, a clear statement that dialogism as exemplified in the novels of Dostoevsky is a matter not of ideological position, still less of novelistic technique, but of the most radical intellectual and even spiritual courage. Here is Frank on *The Idiot*:

> With an integrity that cannot be too highly praised, Dostoevsky fearlessly submits his *own* most hallowed convictions to the same test that he had used for those of the Nihilists – the test of what they would mean for human life if taken seriously and literally, and lived out to their full extent . . . With exemplary honesty, he portrays the moral extremism of his own eschatological ideal, incarnated by [Prince Myshkin], as being equally incompatible with the normal demands of ordinary social life, and constituting just as much of a disruptive scandal as the appearance of Christ himself among the complacently respectable Pharisees. (p. 341)

What Frank describes here is, on a larger scale, the same phenomenon that Bakhtin calls dialogism. But implicit in Frank's account is what Bakhtin leaves out: that to the degree that Dostoevskian dialogism grows out of Dostoevsky's own moral character, out of his ideals, and out of his being as a writer, it is only distantly imitable.

Although Frank is a biographer, it is literary biography he writes, as he warned his readers as early as the preface to the first volume: 'Anyone who seeks a conventional biography in the following pages will be sorely disappointed . . . I do not go from the life to the work, but rather the other way round. My purpose is to interpret Dostoevsky's art.' These rather austere aims are modified in the second volume, in which Frank concedes that what he is actually trying to do is to fuse biography and social-cultural history with literary criticism.[5] Nevertheless, in each of the volumes there is a goodly amount of literary-critical commentary, with Dostoevsky's more substantial books getting chapters to themselves.

Frank is a literary theorist in his own right, author of the influential essay 'Spatial Form in the Modern Novel' (1945), in which he applies the modernist theory of *montage* to the study of prose fiction, showing that many modern novels are better understood as juxtaposing their narrative elements in space than as unrolling them in time.[6] His affiliations are to American New Criticism, Russian Formalism and, to an extent, to the literary Structuralism of Gérard Genette. Though the seams inevitably show, he is, on the whole, singularly successful at working his rather ahistorical formal analyses of texts into the larger historical and cultural project.

In the first volume of the biography, Frank called into serious doubt Freud's account of the origins of Dostoevsky's epilepsy by showing that Freud got many of the facts of the case wrong. But Frank's scepticism about psychoanalysis and other grand theories of the inner life has its drawbacks. We do not get from him, for instance, any truly searching exploration of the intertwining of pity and cruelty characteristic of Dostoevsky's darker characters. At one point he does remark that the subconscious in Dostoevsky is 'usually moral' (that is to say, the messages that come to Dostoevsky's characters in their dreams or in sudden wellings up of feeling are usually to be trusted). But he does not follow up the implications of this assertion, which seems to me to make Dostoevsky less disturbing than he truly is. (p. 145) (It is hard to know how many exceptions Frank allows himself with 'usually': is Svidrigailov, for instance, one of the exceptions?)

In the biographical sections of the book the reader misses a sense of the growth and development of Dostoevsky the man. But then, as Sidney Monas has pointed out, the notion of steady growth is as foreign to Dostoevsky's imagination as it is fundamental to Tolstoy's. Dostoevsky's novels are essentially scenic in construction, moving from one crisis to the next. Perhaps the same is true of his life.

The Miraculous Years has its *longueurs*. To support his claim that Dostoevsky was not only an innovator in the novel but a great technician too, Frank feels obliged to demonstrate at sometimes unnecessary length how minor scenes contribute to the whole. He assumes, without explaining why, that Dostoevsky's characters have real-life models and spends pages speculating on who these models might be. While he is adept at keeping several strands of narrative going at the same time (the masters of the nineteenth-century novel stand him in good stead here), his use of the device of foreshadowing – ending a chapter by hinting at what is to follow – tends to be mechanical. The index is comprehensive, but the addition of a chronological table would have made the volume more friendly as a reference source. (The index to Volume Three, by the way, manages to get most of the page numbers wrong.)

At another level, while Frank is able to show with exemplary clarity why Dostoevsky chose to shape Stavrogin in the mould of 'the doomed and glamorous Russian Byronic dandy' of Pushkin, he does not look critically enough at Dostoevsky's claim that avatars of the dandy in the 1870s continue to attest to subterranean movements in the national psyche. (p. 467) Dostoevsky's historical intuitions were usually right, but in this case history does not seem to bear him out.

But these are quibbles. In his larger aim of elucidating the setting within which Dostoevsky wrote – personal on the one hand, social, historical, cultural, literary, and philosophical on the other – Frank succeeds triumphantly.

I

IN 1986 JOSEPH BRODSKY published *Less than One*, a book of essays. Some of the essays were translated from the Russian, others he wrote directly in English. In two cases the English matrix had a symbolic importance to him: in a heartfelt homage to W. H. Auden, who did much to smooth his path for him when he quit Russia in 1972, and whom he regarded as the greatest poet in English of the century; and in his memoir of his parents, whom he had to leave behind in Leningrad, and who, despite repeated petitions to the Soviet-era authorities, were never granted permission to visit him. He chose English, he explained, to honour them in a language of freedom.

Less than One is an outstanding book in its own right, worthy to stand beside Brodsky's principal collections of verse, *A Part of Speech* (1980) and *To Urania* (1988). It includes magisterial essays on Osip Mandelstam, Anna Akhmatova, and Marina Tsvetaeva, the poets of the generation before Brodsky to whom he felt closest, as well as two gems of autobiographical recreation: the memoir of his parents and the title essay, 'Less than One', on growing up amid the stupefying boredom of Leningrad of the 1950s. There are also travel essays. A trip to Istanbul, for instance, gives rise to thoughts on the Second and Third Romes, namely Constantinople/ Byzantium and Moscow, and thus on the meaning of the West to Westernising Russians like himself. Finally, there are two of the virtuoso literary-critical essays which later became Brodsky's stock in trade, in which he explicates ('unpacks') individual poems particularly dear to him.

In 1995 came *On Grief and Reason: Essays*, which collects a further twenty-one pieces. Of these, a number are without question on a par with the best of the earlier work. In 'Spoils of War', for instance – an essay classical in form, light in touch – Brodsky continues the amusing and sometimes poignant story of his youth, using those traces of the West – corned-beef cans and short-wave radios as well as movies and jazz music – that found their way through the Iron Curtain to explore the meaning of the West to Russians. Given the imaginative intensity with which they pored over these artefacts, Brodsky suggests, Russians of his generation were 'the real Westerners, perhaps the only ones'.[1]

In his autobiographical journeyings Brodsky never reached the 1960s, the time of his notorious trial on charges of social parasitism and his sentencing to corrective labour in the Russian far north. This silence was, in all likelihood, deliberate: a refusal to exhibit his wounds was always one of his more admirable traits ('At all costs try to avoid granting yourself the status of the victim,' he advises an audience of students). (*On Grief*, p. 144)

Other essays also continue where *Less than One* left off. The dialogue with Auden begun in 'To Please a Shadow' is carried on in 'Letter to Horace'; while the long analytical essays on Thomas Hardy and Robert Frost can stand beside the earlier readings of poems by Tsvetaeva and Auden.

Nevertheless, as a whole, *On Grief and Reason* is not as strong as *Less than One*. Only two of the essays – 'Homage to Marcus Aurelius' (1994) and 'Letter to Horace' (1995) – mark a clear advance in, and deepening of, Brodsky's thought. Several are little more than makeweights: a jaundiced memoir of a writers' conference ('After a Journey'), for instance, from which Brodsky emerges less than creditably, and the texts of a couple of commencement addresses. More tellingly, what in earlier essays had seemed no more than passing quirks now reveal themselves as settled elements of a systematic Brodskian philosophy of language.

II

Brodsky's system can best be illustrated from the essay on Thomas Hardy. Brodsky regards Hardy as a neglected major poet, 'seldom taught, less read', particularly in America, cast out by fashion-minded critics into the limbo of 'premodernism'. (*On Grief*, pp. 373, 315, 313)

It is certainly true that modern criticism has had little of interest to say about Hardy. Nevertheless, despite what Brodsky says, ordinary readers and (particularly) poets have never deserted him. John Crowe Ransom edited a selection of Hardy's verse in 1960. Hardy dominates Philip Larkin's widely read *Oxford Book of Twentieth-Century English Verse* (1973) with 27 pages as opposed to 19 for Yeats, 16 for Auden and a mere 9 for Eliot. Nor did the Modernist avant-garde dismiss Hardy *en bloc*. Ezra Pound, for instance, tirelessly recommended him to younger poets. 'Nobody has taught me anything about writing since Thomas Hardy died,' he remarked in 1934.[2]

Brodsky's claim that Hardy is a neglected poet is part of his attack on the French-oriented modernism of the Pound–Eliot school, and on all the revolutionary -isms of the first decades of the twentieth century, which, to his mind, pointed literature in a false direction. He wishes to reclaim leading positions in Anglo-American letters for Hardy and Frost and in general for those poets who built upon, rather than broke with, traditional poetics. Thus he rejects the influential anti-naturalist poetics of Viktor Shklovsky, based on unabashed artificiality, on the foregrounding of the poetic device. 'This is where modernism goofed,' he says. Genuinely modern aesthetics – the aesthetics of Hardy, Frost and later Auden – uses traditional forms because form, as camouflage, allows the writer 'to land a better punch when and where it's least expected'. (*On Grief*, p. 322)

(Everyday, common-sense language of this kind is prominent in the literary essays in *On Grief and Reason*, which appear to have had their origin as lectures to classes of undergraduates. Brodsky's readiness to operate at his audience's linguistic level has its unfortunate side, including an eagerness to use youthful slang.)

Strong poets have always created their own lineage and, in the process, rewritten the history of poetry. Brodsky is no exception. What he finds in Hardy is, to a degree, what he wants readers to find in himself; his reading of Hardy is most compelling when in veiled fashion it describes his own practices or ambitions. His suggestion – dropped almost in passing – that the germ of Hardy's famous poem 'The Convergence of the Twain' (on the sinking of the *Titanic*) probably lay in the word 'maiden' (as in the phrase 'maiden voyage'), which then generated the central conceit of the poem, ship and iceberg as fated lovers, is a stroke of genius, but beyond that gives an insight into Brodsky's own creative habits. (*On Grief*, p. 352)

Behind 'The Convergence of the Twain' Brodsky points to the presence of the Schopenhauer of *The World as Will and Idea*: ship and iceberg collide at the behest of a blind metaphysical force devoid of any ultimate purpose, a force which Brodsky calls 'the phenomenal world's inner essence'. In itself this suggestion is not novel: whether or not Hardy had Schopenhauer in mind, Schopenhauer's brand of pessimistic determinism was clearly congenial to him. But Brodsky goes further: he recommends to his audience that they read Schopenhauer, 'not so much for Mr. Hardy's sake as for your own'. Schopenhauer's Will is thus attractive not only to Brodsky's Hardy but to Brodsky himself. (*On Grief*, p. 347)

In fact, through his reading of five Hardy poems, Brodsky intends to reveal Hardy as no more than a vehicle for a Schopenhauerian Will acting through language, more like a scribe used by language than an autonomous user. In certain lines of 'The Darkling Thrush', 'language flows into the human domain from the realm of nonhuman truths and dependencies [and] is ultimately the voice of inanimate matter'. While this may not have been what Hardy intended, 'it was what this line was after in Thomas Hardy, and he responded'. Thus what we take to be creativity may be 'nothing more (or less) than matter's attempts to articulate itself'. (*On Grief*, pp. 333, 310)

What is here called the voice of inanimate matter more often becomes, in Brodsky's essays, the voice of language, the voice of poetry, or the voice of a specific metre. Brodsky is resolutely anti-Freudian in the sense that he is not interested in the notion of a personal unconscious. Thus to him the language that speaks through poets has a truly metaphysical status. And as it sometimes spoke through Hardy, Brodsky makes it clear, language is capable of speaking through every real poet, including himself. In a disconcerting way, Brodsky here finds himself not at all far from the kind of reductive critique which claims that speakers are little more than the mouthpieces of hegemonic discourses or ideologies. The difference is that, while it is accepted that these discourses and ideologies change with the historical times, Brodsky's language – the time-marked and time-marking language of poetry – is a force operating through and within time but outside history. 'Prosody . . . is simply a repository of time within language'; 'Language is older than state and . . . prosody always survives history.'[3]

Brodsky is unequivocal in taking away control of the larger-scale history and development of poetry from poets themselves and handing it to a metaphysical language – language as will and idea. In Hardy's poetry, for instance, having pointed acutely to a certain absence of a detectable speaking voice, an 'audial neutrality', he suggests that this apparently negative attribute would turn out to have great importance to twentieth-century poetry – would, indeed, make Hardy 'prophetic' of Auden. But, Brodsky maintains, it was not so much the case that Auden or any other of Hardy's successors *imitated* him as that Hardy's neutrality of voice became 'what the future [of English poetry] liked'. (*On Grief*, p. 322)

For an idea so fundamental to his philosophy of poetry, it is odd that the experience of being spoken through by language figures so seldom in Brodsky's own poetry. In only one or two poems, and there only fleetingly, does Brodsky directly thematise that experience (of course, he may claim that the experience is *embodied* in all his poems). One explanation might be that the experience is more appropriately treated at a dispassionate remove in discursive prose. A more interesting explanation would be that the meta-poetical theme of poetry reflecting on the conditions of its own existence is absent precisely because, as an attempt on the part of the poet to understand and thus to master the force animating him, it strikes Brodsky as not only impious but futile as well.

But even granting the claim that poetry is written in a state of possession by a higher force, there remains something strange, even eccentric, in the elevation of prosody in particular to metaphysical status. 'Verse meters in themselves are kinds of spiritual magnitudes for which nothing can be substituted,' writes Brodsky. (*Less than One*, p. 141) They are 'a means of restructuring time'. (*On Grief*, p. 418) What precisely does it mean to restructure time? How thorough is that restructuring? How long does it last? Brodsky never explains fully, or fully enough. He comes closest in the essay on Mandelstam in *Less than One*, where the time that utters itself through Mandelstam confronts the 'mute space' of Stalin; but even there the core of the notion remains mysterious and perhaps even mystical. Nevertheless, when Brodsky says, in *On Grief and Reason*, that 'language . . . uses a human being, not the other way around', he would seem to have the metres of poetry above all in mind; and when – particularly in his lectures to students – he pleads for the educative and even redemptive function of poetry ('love is a metaphysical affair whose goal is either accomplishing or liberating one's soul . . . [and] that is and always has been the core of lyric poetry'), it is submission to the rhythms of poetry he is alluding to. (*On Grief*, p. 87)

If I am right, then Brodsky's position is not far from that of the educationists of ancient Athens, who prescribed for students (men only, not women) a tripartite curriculum of music (intended to make the soul rhythmical and harmonious), poetry and gymnastics. Plato collapsed these three parts into two, music absorbing poetry and becoming the principal mental/spiritual discipline. Those powers that Brodsky claims for poetry would seem to belong less to poetry than to music. For instance, time is the medium of music more clearly than it is the medium of poetry: we read poetry on the printed page as fast as we like – usually faster than we ought to – whereas we listen to music in its own time. Music thus structures the time in which it is performed, lending it purposive form, more clearly than poetry does. So why does Brodsky not make his case for poetry along Plato's lines, as a species of music?

The answer is, of course, that, while the technical language of prosody may derive from the technical language of music, poetry is not a species of music. Specifically, because it works through words, not sounds, poetry has a semantic dimension; whereas the semantic dimension of music is at most connotational and therefore secondary.

Since antique times we have had a well-developed account, borrowed from music, of the phonics of poetry. We also have scores of theories of the semantics of poetry, of poetry as a kind of language with special rules of meaning. What we lack is any widely accepted theory which marries the two. The last critics in America who believed they had such a theory were the New Critics; their rather arid style of reading ran out in the sands in the early 1960s. Since then poetry, and lyric poetry in particular, has become an embarrassment to the critical profession, or at least to the academic arm of that profession. None of the schools of criticism that rule the academy wants to deal with poetry in its own right; in practice it is read as if it were prose with ragged right-hand margins.

In 'An Immodest Proposal' (1991), a plea for a federally sub-sidised programme to distribute millions of cheap anthologies of American poetry, Brodsky suggests that lines like 'No memory of having starred / Atones for later disregard / Or keeps the end from being hard' (Robert Frost) ought to enter the bloodstream of every citizen, not just because they constitute a lapidary *memento mori*, and not just because they exemplify language at its purest and most powerful, but because, in absorbing them and making them our own, we work toward an evolutionary goal: 'The purpose of evolution, believe it or not, is beauty.' (*On Grief*, p. 207)

Perhaps. But what if we experiment? What if we rewrite Frost's lines thus: 'Memories of having starred / Atone for later disregard / And keep the end from being hard'? At a purely metrical level the revision is not, to my ear, inferior to Frost's original. However, its meaning is opposite. Would these lines, in Brodsky's eyes, qualify to enter the bloodstream of the nation? The answer is: no – the lines are in a telling sense false. But to show how and why they are false requires a poetics with an historical dimension, capable of explaining why it is that Frost's original, coming into being at the moment in history when it does, carves out for itself a place in time ('restructures time'), whereas the alternative, the parody, cannot do so. What is required, therefore, is a means of treating prosody and semantics together in a unified yet also diachronic way. For a teacher (and Brodsky clearly thinks of himself as a teacher) to assert that the genuine poem restructures time means little until he can show why the fake does not.

In sum, then, there are two sides to Brodsky's critical poetics. On the one hand there is a metaphysical superstructure in which the language-Muse speaks through the medium of the poet and thereby accomplishes world-historical (evolutionary) goals of its own. On the other there is a body of insights into and intuitions about how certain poems in English, Russian and (to a lesser extent) German actually work. The poems Brodsky chooses are clearly poems he loves; his comments on them are always intelligent, often penetrating, sometimes dazzling. I doubt that Mandelstam (in *Less than One*) or Hardy (in *On Grief*) have ever had a more sympathetic, attentive, co-creative reader. Fortunately the metaphysical superstructure of Brodsky's system can be detached and laid aside, leaving us with a set of critical readings which in their ambitiousness and their fineness of detail put contemporary academic criticism of poetry to shame.

Can academic critics take a lesson from Brodsky? I fear not. To operate at his level, one has to live with and by the great poets of the past, and perhaps be visited by the Muse as well. Can Brodsky take a lesson from the academy? Yes: not to publish your lecture notes verbatim, unrevised and uncondensed, quips and asides included. The lectures on Frost, Hardy and Rilke could with advantage be cut by ten pages each.

III

Though *On Grief and Reason* intermittently alludes to, and

sometimes directly addresses, Brodsky's own exile/immigrant status, it does not, except in an odd and inconclusive exercise on the spy Kim Philby, address politics pure and simple. At the risk of oversimplifying, one can say that Brodsky despairs of politics and looks to literature for redemption.

Thus, in an open letter to Vaclav Havel, Brodsky suggests that Havel drop the pretence that Communism in Central Europe was imposed from abroad and acknowledge that it was the result of 'an extraordinary anthropological backslide' whose basis was no more and no less than original sin. As President of the Czech state, Havel would be well advised to operate on the premise that man is inherently evil; the re-education of the Czech public might begin with doses of Proust, Kafka, Faulkner and Camus in the daily papers. (*On Grief*, pp. 218–22)

(Elsewhere Brodsky criticises Aleksandr Solzhenitsyn on the same grounds: for refusing to accept what his senses plainly tell him, that humankind is 'radically bad.' *Less than One*, p. 299)

In his Nobel Prize lecture, Brodsky sketches out an aesthetic credo on the basis of which an ethical public life might be built. Aesthetics, he says, is the mother of ethics, in the sense that making fine aesthetic discriminations teaches one to make fine ethical discriminations. Good art is thus on the side of the good. Evil, on the other hand, 'especially political evil, is always a bad stylist'. (*On Grief*, p. 49) (At moments like this Brodsky finds himself closer to his illustrious Russo-American precursor, the patrician Vladimir Nabokov, than he might have wished to be.)

Entering into dialogue with great literature, Brodsky continues, fosters in the reading subject 'a sense of uniqueness, of individuality, of separateness – thus turning him from a social animal into an autonomous "I"'. (*On Grief*, p. 46) Earlier, in *Less than One* Brodsky had commended Russian poetry for 'set[ting] an example of moral purity and firmness' in the Soviet era, not least by preserving classical literary forms. (p. 142) Now he rejects the nihilism of postmodernism, 'the poetics of ruin and debris, of minimalism, of choked breath', holding up instead the example of those poets of his generation who, in the wake of the Holocaust and the Gulag, took it as their task to reconstruct world culture and hence to rebuild human dignity. (*On Grief*, p. 56)

It is not Brodsky's manner to attack, discuss, or even mention the names of his philosophical opponents. Thus one can only guess at his response to arguments that artworks (or 'texts') construct communities of readers as much as they construct individuals, that an emphasis such as his on a highly individualistic relation between reader and text is historically and culturally bounded, and that what he (following Mandelstam) calls 'world culture' is merely the high culture of Western Europe in a particular phase of its history. There can be no doubt, however, that he would have rejected them.

IV

The prestige of the poet figure in Russia since Pushkin, the example of the great poets in keeping the flame of individual integrity alive during Stalin's dark night, as well as deeply embedded traditions of reading and memorising poetry, cheap editions of the classics and the near-sacred status of forbidden texts in the *samizdat* phase – these and other factors contributed to the persistence in Russia, before the great opening up of the 1990s, of a large, committed, and informed public for poetry. The linguistically oriented bias of literary studies there – in part a continuation of the Formalist advances of the 1920s, in part a self-protective reaction to the ban, after 1934, on literary criticism not in line with Socialist-realist dogma – further nurtured an analytic discourse hard to match in the West in its level of technical sophistication.

Comments on Brodsky by his Russian contemporaries – fellow poets, disciples, rivals – as collected by Valentina Polukhina four years before Brodsky's death in 1996, prove that even after a quarter of a century abroad he was still read and judged in Russia as a Russian poet.[4]

Brodsky's greatest achievement, says the poet Olga Sedakova, was to have 'placed a full stop at the end of [the Soviet] literary epoch'. (p. 247) He did so by bringing back to Russian letters a quality crushed, in the name of optimism, by the Soviet culture industry: a tragic perception of life. Furthermore, he fertilised Russian poetry by importing new forms from England and America. For this he deserves to stand beside Pushkin. Elena Shvarts, Brodsky's younger contemporary and perhaps his main rival, concurs: he brought 'a completely new musicality and even a new form of thought' to Russian poetry. (Shvarts is not so kind to Brodsky the essayist, whom she calls 'a brilliant sophist'.) (pp. 222, 221)

Brodsky's fellow Russians are particularly illuminating on technical features of his verse. Brodsky, claims Yevgeny Rein, found metrical means to embody 'the way time flows past and away from you'. This 'merging of [the] poetry with the movement of time' is 'metaphysically' Brodsky's greatest achievement. (p. 63) To the Lithuanian poet Tomas Venclova, Brodsky's 'giant linguistic and cultural reach, his syntax, his thoughts that transcend the limits of the stanza', make of his poetry 'a spiritual exercise [which] extends the reach of [the reader's] soul'. (p. 278)

There is thus no doubt that Brodsky in exile remained a powerful presence on the Russian stage. Receptive as his fellow writers are to his innovations, however, all except Rein seem sceptical about the full metaphysical baggage behind them, a metaphysics that makes the poet the voice of an hypostatised Language. Lev Loseff dismisses this 'idolisation' of language out of hand, attributing it to Brodsky's lack of formal education in linguistics. (p. 123)

In Russia Brodsky has not managed to make himself a well-loved poet, as (say) Pasternak was well loved. Russians look in vain to him, says Venclova, for 'warmth . . . all-forgivingness, tearfulness, tender-heartedness, or cheeriness'. 'He does not believe in man's inherent goodness; nor does he see nature as . . . made in the image of God.' (p. 283) The poet Viktor Krivulin expresses doubts about the very un-Russian irony that became habitual in Brodsky's later poetry. Brodsky cultivates irony, suggests Krivulin, to protect himself from ideas or situations he finds uncomfortable. 'A fear of openness, possibly a desire not to be open . . . has grown deeper so that every poetic statement already exists inherently as an object for analysis and the following statement springs from that analysis.' (p. 187)

Roy Fisher, one of Brodsky's best English commentators, points to something analogous in the texture of Brodsky's self-translations from Russian, which he criticises as 'busy' in a musical sense, with 'lots of little notes and pauses'. 'Something is running about in the way of the poetry.' (p. 300)

This 'busyness', together with a continual ironic backtracking, became a feature of Brodsky's prose as much as of his verse. His logic acquired a jagged, spiky quality: trains of thought have no time to develop before being halted, questioned, cast in doubt, in qualifications that are in turn, with mannered irony, interrogated and qualified. There is a continual shuttling back and forth between colloquial and formal diction; and when a *bon mot* is in the offing, Brodsky can be trusted to scamper after it. In his fascination with the echo chamber of the English language, he is again not unlike Nabokov, though Nabokov's linguistic imagination was more disciplined (also, perhaps, more trammelled). The problem of consistency of tone becomes particularly marked in essays that have their origin in public addresses, where, as if in an effort to suppress the habitual sideways movement of his thought, Brodsky goes in for large generalisations and hollow lecture-hall prose.

Brodsky's difficulties here may in part be temperamental – public occasions clearly did not fire his imagination – but they are also linguistic. Brodsky, David Bethea has observed, never quite succeeded in commanding the 'quasi-civic' level of American discourse, as he never entirely commanded the nuances of ironic humour, perhaps the last level of English to be mastered by foreigners.[5]

An alternative approach to Brodsky's problem with tone is to ask whether his imagined interlocutors are always adequate to him. In his lectures and addresses there seems to be an element of speaking down that leads him not only to simplify his matter but also to wisecrack and generally to flatten his emotional and intellectual range; whereas, once he is alone with a subject equal to him, this uneasiness of tone vanishes.

We see Brodsky truly rising to his subject in the two Roman essays in *On Grief and Reason*. In emotional reach, the essay on Marcus Aurelius is one of Brodsky's most ambitious, as though the nobility of his interlocutor frees him to explore a certain melancholy grandeur. Like the Polish poet Zbigniew Herbert, with whose stance of stoic pessimism in public affairs he has more than a little in common, Brodsky looks to Marcus as the one Roman ruler with whom some kind of communion across the ages is possible. 'You were one of the best men that ever lived, and you were obsessed with your duty because you were obsessed with virtue,' he writes movingly. Wistfully he adds that we ought always to have rulers who, like Marcus, have 'a detectable melancholic streak'. (*On Grief*, pp. 291, 294)

The finest essay in the collection is similarly elegiac. It takes the form of a letter from Brodsky the Russian or, in Roman terms, the

Hyperborean, to Horace in the Underworld. To Brodsky, Horace is, if not his favourite Roman poet (Ovid holds that place), then at least the great poet of 'melancholic equipoise'. (*On Grief*, p. 235). Brodsky plays with the conceit that Quintus Horatius Flaccus has just completed a spell on earth in the guise of Wystan Hugh Auden, and that Horace, Auden, and Joseph Brodsky himself are thus the same poetic temperament, if not the same person, reborn in successive Pythagorean metamorphoses. His prose attains new and complex, bitter-sweet tones as he meditates on the death of the poet, on the extinction of the man and his survival in the echo of the poetic metres he has served.

13   J. L. Borges, *Collected Fictions*

I

IN 1961 the directors of six leading Western publishing houses (Gallimard, Einaudi, Rowohlt, Seix Barral, Grove, and Weidenfeld & Nicolson) met at a resort in the Balearic Islands to plan a literary prize that would single out writers who were actively transforming the world literary landscape, and eventually rival the Nobel Prize in prestige. The first International Publishers' Prize (also known as the Prix Formentor) was split between Samuel Beckett and Jorge Luis Borges. That same year the Nobel Prize was awarded to the Yugoslav Ivo Andrić, a substantial novelist but no innovator. (Beckett won the Nobel in 1969. Borges never won it – his advocates claimed that his politics scuppered him.)

The publicity surrounding the Prix Formentor catapulted Borges on to the world stage. In the United States, Grove Press brought out seventeen stories under the title *Ficciones*. New Directions followed with *Labyrinths*, twenty-three stories – some overlapping the *Ficciones*, but in alternative translations – as well as essays and parables. Translation into other languages proceeded apace.

Besides his native Argentina, there was one country in which the name Borges was already well known. The French critic and editor Roger Caillois had spent the years 1939–45 in exile in Buenos Aires. After the war he promoted Borges in France, bringing out *Ficciones* in 1951 and *Labyrinthes* in 1953 (the latter collection substantially different from the New Directions *Labyrinths* – the Borges bibliography constitutes a labyrinth in its own right). In the 1950s Borges was more highly regarded, and perhaps more widely read, in France than in Argentina. In this respect his career curiously parallels that of his forerunner in speculative fiction, Edgar Allan Poe, championed by Baudelaire and enthusiastically taken up by the French public.

The Borges of 1961 was already in his sixties. The stories that had made him famous had been written in the 1930s and 1940s. He had lost his creative drive and had furthermore become suspicious of these earlier, 'baroque' pieces. Though he lived until 1986, he would only fitfully reproduce their intellectual daring and intensity.

In Argentina Borges had by 1960 been recognised, along with Ernesto Sábato and Julio Cortázar, as a leading light of his literary generation. During the first regime of Juan Perón (1946–55) he had become somewhat of a whipping boy of the press, denounced as *extranjerizante* (foreign-loving), a lackey of the landowning elite and of international capital. Soon after Perón's inauguration he was ostentatiously dismissed from his job in the city library and 'promoted' to be inspector of poultry and rabbits at the municipal market. After the fall of Perón it became fashionable again to read him; but his support for unpopular causes (the Bay of Pigs invasion of Cuba, for instance) made him vulnerable to denunciation from the Left as well as by nationalists and populists.

His influence on Latin American letters – where writers have traditionally turned to Europe for their models – has been extensive. He, more than anyone, renovated the language of fiction and thus opened the way to a remarkable generation of Spanish-American novelists. Gabriel Garcia Márquez, Carlos

Fuentes, José Donoso and Mario Vargas Llosa have all acknowledged a debt to him. 'The only thing I bought [in Buenos Aires] was Borges's *Complete Works*,' said Garcia Márquez. 'I carry them in my suitcase; I am going to read them every day, and he is [for political reasons] a writer I detest.'[1]

For a decade after Borges's death in 1986, his literary estate remained in a state of confusion as various parties contested the terms of his will. Happily that confusion has now been resolved, and the first fruits in English are a *Collected Fictions*, newly translated by Andrew Hurley.[2] This volume brings together Borges's early stories *A Universal History of Iniquity* (1935), the *Fictions* of 1944 (which include the stories of *The Garden of Forking Paths*, 1941), *The Aleph* (1949), the prose pieces of *The Maker* (*El hacedor*, previously translated as *Dreamtigers*) (1960), five short prose pieces from *In Praise of Darkness* (1969), *Brodie's Report* (1970), *The Book of Sand* (1975) and four late stories, collected here under the title 'Shakespeare's Memory' (1983).

Of the hundred-odd pieces in the volume, ranging in length from a single paragraph to a dozen pages, only the last four have not hitherto been available in English. The notes appended by Hurley, while valuable in themselves, are limited in scope, 'intended only to supply information that a Latin American (and especially Argentine or Uruguayan) reader would have and that would color or determine his or her reading of the stories'. (*CF*, p. 520) For the rest, the reader who has difficulty with this learned and allusive writer is directed to *A Dictionary of Borges* by Evelyn Fishburn and Psiche Hughes (London: Duckworth, 1990), a commendable work of reference which, however, fails to rise to the challenge of providing an entry for J.L. Borges, a character – fictional? real? – who appears in the story 'Borges and I' and numerous other pieces.

The *Collected Fictions* – the first of three Borges volumes published by Viking in 1999 – is based on the Spanish *Obras completas* of 1989.[3] As an edition without scholarly apparatus, it does not aspire to rival the French *Oeuvres complètes*, scrupulously edited in two volumes for Gallimard's Bibliothèque de la Pléiade by Jean-Pierre Bernès, which not only attempts to collect the totality of Borges's writings (including journalism, reviews and other ephemera), but, more importantly, goes a long way in tracking the revisions which Borges – himself a fussy editor – carried out on successive printings of his own texts ('[Borges's] habit of changing texts from edition to edition, of suppressing, or excising, sometimes reintroducing in modified form, words, phrases, lines . . . has landed any potential bibliographer with a lifetime's toil,' remarks Borges's biographer James Woodall).[4]

II

Jorge Luis Borges was born in 1899 into a prosperous middle-class family, in a Buenos Aires where Spanish – to say nothing of Italian – descent was not deemed a social asset. One of his grandmothers was from England; the family chose to stress their English affiliations and to bring up the children speaking English as well as Spanish. Borges remained a lifelong anglophile. Curiously for a writer with an avant-garde reputation, his own reading seemed to stop around 1920. His taste in English-language fiction was for Stevenson, Chesterton, Kipling, Wells; he often referred to himself as '*un ser victoriano*', a Victorian. (Woodall, p. xxix)

Englishness was one part of Borges's self-fashioning, Jewishness another. He invoked a rather hypothetical Sephardic strain on his mother's side to explain his interest in the Kabbalah and, more interestingly, to present himself as an outsider to Western culture, with an outsider's freedom to criticise and innovate. (Indeed, one might add, to pillage whole libraries for citations.)

In 1914 the Borges family travelled to Switzerland to seek a cure for Borges senior's eye condition (detached retinas, a condition inherited by his son). Trapped in Europe by the war, the children received a French-language education. The young Borges also taught himself German and read Schopenhauer, who came to exert a lasting influence on his thought. German led him to the new Expressionist poets, painters, and film-makers, and thus to forays into mysticism, thought transmission, double personalities, the fourth dimension, and so forth.

After a spell in Spain, Borges returned to Argentina in 1921 an enthusiast for *Ultraismo*, the Spanish cousin of Imagism. Yet even in his rather conventional youthful radicalism there are flashes of originality – for instance, when he dreams up a language in which one word will stand simultaneously for sunset and the sound of cattle bells.

In 1931 the wealthy patroness of the arts Victoria Ocampo launched the magazine *Sur* and threw open its pages to Borges. Ocampo's inclinations were European and internationalist; in his years as chief contributor to *Sur* Borges worked his way beyond the rather tired issues of Argentine literary debate (naturalism versus modernism, Europeanism versus nativism). The stories that make up *The Garden of Forking Paths* – stories that mark the beginning of his major period – appeared in *Sur* in a burst between 1939 and 1941.

'Pierre Menard', the earliest of the group, is, as fiction, the least satisfactory: a cross between spoof scholarly essay and *conte philosophique*. Borges excluded the piece from his *Personal Anthology* of 1968. Nevertheless, its intellectual daring is remarkable. Pierre Menard, minor contemporary of Paul Valéry, absorbs himself totally in the world of Cervantes so as to be able to write (*not* rewrite) *Don Quixote* word for word.

The ideas on which 'Pierre Menard' is built can be found in David Hume (the past, including the age of Cervantes, has no existence except as a succession of present mental states). What Borges achieves is to invent a vehicle (imperfect in this case, but rapidly perfected in the stories that follow) in which the paradoxes of philosophical scepticism can be elegantly staged and followed to their vertiginous conclusions.

The finest of the stories of *The Garden of Forking Paths* are 'Tlön, Uqbar, Orbis Tertius' and 'The Library of Babel' — finest in the sense that the philosophical argument folds discreetly into the narrative, and the fiction takes its course with the certainty of a game of chess in which the reader is always a move behind the author. The technical innovation on which these fictions rest, and which allows them their swift pace — the reader is outflanked and overwhelmed by his opponent before he knows where he is — is that they use as model the anatomy or critical essay, rather than the tale: with narrative exposition reduced to a bare minimum, the action can be condensed to an exploration of the implications of a hypothetical situation (an infinite library, for instance).

In interviews given in the 1960s Borges suggested that, besides exploring the intellectual possibilities of inventing a world by writing a total description of it, 'Tlön' explores the 'dismay' of a narrator 'who feels that his everyday world . . . his past . . . [and] the past of his forefathers . . . [are] slipping away from him'. Thus the hidden subject of the story is 'a man who is being drowned in a new and overwhelming world that he cannot make out'.[5] Like all authors' readings of their own work, this one has its own interest. But as an account of 'Tlön' it misses something important: the excitement, even creative triumph, however sombre its shading, with which the narrator records the stages by which an ideal universe takes over a real one, the takeover being capped, in a turn of the screw of paradox characteristic of Borges, by the realisation that the universe of which we are part is more than likely already a simulacrum, perhaps a simulacrum of simulacra going on to infinity. Revisiting his 1940 story a quarter of a century later, Borges finds in it an emotional colouring that belongs to his older, more pessimistic self.

Yet to conclude that Borges misreads his story is to miss the Borgesian (or Menardian) point. There is no Tlön, just as there is no 1940, outside the conceptions of Tlön and 1940 that humankind collectively holds in the present. Just as the all-comprehending encyclopedia of Orbis Tertius takes over the universe, our fictions of the fictions of the past take over these fictions. (Gnostic cosmology, in which Borges was deeply read, proposes that the universe in which we believe we live is the work of a minor creator nested within a universe which is the handiwork of a slightly less minor creator who is nested within another universe, and so on 365 times.)

Of the *Fictions* of 1944, 'Funes, His Memory' is the most astonishing. Ireneo Funes, an untutored country boy, is possessed of an infinite memory. Nothing escapes him; all of his sensory experience, past and present, persists in his mind; drowned in particulars, unable to forget even the changing formations of all the clouds he has seen, he cannot form general ideas, and therefore – paradoxically, for a creature who is almost pure mind – cannot *think*.

'Funes' follows the by now familiar Borgesian pattern of pushing a *donnée* to its dizzying conclusions. What is new in the story is a confidence with which Borges embeds his Funes in a recognisable Argentine social reality, as well as a touch of human pity for the afflicted boy, 'the solitary, lucid spectator of a multiform, momentaneous, and almost unbearably precise world'. (*CF*, p. 137)

It is not hard to see why daringly idealistic fictions about worlds created by language or characters enclosed in texts should have found resonance in a generation of French intellectuals who had just discovered the structural linguistics of Ferdinand de Saussure, to whom language is a self-regulating field within which the human subject functions without power, more spoken by language than speaking it, and the past ('diachrony') is reducible to a series of superposed present ('synchronic') states. What Borges's French readers found startling – or perhaps just piquant – was that he had found a way to *textualité* along routes of his own devising. (In fact there is reason to believe that Borges found his way there via Schopenhauer and, particularly, Fritz Mauthner [1849–1923]. Mauthner is little read nowadays; there is no entry for him in Fishburn and Hughes's *Dictionary of Borges*, despite the fact that Borges alludes to him several times.)

The three collections that comprise Borges's middle and major period – *The Garden of Forking Paths*, *Fictions*, and *The Aleph* – were followed in 1952 by *Other Inquisitions*, a mosaic of pieces culled from his critical writing. The fact that many of these pieces, with their vast erudition in a range of languages, first appeared in newspapers says much for the upper reaches of the Buenos Aires press. Many of the ideas explored in the fiction can be found half-grown here, not yet ready to show their teeth.

Reading the essays side by side with the fictions prompts what is perhaps the central question about Borges: what do the operations of fiction offer this scholar-writer that enable him to take ideas into reaches where the discursive essay, as a mode of writing, fails him? Borges's own answer, following Coleridge, is that the poetic imagination enables the writer to join himself to the universal creative principle; following Schopenhauer, he would add that this principle has the nature of Will rather than (as Plato would say) of Reason. 'In the course of a lifetime dedicated less to living than to reading, I have been able to verify repeatedly that aims and literary theories are nothing but stimuli; the finished work frequently ignores and even contradicts them.'[6]

Yet it would be obtuse not to hear, in pronouncements like this one, tones of parody and self-parody. The voices that speak the *Other Inquisitions* are much like the voices of the narrators of the fictions; behind the essays is a persona whom Borges had already begun to call 'Borges'. Which Borges is real, which is the other in the mirror, remains dark. The essays allow the one Borges to dramatise the other. In practical terms, this puts in question the distinction between fiction and non-fiction used by Borges's American publishers (see note 3).

El hacedor (1960) is a compendium of prose and verse, from which the Viking *Collected Fictions* drops the verse. The title alludes – rather cryptically, for a Spanish-speaking audience – to the archaic English 'maker', or poet, which is the word that Hurley takes over; Mildred Boyer and Harold Morland, in their 1964 translation, retitle the book *Dreamtigers*. Borges called it 'my most personal work, and to my taste, maybe the best'. (Woodall, p. 188) There is a touch of defiance in this pronouncement, since nothing in the collection measures up to the best of the fictions of the period 1939–49. But by 1960 Borges had already begun to put a distance between himself and what he would later, disparagingly, call 'labyrinths and mirrors and tigers and all that'.[7]

The truth was that the Prix Formentor of 1961 caught Borges in the middle of a long creative slump. His newfound fame brought invitations to lecture, which he was happy to accept. Accompanied by his mother, he travelled widely. From the North American lecture circuit he began to enjoy a steady income. Rarely did he refuse interviews; he became, in fact, garrulous. He searched actively for a wife, found one, and for three years, in his late sixties, suffered an unhappy marriage.

In 1967 Borges met the American translator Norman Thomas di Giovanni. An association developed: not only did di Giovanni translate, or collaborate with Borges to translate, a number of works, and help with his business affairs, but he also coaxed Borges back into writing fiction. The fruits can be seen in the eleven stories of *Brodie's Report* (1970). The mirrors and labyrinths are gone. The settings are the Argentine pampas or the outskirts of Buenos Aires, the language is simpler, the plots are more conventional (in his foreword Borges points to Kipling as a model). Borges was proudest of 'The Interloper', but 'The Gospel according to St Mark', in which a student, having introduced the Christian gospel to a backlands gaucho family, is accepted as their saviour and solemnly crucified, is as good. With its concentration on jealousy, physical bravery, and laconically treated violence, *Brodie's Report* is the most defiantly masculine of Borges's collections.

The Book of Sand (1975) and 'Shakespeare's Memory' (1983) recycle old themes (the *Doppelgänger*, possession, the interpenetration of universes) as well as exploring Germanic mythology, a new interest of Borges's. There is much tired writing in them; they add nothing to his stature.

III

Borges's gnosticism – his sense that the ultimate God is beyond good and evil, and infinitely remote from creation – is deeply felt. But the sense of dread that informs his work is metaphysical rather than religious in nature: at its base are vertiginous glimpses of the collapse of all structures of meaning, including language itself, flashing intimations that the very self that speaks has no real existence.

In the fiction that responds to this dread, the ethical and the aesthetic are tightly wound together: the light but remorseless tread of the logic of his parables, the lapidary concision of his language, the gradual tightening of paradox, are stylistic traces of a stoical self-control that stares back into the abysses of thought without the Gothic hysteria of a Poe.

Borges has been criticised for falling back on the aesthetic for salvation. Harold Bloom, for instance, suggests that Borges would have been a greater writer if he had exercised a less iron control over his creative impulse – a control whose purpose Bloom sees as self-protective. 'What Borges lacks, despite the illusive cunning of his labyrinths, is precisely the extravagance of the romancer . . . [He] has never been reckless enough to lose himself in a story, to our loss, if not to his.'[8]

I am not sure that these strictures take adequately into account those stories of Borges's that focus on the confrontation with death. 'The South' – which ends with the hero accepting the challenge to a knife duel he is sure to lose – is the most haunting of these; but there are several other more realistic tales of gaucho or hoodlum life in which characters, following an unarticulated stoic ethic, choose death rather than loss of honour, recovering themselves from disgrace and discovering their truth in the same moment. These stories, laconic in expression and sometimes brutal in content, reveal the attractions of a life of action for their bookish and rather timid author. They also show Borges trying to situate himself more forthrightly in an Argentine literary tradition and contribute to Argentine national myth-making.

The word 'camel', observes Borges in a lecture entitled 'The Argentine Writer and Tradition' (1953), does not occur in the Koran. The lesson? That 'we can believe in the possibility of being Argentine without abounding in local colour'.[9] But his own later stories – particularly those collected in *Brodie's Report* – do in fact abound in local colour. They represent a tenacious return to the task that Borges, on his return to Buenos Aires in the 1920s, saw before him: to hold on to the density of culture that was part of his generations-old *criollo* heritage, yet to get beyond mere regionalism and localism. 'There are no legends in this land,' he wrote in 1926. 'That is our disgrace. Our lived reality is grandiose yet the life of our imagination is paltry . . . We must find the poetry, the music, the painting, the religion and the metaphysics appropriate to [the] greatness [of Buenos Aires].'[10]

Set in the seedier Buenos Aires suburbs of the turn of the century, or even further back in time on the Argentine pampas, the later stories can hardly be claimed to confront the reality of modern Argentina. They embrace a romantic, nativistic streak in Argentine nationalism, turning their back both on the enlightened liberalism of the class into which Borges was born and on the new mass culture and mass politics – represented in his lifetime by Perónism – which he held in abhorrence.

IV

Borges's prose is controlled, precise and economical to a degree uncommon in Spanish America. It avoids (as Borges notes with some pride) 'Hispanicisms, Argentinisms, archaisms, and neo-logisms; [it uses] everyday words rather than shocking ones'.[11] In his work up to and including *The Aleph*, the clear surface of his prose is ruffled now and again by unusual, even disturbing verbal collocations. In his late phase such moments are rare.

Although any translator will be challenged to match the simultaneous concision and force of Borges's Spanish and to find renderings for his sometimes riddling metaphors, his language presents no irresolvable problems, except on those occasions when it is coloured – deliberately, one is sure – by English verbal patterns. (Such patterns, as soon as they are reproduced in English translation, of course sink into invisibility.)

There is a set of difficulties of a more practical nature, however, created by the fact that Borges, late in life, acted as his own (co)translator (of *The Aleph* and *Brodie's Report*, as well as of much poetry), and in the process of translating availed himself of the opportunity to do some revising. These revisions can be quite sweeping in scale: half a page of rather dated satire is cut from 'The Aleph', for instance. Borges also felt free to work into his English texts information that the protocols of the craft would constrain any other translator to relegate to footnotes: a cryptic mention of *la revolución de Aparício*, for instance, is expanded to 'a civil war . . . between the Colorados, or Reds, who were in power, and Aparício's Blancos, or Whites'.[12]

But Borges's revisions have a subsidiary purpose as well: to tone down his own Spanish. Resounding trademark adjectives of the middle phase, like *abominable, enigmático, implacable, interminable, notorio, perverso, pérfido, vertiginoso, violento* – are softened: the 'violent [*violento*] flank of the mountain' becomes its 'steep slope', a woman's 'violent [*violenta*] hair' becomes her 'tangled hair' (*CF*, pp. 96, 285).

The justification offered by Borges and di Giovanni for this toning down, and for the general smoothness of their English versions, is that Spanish and English embody 'two quite different ways of looking at the world'. They have tried less to transpose the original Spanish into English, they say, than 'to rethink every sentence in English words', aiming for prose that '[reads] as though . . . written in English'.[13]

Hurley – correctly, to my mind – ignores the example Borges sets. Unfortunately, that cannot be the end of the story. The changes that Borges (as the creative partner in the collaboration) introduces in the process of translating himself can be regarded as authorial revisions capable, at least in theory, of being reintroduced into the Spanish text, and in any event as revisions authorially approved for the stories in their English guise.

Hurley does not, in his brief 'Note on the Translation', address this problem. What he might have said – if one may be allowed to put words in his mouth – is that there are times when editors and translators have a duty to protect Borges from himself. *Pace* the author, the versions of Borges that we want to read are not necessarily those that sound as if English were their native tongue: if there is indeed a proportion of grandiloquence in the originals, the reader may prefer to hear that grandiloquence and discriminate for himself what is authentically Borgesian in it, what native to the Spanish, rather than have the language uniformly muted on his behalf.

There is one respect, however, in which it would be rash not to take Borges's lead, namely when he offers privileged access to his own intentions. *Un alfajor* can be any of a variety of regional sweetmeats. Which did Borges have in mind? A sugared cake, his translation reveals. Hurley pretends not to know this and calls it, vaguely, a 'sweet offering'. (*CF*, p. 277) If one puts one's ear against a certain stone column in Cairo, says Borges, one can hear the *rumor* of the Aleph inside it. 'Rumour', says Hurley, where Borges could have helped with 'hum'. (*CF*, p. 287)

A quick check against Borges–di Giovanni could even have prevented plain errors. The desert nomads need foreigners to do their 'carpentry', says Hurley. (*CF*, p. 288) The word is *albañilería*, masonry.

Borges has had distinguished translators in the past, among them Anthony Kerrigan, Donald A. Yates, and James E. Irby, to say nothing of the collaborative versions with di Giovanni. Nevertheless, there is much to be said for an integral retranslation of the whole of Borges such as Viking has sponsored. Hurley's versions are generally excellent, marked by accuracy of word choice and a confident sense of narrative style. If there is one general weakness, it is that Hurley's feel for the level of formality of English words is not always reliable. This gives rise to colloquial effects for which there is no parallel in the original. Examples: 'the leery light of dawn', where 'wary' is a more appropriate adjective; priests who 'hornswoggle' rather than 'cheat' (*embaucar*) penitents; a taxi that deposits its fare 'a little ways' from the station rather than 'a little way'. (*CF*, pp. 138, 204, 122) Hurley also performs a disturbing revision of his own. In 'The Circular Ruins,' a story about male generative power and male birth, Borges writes, *A todo padre le interesan los hijos que ha procreado*, 'Every father feels concern for the sons he has procreated'. Hurley translates this, 'Every parent feels concern for the children he has procreated.' (*CF*, p. 100)

14   A.S. Byatt

I

IN THE 1970s A.S. Byatt (born 1936) embarked on a major project: a sequence of novels that would trace the growth of an Englishwoman of her class and generation and education, a woman who would and would not be herself, from the drab early 1950s through the cultural revolution of the 1960s.

Byatt planned four novels. *The Virgin in the Garden* (1978) follows the struggles of her heroine, Frederica Potter, also born 1936, to shed the sexual morality of her parents and the narrow lifestyle imposed by the austerities of the postwar years. 1953, she feels, ought to be the first year of a happier era. Years will pass before she can recognise to what an extent the new Elizabethan Age is underpinned by fake ceremony and mere nostalgia.

Still Life (1985) takes Frederica through her Cambridge years. Although the novel contains *tours de force* of realistic description – performed, one guesses, as a tribute to the great English realists – it is very much a novel of ideas, assembling intersecting circles of characters whose conversations allow Byatt to explore the Zeitgeist of the England of the late 1950s. It ends in 1958, with Frederica in the arms of Nigel Reiver, visiting for the first time the wilder shores of love.

Babel Tower (1995), the third in the as yet (1999) unfinished series, opens six years later. The marriage with Nigel is not going well. Cooped up with his horsy sisters and odious housekeeper in a house in the Home Counties, Frederica feels stifled. She would like to see her old college friends, now making names for themselves on the buzzing London cultural scene, but Nigel doesn't like them. When they write to her, he intercepts their letters. An ex-commando, he has no scruples about roughing her up in ways that leave no telltale marks. She becomes a virtual prisoner.

Frederica flees to London with her four-year-old son. Nigel pursues, leaving a trail of violence in his wake, demanding her back, or, if not her, then the child.

At the ever-so-polite cocktail parties that Frederica begins to frequent, the talk is dominated by men; the women huddle in corners exchanging notes on anti-depressants. It is this kind of future, as much as marital violence, that Frederica resolves to escape.

Frederica has been brought up in 'that tolerant, non-conformist, cautiously sceptical tradition that requires you . . . to look for the good and the bad in everything'.[1] Though she fears and hates her husband, she is unnerved by her own hatred; her urge to cut all ties is held in check by a puritanical determination to be fair. Furthermore, she continues to be fascinated by him. Even at the divorce trial she feels a hot rush of desire.

It is the Lawrentian flavour of her response ('the dark dark look, the intentness that always stirs her') which, to Frederica, identifies it as a symptom not of a merely individual masochistic dependence, but of a sexual pathology afflicting a generation of young women who came to maturity in the 1950s taking as gospel Lawrence's fictions of women who abnegated the intellect to find salvation in the service of the phallus. 'That was our myth,' thinks Frederica –

'that the body is truth. Lady Chatterley hated *words* . . . [whereas] I cannot do without them.' (*Babel Tower*, pp. 241, 129)

Just as, in *The Virgin in the Garden*, Frederica and her sister had felt Lawrence's Brangwen sisters, Ursula and Gudrun, thrust upon them as role-models, so in *Babel Tower* she finds herself resisting the model of Connie Chatterley. The trial scene that ends the novel parodies the famous obscenity trial of 1961; but this is not the only way in which *Lady Chatterley's Lover* looms over *Babel Tower*. In making a new life for herself as a woman and a sexual being in the 1960s, Frederica has to question and in many respects repudiate her earlier moral education, an education imbibed from parents and teachers who had sat at the feet of Lawrence's influential champion at Cambridge, F.R. Leavis.

The conflict between Frederica and Nigel comes to a head in a divorce hearing, an extended scene into which Byatt throws all her considerable resources as a writer. The hearing is a chastening experience for Frederica, who, under the remorseless interrogation of her husband's lawyer, backed by a private detective hired to spy on her and Reiver sisters prepared to perjure themselves, emerges before the court as a selfish, promiscuous woman, unfit to care for her son.

Yet there is a surprise to come. Dominated though it may be by men from the public-school network, men who might be expected to gang up against a woman who has not only bucked the system but, coming from the north of England, from a different class and a different political tradition, has never really been part of that system, the court, in its patriarchal wisdom, and to the rage of the Reiver family, decides that a child belongs with its mother.

Frederica's son is anything but cute. Fiercely he demands that she subordinate her happiness to his. For her part, Frederica – who to her secret shame had planned to abscond without him – slowly discovers the centrality of motherhood to her life, 'a love so violent that it is almost its opposite'. (p. 237)

Frederica spends a lot of her time reading stories to her son, stories that pay him the compliment of taking him seriously as a moral intelligence. What Byatt has to say via these stories – often given *in extenso* in the text – is interesting and challenging in times when the orthodoxy in educational circles is that young children should not be exposed to disturbing material. Just as she is in favour of Racine in secondary school, Byatt is in favour of tales of magic and terror, of heroism and resourcefulness, for under-fives. The education of the imagination comes first: it is because the creative imagination is still alive among the writers and painters and scientists with whom Frederica chooses to cast her lot that they are better people than Nigel, his Shires family and his business friends.

In this respect Byatt belongs squarely in a liberal-humanist Arnoldian tradition. In times of crisis, her people do not go into therapy. Salvation is a matter of private wrestling; the best aids are applied intelligence, hard work and a knowledge of the classics, preferably in several languages. In the struggle of life happiness is not the ultimate prize but self-improvement; childhood is not an island of joy but a time of preparation.

Yet all is not as simple or as puritanically grim as that. At the very moment when Frederica and her closest woman friend agree that their own childhood was a hell of inauthenticity, the key poem on childhood, for people of English culture, comes unbidden to mind: Wordsworth's ode 'Intimations of Immortality', with its evocation of 'those shadowy recollections' from our childhood years which 'Are yet the fountain-light of all our day, / Are yet a master-light of all our seeing'.

A telling moment, as the voice of their culture speaks through the two women. Byatt evokes another such moment when a friend of Frederica's, tramping through the countryside, experiences what he calls 'the *English* feeling', a feeling of belonging to a soil that his ancestors have been born out of and buried in for thousands of years, yet nuanced and coloured by lines of verse so well remembered that 'like turf and stones, [they] are part of the matter of the mind'. (p. 20)

II

Though a brilliant student at Cambridge, Frederica has resisted becoming a teacher. Now the need to make a living in London forces her to take on evening teaching and extend her horizons. She reads Nietzsche and Freud, begins to see how insular her typically British education has been. She reads the great European novelists, from Flaubert to Mann, while putting behind her some of the writers who have formed her outlook. Lawrence and E.M. Forster now seem to her latterday religious writers, trying to elevate the Novel to where the Bible used to be. (T.S. Eliot, another formative influence on the youthful Frederica, is more kindly treated.) The unified self begins to look like an outmoded goal; she prefers that the various identities, linguistic, intellectual, sexual, which make her up be left 'juxtaposed but divided'. She has a presentiment of the kind of art-work in which such a self as hers might express itself: 'an art-form of fragments, juxtaposed, not interwoven, not "organically" spiralling up like a tree or a shell, but constructed brick by brick, layer by layer'. (pp. 318, 363)

Taking a lead from William Burroughs, Frederica experiments idly with cutting up her husband's divorce lawyer's letters and rearranging the fragments. She enjoys the effect so much that she does cut-ups of Lawrence and Forster too. Her notebooks become a mosaic of diary entries and quotations from writers of the day (Allen Ginsberg, Samuel Beckett, R.D. Laing, William Blake,

Nietzsche, Norman O. Brown) as well as from the newspapers. They take on an avant-garde, even Parisian tone.

Frederica calls her textual experiments 'laminations'; the theory of laminations had already been set out in *The Virgin in the Garden*. An ambition grows in her to turn her notebooks into 'a coherently incoherent work', a 'plait of voices' from the 'many women in one' of whom she is made. (*Babel Tower*, p. 466) The implicit promise is that in the fourth volume Frederica will grow into a writer. (The main character in Doris' Lessing's *The Golden Notebook*, published in 1962, also wrote in a layered set of notebooks corresponding to her various identities: dissatisfaction with the organic novel as much as with the organic, integrated self was clearly in the air.)

Like the occasionally essayistic *Still Life*, *Babel Tower* is a novel of ideas, and many of its situations are contrived as frameworks for the discussion of ideas. Not only does the new Parisian structuralism come up, but advances in the sciences: in genetics, biochemistry, animal psychology, linguistics, computer science. To an extent these conversations bring to life the intellectual excitement of the mid-1960s. But much of the material is now so outdated as to be of historical interest only. Byatt's motive for preserving it at length is unclear.

Frederica's attitude toward the new fashions of thought remains cautious. 'In a world where most intellectuals are proclaiming the death of coherence,' comments her author in one of her more magisterial interventions, 'Frederica is an intellectual at large . . . driven by curiosity, by a pleasure in coherence, by making connections.' (p. 383) The promise is thus that Frederica will outgrow the 1960s as she outgrew the 1950s.

The *Bildung* of Frederica continues on the personal front too. There is no shortage of men in her life. But, having spent the first novel of the series trying to lose her virginity, and the second having friendly sex with fellow students, she is now learning to enjoy the companionship of men without sleeping with them. In 1953 she had acted Elizabeth I in a play celebrating the coronation of Elizabeth II. Now she begins to appreciate the power of separateness, the power of the Virgin Queen.

In her restless intelligence and scrupulousness of mind, and her steadily growing sense of herself as a being formed not only by books but by the larger narratives of family history and national history, the Frederica of *Babel Tower* is one of the more interesting characters-in-progress in contemporary fiction, both as woman and as social type, even if one sometimes wonders whether her author has not given her an historical self-awareness beyond her years.

III

One of the tensions in Byatt's work since the 1980s is that, formed though she has been, as writer and as woman, by the inter-penetration of natural landscape and literary tradition that makes up 'the English feeling', she has had to confront the exhaustion of that tradition as a resource for the practising novelist.

Her more recent fiction shows a great deal of textual variety (embedded stories and documents and so forth) and plays with some of the devices of postmodernism. Nevertheless, it continually falls back on the close social observation and moral attentiveness of the great English realists. Though *Babel Tower* shows Frederica (whom it is impossible not to read, in this respect, as a stand-in for Byatt) reflecting (rather tentatively) on the poststructuralist critique of realism, it is hard to see that this critique has had any thoroughgoing effect on Byatt's own fictional language. In *Still Life* she quoted William Carlos Williams with approval: 'No ideas but in things.'[2] In her respect for the truth of accurate observation, Byatt has been formed by Pound (what are Pound's *Cantos* but 'laminations'?) and Williams: her practice is modernist rather than postmodernist.

In an interview from the years when she was writing *Still Life*, Byatt listed some of the features she admired in George Eliot's novels: their 'large number of characters, wide cultural relevance, complex language'. 'It's important for a writer to have a large canvas and plenty of characters,' she emphasised.[3] *Babel Tower* is a recognisably late-twentieth-century novel. Nevertheless here, as in the earlier two books, Byatt aspires to a large canvas, wide cultural relevance (*cultural*, not social: her social range is rather limited), and, by no means least, plenitude of characters. This plenitude is not always a boon. *Babel Tower* has over a hundred characters: one hundred names to remember, one hundred roles, most of them minor. I doubt that even Dickens wrote as many names into a single novel; and Dickens's minor names are thumbnail sketches in their own right, whereas Byatt's could come straight out of the telephone directory.

Mark Twain remarked that, when an American writer does not know how to end a story, he shoots everyone in sight. When Byatt does not know what to do next, she trots a set of new characters on to the stage.

IV

By dint of some rather contrived plotting, Byatt has Frederica attend a trial at law in which the author of a book named *Babbletower* is being prosecuted for obscenity. *Babbletower* is an anti-utopian fiction with a strong debt to the Sade of *120 Days of Sodom*, aimed at all utopian projects spawned by the Enlightenment, from Fourier's to Mao's. It follows the progress of an ideal community in France from its beginnings (dismantling of family ties, reconstruction of language) to its degeneration into a savage tyranny, with the children revealing themselves to be no less proficient in evil than the adults.

Byatt is able to use the occasion of the trial for some tepid satire on the vanity and muddleheadedness of typical 1960s intellectuals who appear as expert witnesses for the defence. Apart from this, the incorporation of whole chapters of this fictive book, written in a mannered, pseudo-archaic, soft-porn prose so stickily rich as to be almost unreadable, constitutes a sorry miscalculation on Byatt's part. *Babel Tower* is in fact far too long a book, at 622 pages, for its material.

Byatt is a gifted literary ventriloquist, as she proved in *Possession* (1990), where she created the lovers Randolph Henry Ash and Christabel LaMotte by the herculean means of forging a body of poems and letters for each. But *Possession* was a highbrow detective story and satire of academic manners, a considerably less ambitious project than the tetralogy. Because the realism of *Possession* was purely textual, a matter of imitating surfaces, such real-world questions as why an academic industry should be devoted to such mediocre and derivative creative spirits as Ash and LaMotte could be finessed.

Is *Babbletower* just another a piece of literary ventriloquism, carried this time to tedious lengths? Byatt makes the question hard to answer by failing to reproduce (or, more accurately, to produce) the key passage for the prosecution, a passage in which – we are to understand – a woman is put to death with particularly repulsive sadistic salaciousness. Why recount at length, in a work of fiction, the trial of another work of fiction whose substantial offence is not only fictive but a matter of hearsay?

V

Byatt's own *Babel Tower* winds down in 1967 with the smoke of catastrophe in the air. The newspapers are full of the Moors Murders and Vietnam. 'Happenings' take place involving blood orgies and the burning of 'skoob' towers ('books' back to front). The prophecy of *Babbletower*, the bad twin of *Babel Tower*, seems on the point of coming true: that energy without restraint leads ineluctably to apocalypse.

Frederica, in her periodisation of history, had thought of herself as a child of the 1930s and 1940s, the grey era which had ended, symbolically, with the accession of Elizabeth II in 1953. Her generation had grown up 'politically placid'. (*Still Life*, p. 300) Now, in 1967, she must face up to the reality of the new age, an age not only of turbulence in the arts and exciting advances in the sciences, but of nuclear power plants on the Yorkshire moors and 'lifeless lakes where no bird sings', of a blighted countryside in which 'the English feeling' as she has known it will have a hard time surviving. (*Babel Tower*, p. 60)

On the brink of the fourth decade of her life, Frederica looks in two directions: towards a past whose shaping of her she has a duty to understand; and towards a present with which, after her Rip van Winkle years in the countryside, she has to catch up. The intellectual equipment with which Byatt has endowed Frederica to perform these tasks is critical rather than creative. If the spectacle of Frederica wrestling with the past is more arresting than Frederica engaging with the present, this is because Byatt does not yet, in the third of the four volumes, seem to have decided whether Frederica has it in her to be creative – in her own terms, to write the book of laminations – or whether she will simply continue to subject the world around her to the operations of a sophisticated but rather passive critical intelligence.

15   Caryl Phillips

I

OVER THE COURSE of three centuries the slave trade shipped some eleven million unwilling people from Africa to the New World – the greatest forced population movement that we know of before the twentieth century. Two-fifths of them went to the plantations of the West Indies, which made up the hard-core area of slavery in the Americas. In comparison, the English-speaking North American mainland received only 5 per cent.

Britain (as well as Spain, France and Holland) transported Africans to the Caribbean to work its colonial plantations, sending out its own people, many of them undesirables or misfits, to oversee their labour. Planter society became notorious for its dissoluteness, its indolence, its philistinism and its snobbishness – a snobbishness that turned on money and on race. It left behind a legacy of racial prejudice based on minute gradations of skin pigmentation, 'white, fusty, musty, dusty, tea, coffee, cocoa, light black, black, dark black,' says V.S. Naipaul, reciting a familiar Caribbean colour litany.[1]

Out of plantation practice and the rationale that sustained it there grew a corpus of colonial lore about black mentality and the black body that we can properly call racist. Eric Williams may go too far in claiming that, far from slavery being born from racism, racism itself was a consequence of slavery – nineteenth-century European ethnography and racial science would make their own huge contribution to the theory of racism – but Williams is certainly right to point to the Americas, and the West Indies in particular, as a forcing-bed for racist thought.[2] In that sense, as the West wrestles today with its racist inheritance, it continues to live in the long shadow of slavery.

The slave ships sailing to the New World bore the first wave of the African diaspora. Then, as the sugar-based economies of the islands began to falter in the early nineteenth century and as the European powers emancipated their slaves, that wave was succeeded by a second, more complex set of migrations continuing into the present: from one island to another; from the islands to the American mainland; from the islands to the former metropolitan ('mother') countries; from the islands to Africa; and from America or Europe or Africa back to the islands. (The spectacular migrations of Cubans and Haitians to the mainland in recent years have obscured the fact that shifts of population have long been a feature of Caribbean demography.)

It is against this historical background of unsettledness and unsettlement, of Eurafrican hybridity and minutely fractured racial consciousness, of incomplete independence and ambivalence about models to follow in the future ('Eventually, the masters left, in a kind of way,' writes Jamaica Kincaid; 'eventually, the slaves were freed, in a kind of way'), that the preoccupations of many of the great Caribbean writers of this century, including Aimé Césaire, Naipaul, and Derek Walcott, need to be seen.[3]

II

Caryl Phillips was born in 1958 on the island of St Kitts (population

45,000) but was taken to Britain as a child (the three loci of his genealogy are thus the three apices of the transatlantic slave trade: West Africa, the Caribbean, Britain). St Kitts of the 1950s was, as it still is, a typical migration society, its economy dependent on remittances sent home by the labour it exported. Phillips calls such islands 'Third Worlds within the Third World'.[4]

Britain of the 1960s was rife with anti-black feeling; in 1962 legislation with a transparently racist basis was passed to make immigration from the ex-colonies more difficult. In an autobiographical essay, Phillips has described the contradictions of growing up 'feeling British, while being constantly told in many subtle and unsubtle ways that I did not belong'.[5] His first novel, *The Final Passage* (1985) – for an unsettled West Indian the title reverberates with irony – draws upon the immigrant's multifarious experience of cold-shouldering behaviour, subtle and unsubtle, conscious and unconscious, on the part of the natives. Of a white social worker, for instance, he writes, 'When she talked . . . she always swallowed just before or just after the word coloured, as if ashamed of it . . . [The word] always got caught just beneath the centre of her tongue and created more saliva than the rest of the words in the sentence put together.'[6]

Yet Phillips has also written sensitively about white characters, most notably in the story 'Higher Ground' (in the novel of the same name) and in the novella 'Somewhere in England' (in *Crossing the River*, 1993). In the latter, the central character is an Englishwoman living through the Second World War in the obscurity of the provinces, coping with a domineering mother, a petty crook of a husband, neighbours who ostracise her when she falls in love with a coloured American serviceman, and a social-welfare bureaucracy that removes their child from her on the grounds that it is a GI baby. In her levelheadedness, loyalty, calm competence and independence of mind (she sees through the war propaganda with which the country is deluged and particularly dislikes 'that fat bastard Churchill'), she exemplifies the heroism of daily life at its most muted; but there is a solitariness, a bleakness, an untouchableness to her as well which is a feature of Phillips's more deeply felt women.[7]

Even the novel *Cambridge* (1991) is not unsympathetic toward its white central character, opinionated and prejudiced though she may be. *Cambridge* is set on an island that looks suspiciously like St Kitts, in the first half of the nineteenth century. Its main character is a young woman sent out from England to report on conditions on her father's sugar plantation. It is hoped that on her return to England she will lecture to ladies' associations on the realities of plantation life, rebutting anti-slavery agitation.

Her first impression of slave life on the island is a rosy one: happy and hedonistic, with ample food and much singing and dancing. As she is absorbed into planter society, she comes to admire what she thinks of as the energy of the plantation managers, and to develop typically colonial nightmares of being cast adrift in an ocean of black bodies.

After a reckless and sordid affair with one of the managers, however, followed by a stillbirth, her mind begins to unravel. The prim, careful language of her journal loosens up as structures of control and self-control – the patriarchal order embedded within her – crumble, and by the time the novel ends she is teetering on a knife edge between madness and a potentially real psychic engagement with the Caribbean.

Cambridge itself is not a particularly good book – the last sections are schematically plotted and betray signs of hasty writing – but it does show Phillips, by 1991, extending the compass of oppression to include the white woman, particularly the white daughter figure.

Phillips has written a number of other stories set in the slave era, marked (though not in all cases) by a finely judged balance between, on the one hand, linguistic and historical immersion in the period, and, on the other, a retrospective modern awareness of what was at stake.

The best of these pieces is 'The Pagan Coast' (in *Crossing the River*), set in the 1830s. 'The Pagan Coast' is a takeoff of Conrad's *Heart of Darkness*, the role of Kurtz being played by a naïve house slave, Nash Williams, who is set free by his Southern master on condition that he go to Liberia and preach Christianity to the natives. Nash's optimistic vision of Liberia ('the beautiful land of my forefathers . . . the star in the East for the free coloured man') gradually gives way to disillusionment. Missionary work is futile, he declares finally: he discards his Western upbringing, takes three wives, becomes, in effect, an African.

His ex-owner, sponsor (via the American Colonisation Society) and onetime lover, travels to Liberia to reclaim him for civilisation, but arrives too late: 'Nash Williams is dead,' he is told (the words echo Conrad's 'Mistah Kurtz – he dead'). Like Kurtz's trading post, Nash's upriver mission station turns out to be squalid and overgrown, reclaimed by Africa.[8]

The American Colonisation Society in effect asks Nash Williams to live out a hypocritical white project in which Africa will take back to her bosom her troublesome New World children. In its vision of Africa as the solution to America's race problems, the Society came ironically close to the Pan-Africanism of Edward Wilmot Blyden and Marcus Garvey – both West Indians – who saw the black man as spiritually grounded in Africa and advocated a return to African roots. In 'The Cargo Rap' (in *The Higher Ground*, 1995) Phillips satirises the Pan-Africanist elements in the Black Power movement of the 1960s, unveiling a deadpan sense of humour and a talent for unobtrusive comic mimicry that one would not have suspected from his early novels.

'The Cargo Rap' is the monologue of a young African American jailed for armed robbery and suffering under a punitive regime of detention. Phillips uses as his starting point the prison letters of the Black Power activist George Jackson, collected in *Soledad Brother*, but achieves an admirable balance between satire of the prim didacticism of the revolutionary ('I think the African man does not masturbate enough . . . Masturbation is safe, quick and can be practised with little danger to self or others') and compassion for a young man of considerable intellectual passion growing more and more frantic as he sees he may never leave jail alive ('Is there not an attorney who would agree to one day being paid in African crops and fruit?' he writes desperately).[9]

Though it played a large part in the creation of Liberia, the real-life American Colonisation Society had little success in repatriating freed blacks to Africa. Its greatest opponent was Frederick Douglass, who denounced it as a tool of the slaveholders: 'Individuals emigrate, nations never.'

As Douglass makes clear in his way, and Phillips in his, the question is not whether Africa is capable of reabsorbing its children, but how and where the African diaspora must see its future. Phillips's position is more complex than Douglass's because he comes after (indeed, has participated in) the second wave of the diaspora, and thus knows that neither Africa nor the second countries of birth of the diaspora – principally the impoverished islands of the Caribbean – are capable of providing a home for all the lost children. But both Douglass and Phillips claim a future for themselves where they are: in Douglass's case in the United States, in Phillips's in a Europe that includes Britain.

This claim on Europe is implicit in Phillips's stories, but comes out more clearly – and with less nuance – in his essays. 'Black people,' he writes, 'trapped in a hostile and racist Europe, exiled from a politically and economically unreliable Caribbean, are beginning to gather around themselves the values of survival and resistance that have sustained them on two journeys across the Atlantic, and are now fighting for the right to be part of the future of this continent.'[10]

III

Frantz Fanon, interpreter of the black condition, used to recall the advice of one of his teachers: 'Whenever you hear anyone abuse the Jews, pay attention, because he is talking about you.'[11] In *The Nature of Blood* (1997) Phillips follows a winding path through space and time to connect the ages-old persecution of the Jews of Europe with the sufferings of people of African descent. It is an intricately structured work, four stories of persecution and suffering told in parallel. The one that leaves the most abiding impression is the story of Eva Stern, sole survivor of a German Jewish family which perishes in Hitler's death camps. The corpus of literature about the camps is by now so vast, and the ground so well covered, that one would think nothing new can be said about their horrors. Yet pages of Eva's story seem to come straight from hell. Eva herself, drifting haplessly between the brutal reality of camp life and fantasies in which her mother and sister are still with her, kept alive by her care, is a haunting figure.

Liberated in 1945, Eva waits for her case to be processed, annexing one of the camp huts for herself, turning it into a personal prison where she can hold on to the ghosts from her past. Here a kindly British soldier shows an interest in her. She responds with dogged silence, but takes a half-hearted proposal of marriage seriously enough to track him down in England, where she finds he already has a wife and child. Alone in a strange country, dogged by ghosts from the past, she suffers a series of mental breakdowns and suicide attempts. Her therapist, chilling but perceptive, diagnoses her problem as a refusal to forget – as mourning without end, a form of loyalty to the dead.

When Eva climbs out of the cattle-truck at the camp that is meant to be her final destination, there is a suffocating smell of burning all around and the air is full of ash. In Phillips's universe of interpenetrating historical spheres, the smell, the ash, come not only from the camp furnaces but from St Mark's Square in Venice, where three Jewish moneylenders from the nearby town of Portobuffole are being burned alive for (so the allegation against them goes) killing a young Christian boy and using his blood in a devilish Passover ritual.

In Poland, in Eva's life, the year is 1942; in Venice it is 1480. Incited by wandering Franciscan friars, who denounce Jewish usury and exhort Christians to resort instead to the new ecclesiastical loan funds, the *Monti di Pietà*, there has been a rash of attacks on Jews. The atrocities of St Mark's Square mark the peak of these pogroms. After the demise of the worst of the Franciscan agitators, the flames of persecution will die down for a while, only to be fanned again by the Bull *nimis absurdum* (1555) of Pope Paul IV, commanding that the Jews of Christendom be confined to ghettos on the model of the Ghetto Nuovo of Venice, demarcated in 1516. (From Venice the sense of the word *ghetto* as a quarter where Jews live compulsorily spread across Italy and thence into other languages.)

Through this same Venetian ghetto Othello, one-time slave, now professional soldier and commander of the armed forces of Venice, wanders as he explores his new home. The story of Othello, the black ram who offends Venice by tupping the white ewe, is the third of the four narratives of *The Nature of Blood*; through Venice Othello is tenuously linked to the Jews of Portobuffole, as these Jews are linked via their martyrdom to Eva Stern.

In an essay caustically entitled 'A Black European Success', Phillips had earlier sketched his interpretation of Othello. To Phillips, Othello has not inwardly transcended the state of slave-hood and is therefore anxiously preoccupied with showing himself to be as good as his new Venetian masters. 'Othello is an alien, socially and culturally. Life for him is a game in which he does not know the rules.' It is predictable, says Phillips, that when Desdemona seems to betray him he will resort to violence, for violence is 'the first refuge of the desperate'.[12]

There is some conceptual confusion in Phillips's essay, which veers between treating Othello as a real-life historical person on whom Shakespeare is reporting ('There is no evidence [in the text] of Othello having any black friends, eating any African foods, speaking any other language than [the Venetians']), and as a character in a play who is misinterpreted by fellow characters insensitive to the psychic baggage that an ex-slave must bring with him. (p. 51) Now Phillips renders this confusion irrelevant by the expedient of taking over Othello as a character in his own book, where he can make him as socially insecure, and as divorced from his African roots, as he likes.

In principle there is nothing wrong with this recreation of Othello, doomed though it is to produce a figure pettier than Shakespeare's noble Moor – Othello Minor rather than Othello Major. But for reasons that are not clear Phillips does not follow the Othello story through to its calamitous end. The courtship and secret marriage of Othello and Desdemona are given in close and sometimes sensuous detail, but the narrative comes to a halt with the couple installed on the island of Cyprus: no jealousy, no murder, no suicide. Phillips further loads the dice against his Othello by giving him lifeless prose to speak.

Cyprus provides the link to the fourth and last of the novel's narratives. The year is 1946; the British, who hold the League of

Nations mandate over Palestine, are diverting boatloads of Jewish refugees away from Haifa to transit camps in Cyprus. On the island is a doctor named Stephan Stern, Eva's uncle, who has since the 1930s been active in Haganah, the Jewish underground. (Since Phillips keeps Stern's underground activities shadowy, it should be stated that Phillips's fictional Stephan Stern has nothing to do with the historical Abraham Stern, leader of the notorious Stern Gang of terrorists.)

Stephan Stern is seen twice: once on Cyprus, and once in the Tel Aviv of the 1980s, where he meets a young woman, an Ethiopian Jew. The old man and the young woman spend a night (chastely) together; the encounter allows the woman an opportunity to tell the story of her journey to Israel ('When we arrived, and stepped down off the plane, we all kissed the ground. We thanked God for returning us to Zion'), and Stephan an opportunity to hear at first hand of the hardships and the prejudice encountered by those who have ended one diasporic exile only to embark on another.[13]

IV

In the course of little more than a decade, Phillips has progressed from straightforward linear narration and uncomplicated realism to the complex shuttling of voices and intercutting of narrative lines, and even the forays into postmodern alienation affects, which we encounter in *The Nature of Blood*.

Nevertheless, Phillips has yet to essay a truly large fiction. His first two books were indeed novels as the term is generally understood – prose narratives of a certain length with a single main plot – but since then he has preferred to assemble between the same covers three or four short narratives which may either be closely linked, as in *Cambridge*, or may have only glancing contact with each other, as in *Higher Ground*, *Crossing the River*, and *The Nature of Blood*.

One's first inclination is to take the last three books as collections of thematically linked novellas. However, Phillips has made vigorous gestures toward claiming a more integrated status for them. He subtitles *Higher Ground* 'a novel in three parts'; in *Crossing the River* the component narratives are framed by an authorial voice gathering them together as utterances of 'my lost children' (p. 2) (in an interview Phillips goes on to call *Crossing the River* 'a novel . . . fragmentary in form and structure, polyphonic in its voices');[14] while the prefatory material to *The Nature of Blood* refers explicitly to the book as a novel.

At a formal level these claims will hardly stand up. But they do point to the way in which Phillips wants his fictions to be read: as imaginative forays into a single body of history, the history of persecution and victimisation in the West. Even the early and rather skimpy *A State of Independence* (1986), set entirely on a Caribbean island and deploying only West Indian characters, is at its heart an exploration of the residue of slavery embedded in states of dependency that have remained constant in the transition from British colonialism to American neocolonialism. Despite the generic and historical diversity of Phillips's fictions, they constitute a project with a single aim: remembering what the West would like to forget.

16   Salman Rushdie, *The Moor's Last Sigh*

I

THE NOTION OF personal identity has dramatically narrowed in our times. Identity has become in the first place a matter of group identification: of claiming membership of a group, or being claimed by a group. Identity in this sense has hovered as a problem over Salman Rushdie's head for most of his life. India is where his imagination lives. Yet as a British citizen of Muslim ancestry and, since Ayatollah Khomeini's *fatwa*, of indeterminate residence, it has become less and less easy for him to assert, when he writes about India, the country of his birth, that he writes as an insider.

No wonder, then, that the hero of *Midnight's Children* (1981), the book which revolutionised the Indian English novel and brought Rushdie fame, cries out (prophetically, as it emerged): 'Why, alone of all the more-than-five-hundred-million, should I have to bear the burden of history?'[1] 'I [want] to be Clark Kent, not any kind of Superman,' laments the hero of *The Moor's Last Sigh* in similar vein.[2] Or if not Clark Kent, then simply his own, essential, naked self.

The Moor's Last Sigh (1995) is a novel about India and the world, India in the world. Its hero is a young man from Bombay named Moraes Zogoiby, nicknamed by his mother 'the Moor'. But the famous sigh to which the title refers was breathed five centuries ago, in 1492, when Muhammad XI, last Sultan of Andalusia, bade farewell to his kingdom, bringing to an end Arab-Islamic hegemony in Iberia. 1492 was also the year when the Jews of Spain were offered the choice of baptism or expulsion; and when Columbus, financed by the royal conquerors of the Moor, Ferdinand and Isabella, sailed west to discover a new route to the east. A pivotal date, then, for three great religions; for commerce between Europe and the East; and for the Americas.

From Sultan Muhammad, Rushdie creates a line of descent, partly historical, partly fabulous, which leads forward to Moraes, who is destined to return from the east in 1992 to rediscover Andalusia and bring the circle to a close. The first third of this dynastic opus is devoted to Moraes's nearer forebears, starting with his great-grandparents the Da Gamas, wealthy spice exporters based in Cochin in what is now Kerala State. The great-grandfather, a progressive and a nationalist, soon disappears from the stage (Rushdie gives short shrift to characters whose usefulness has ended), but his wife, a devotee of 'England, God, philistinism, the old ways', survives to trouble succeeding generations and to utter the curse that will blight the life of the as yet unborn hero. (p. 18)

Their son Camoens, after flirting with Communism, becomes a Nehru man, dreaming of an independent, unitary India, which will be 'above religion because secular, above class because socialist, above caste because enlightened'. (p. 51) He dies in 1939, though not before he has had a premonition of the violent, conflict-riven India that will in fact emerge.

Camoens's daughter Aurora falls in love with a humble Jewish clerk, Abraham Zogoiby. Neither Jewish nor Christian authorities will solemnise their marriage, so their son Moraes is raised an undefined mixture, 'a jewholic anonymous'. (p. 104) Abandoning the declining Jewish community of Cochin, Abraham transfers the family business to Bombay and settles in a fashionable suburb, where he branches out into more lucrative activities: supplying girls to the city's brothels, smuggling heroin, speculating in property, trafficking in arms and eventually in nuclear weapons.

Abraham is little more than a comic-book villain. His wife Aurora is a more complex character, however, and in many ways the emotional centre of the book. A painter of genius but a distracted mother, she suffers intermittent remorse for not loving her children enough, but prefers finally to see them through the lens of her art. Thus Moraes is worked into a series of paintings of 'Mooristan', a place where (in Aurora's free and easy Indo-Joycean English) 'worlds collide, flow in and out of one another, and washofy away . . . One universe, one dimension, one country, one dream, bumpo'ing into another, or being under, or on top of. Call it Palimpstine.' In these paintings, with increasing desperation, she tries to paint old, tolerant Moorish Spain over India, overlaying or palimpsesting the ugly reality of the present with 'a romantic myth of a plural, hybrid nation'. (pp. 226, 227) Aurora's paintings give a clear hint of what Rushdie is up to in his own 'Palimpstine' project: not overpainting India in the sense of blotting it out with a fantasy alternative, but laying an alternative, promised-land text or texturation over it like gauze.

Besides palimpsesting, Rushdie also experiments with ekphrasis, the conduct of narration through the description of imaginary works of art. (Among well-known instances of ekphrasis in Western literature are the descriptions of shield of Achilles in the *Iliad* and of the frieze on Keats's Grecian urn.) In Rushdie's hands ekphrasis becomes a handy device for recalling the past and fore-shadowing the future. The magical tiles in the Cochin synagogue not only tell the story of the Jews in India but foretell the atom bomb. Aurora's paintings project her son into the past as Boabdil; the entire history of India, from mythic times to the present, is absorbed into a great phantasmagoria on the wall of her bedroom. Scanning it, her father marvels that she has captured 'the great swarm of being itself', but then notes one major lacuna: 'God was absent.' Through paintings whose only existence, paradoxically, is in words, the darkly prophetic historical imagination of Aurora, her 'Cassandran fears for the nation', dominate the book. Her last painting, which gives the book its title, shows her son 'lost in limbo like a wandering shade: a portrait of a soul in Hell'. (pp. 59, 60, 236, 315–16).

II

Moraes labours under the curse of two witch-grandmothers, so it is no surprise that he is born a freak, with a clublike right hand and an accelerated metabolism that dooms him to grow and to age 'double-quick', twice as fast as ordinary mortals. (p. 143) Kept apart from other children, he receives his sexual initiation at the hands of an attractive governess and discovers he is a born storyteller: telling stories gives him an erection.

When he ventures into the world, he is soon caught in the toils of the beautiful but evil rival artist Uma Sarasvati. A pawn in the war between this demon mistress and his mother, Moraes first finds himself expelled from his parental home and then – after some complicated stage business – in jail accused of Uma's murder. Released, he joins the Bombay underworld as a strikebreaker and enforcer in the pay of one Raman Fielding, boss of a Hindu paramilitary group whose offduty evenings sound like Brownshirt get-togethers in Munich, with 'arm-wrestling and mat-wrestling . . . [until] lubricated by beer and rum, the assembled company would arrive at a point of sweaty, brawling, raucous, and finally exhausted nakedness'. (p. 300)

Moraes's grandfather Camoens had believed in Nehru but not

in Gandhi. In the village India to which Gandhi appealed, Camoens saw forces brewing that spelled trouble for India's minorities: 'In the city we are for secular India but the village is for Ram . . . In the end I am afraid the villagers will march on the cities and people like us will have to lock our doors and there will come a Battering Ram.' (pp. 55–6). His prophecy begins to fulfil itself in Moraes's lifetime when the doors of the Babri mosque at Ayodhya are battered down by a crowd of fanatical Hindus.

Camoens is prescient but ineffectual. Aurora, an activist as well as an artist, is the only Da Gama with the strength to confront the dark, intolerant forces of village India. When the festival procession of the elephant-headed god Ganesha, an annual show of Hindu-fundamentalist triumphalism, passes by their home, she dances in view of the celebrants, dancing *against* the god, though, alas, her dance is read by them as part of the spectacle (Hinduism notoriously absorbs its rivals). Every year she dances on the hillside; dancing at the age of sixty-three, she slips and falls to her death.

Raman Fielding, rising star of the Hindu movement, is a caricature of Bal Thackeray, Bombay leader of the fundamentalist Shiv Shena Party. Closely linked with Bombay's criminal underworld, Fielding is 'against unions . . . against working women, in favour of sati, against poverty and in favour of wealth . . . against "immigrants" to the city . . . against the corruption of the Congress [Party] and for "direct action", by which he meant paramilitary activity in support of his political aims'. (pp. 298-9) He looks forward to a theocracy in which his particular variant of Hinduism will predominate.

If Rushdie's *Satanic Verses* outraged the dour literalists within Islam, then *The Moor's Last Sigh* is aimed at the fascist-populist element within the Hindu political movement. On Raman Fielding Rushdie lavishes some of his most stinging satirical prose: 'In his low cane chair with his great belly slung across his knees like a burglar's sack, with his frog's croak of a voice bursting through his fat frog's lips and his little dart of a tongue licking at the edges of his mouth, with his hooded froggy eyes gazing greedily down upon the little beedi-rolls of money with which his quaking petitioners sought to pacify him . . . he was indeed a Frog King.' (p. 232)

(The microscopic scrutiny given by commentators to the text of *The Satanic Verses*, particularly to its offending passages, and the wealth of religious and cultural reference thereby uncovered, has alerted us to how superficial a non-Muslim reading of that book must be. Similarly, when it comes to political infighting in India, or to the Bombay social and cultural scene, the non-Indian reader of *The Moor's Last Sigh* can have at most an overhearing role: jokes are being made, satiric barbs being cast, which only an insider will appreciate.)

The underworld struggle between Fielding and Moraes's father culminates in the murder of Fielding and the destruction of half of Bombay. Sick of this new barbarism, Moraes retreats to Andalusia, there to confront another monster of evil, Vasco Miranda. Miranda is a Goan painter (another Indo-Iberian connection) who has made a fortune selling kitsch to Westerners. Obsessively jealous of Aurora, he has stolen her Moor paintings; to reclaim them, Moraes has to find his way into Miranda's Daliesque fortress. Here Miranda captures him, imprisons him and allows him to live only as long as (shades of Sheherazade) he keeps writing the story of his life.

Locked up with Moraes is a beautiful Japanese picture restorer named Aoi Uë (her name all vowels, as the Moor's in Arabic is all consonants: would that they had found each other earlier, he thinks). Aoi perishes; Moraes, with Miranda's blood on his hands, escapes. It is 1993, he is thirty-six years old, but his inner clock says he is seventy-two and ready to die.

III

The final chapters of the book, and the opening chapter, to which they loop back, are packed (or palimpsested) with historical allusions. Moraes is not only Muhammad XI (Abu-'Abd-Allah, or Boabdil, in the Spanish corruption of his name): he is Dante in an infernal maze of tourists, and also Martin Luther, looking for doors on which to nail the pages of his life-story, as well as Jesus on the Mount of Olives, waiting for his persecutors to arrive. It is hard to avoid the impression that all the left-over analogues of the Moor fable from Rushdie's notebooks have been poured into these chapters, which are as a result frantic and overwritten. Some of the historical parallels fall flat (Moraes is no Luther: the hounds on his trail are the Spanish police, who suspect a homicide, not the bishops of Hindu orthodoxy, who couldn't care less what he gets up to in Spain), while elementary rules of the novelist's craft, like not introducing new characters in the last pages, are ignored (Aoi is the case in point).

Nor is this the worst. As if unsure that the import of the Boabdil/Moraes parallel has come across, Rushdie, in what sounds very much like *propria persona*, glosses it as follows: Granada, in particular the Alhambra, is a 'monument to a lost possibility', a 'testament . . . to that most profound of our needs . . . for putting an end to frontiers, for the dropping of boundaries of the self'. (p. 433) With all respect due to the author, one must demur. The palimpsesting of Moraes over Boabdil supports a less trite, more provocative thesis: that the Arab penetration of Iberia, like the later Iberian penetration of India, led to a creative mingling of peoples and cultures; that the victory of Christian intolerance in Spain was a tragic turn in history; and that Hindu intolerance in India bodes as ill for the world as did the sixteenth-century Inquisition in Spain. (Fleshing out the thesis in this way depends, however, on ignoring the fact that the historical Boabdil was a timorous and indecisive man, dominated by his mother and duped by Ferdinand.)

Rushdie pursues palimpsesting with considerable vigour as a novelistic, historiographical and autobiographical device. Thus Granada, Boabdil's lost capital, is also Bombay, 'inexhaustible Bombay of excess', the sighed-for home of Moraes as well as of the author over whose person he is written. (p. 193) Both are cities from which a regenerative cross-fertilisation of cultures might have taken place, but for ethnic/religious intolerance. But occasionally palimpsesting descends to mere postmodernist frivolousness: 'Had I accidentally slipped from one page, one book of life on to another,' Moraes wonders, unable to believe he is in jail. (p. 285) Yet at other moments Moraes expresses a hunger for the real: 'How,' he asks himself, looking back in bafflement, 'trapped as we were . . . in the fancy-dress, weeping-Arab kitsch of the superficial, could we have penetrated to the full sensual truth of the lost mother below? How could we have lived authentic lives?' (pp. 184–5)

Here Moraes articulates a passionate but fearful attachment to his mother – whom he elsewhere calls 'my Nemesis, my foe beyond the grave' – and through her to a 'Mother India who loved and betrayed and ate and destroyed and again loved her children, and with whom the children's passionate conjoining and eternal quarrel stretched long beyond the grave'. (pp. 45, 60–1) The conflicted attachment touched on here is the saddest note in the book, but remains a submerged, barely explored element of Moraes's make-up.

Moraes's yearning for authenticity expresses itself most clearly in his dream of peeling off his skin and going into the world naked 'like an anatomy illustration from *Encyclopaedia Britannica* . . . set free from the otherwise inescapable jails of colour, race and clan'. (p. 136) Alas, he proceeds, in a complex joke that conflates Indian Indians, whom Columbus set off to find, with American Indians, the Indians he in fact found, 'in Indian country there was no room for a man who didn't want to belong to a tribe, who dreamed . . . of peeling off his skin and revealing his secret identity – the secret, that is, of the identity of all men – of standing before the war-painted braves to unveil the flayed and naked unity of the flesh.' (p. 414)

If this does not mark a crisis in Rushdie's thinking – a longing for the pages of history to stop turning, or at least no longer to turn 'double-quick', for the ultimate self to emerge from the parade of fictional identities, fictions of the self – then at least it marks a crisis for the Moor persona, the prince in exile, no longer young, confronting the overriding truth uniting mankind: we are all going to die.

IV

Like *Midnight's Children* (1981), *Shame* (1983) and *The Satanic Verses* (1989), *The Moor's Last Sigh* is a novel with large ambitions composed on a large scale. Its structure is, however, anything but sturdy. Aside from the dynastic prelude set in Cochin and the last fifty pages set in Spain, the body of the book belongs to Moraes's life in Bombay. But instead of the interwoven development of character, theme and action characteristic of the middle section of what we may call the classic novel, we find in the middle section of Rushdie's novel only fitful and episodic progress. New actors are introduced with enough inventiveness and wealth of detail to justify major roles; yet all too often their contribution to the action turns out to be slight, and they slip (or are slipped) out of the picture almost whimsically.

To complaints of this kind – which have been voiced in respect of the earlier novels as well – defenders of Rushdie have responded by arguing that he operates, and should therefore be read, within a double narrative tradition: of the Western novel (with its sub-genre the anti-novel *à la Tristram Shandy*), and of Eastern story-cycles like the *Panchatantra*, with their chainlike linking of self-contained shorter narratives. To such critics, Rushdie is a multi-cultural writer not merely in the weak sense of having roots in more than one culture, but in the strong sense of using one literary tradition to renew another.

It is not easy to counter this defence in its general form. But as a test case let us take the episode in *The Moor's Last Sigh* in which Abraham Zogoiby, in a fit of enthusiasm for the modern, impersonal, 'management' style in business, adopts a young go-getter named Adam in place of Moraes as his son and heir. For some fifteen pages Adam occupies centre stage. Then he is dropped from the book. The episode peters out and has no consequences. I would hazard a guess that the reason why Adam disappears is not that Rushdie is following a particular narrative model but that he is only half-heartedly committed to satirising the business school ethos; he abandons this particular narrative strand for no better reason than that it is leading nowhere.

Characters such as Vasco Miranda, Uma Sarasvati, or even Abraham Zogoiby himself, create a comparable problem. In their extravagant villainy they seem to come straight out of the enter-tainment factories of Hollywood or Bollywood. But, it might be argued, is this necessarily a drawback? In so palimpsested a novel as *The Moor's Last Sigh*, why should the popular storytelling media of today not contribute to the textual layering? And are traditional folktales not full of unmotivated evil anyway?

If we want to read *The Moor's Last Sigh* as a mix of genres and a play of textuality, we must accept the consequences, however. When Moraes, in prison, wonders whether he is on the wrong page, he moves into a dimension in which not only the walls of his cell but he himself consist simply of words. In this purely textual dimension, Moraes's lament that he is trapped within 'colour, caste, sect' and his longing for an authentic life outside them cannot be taken fully seriously. For if a creature of words wants to escape the inessential determinants of his life, all he need do is storytell his way out of them.

V

In fact Rushdie is far from being a programmatic metafictional postmodernist. The most obvious proof is that he is disinclined to treat the historical record as just one story among many. We see this in handling of the two histories out of which Moraes's story grows: of the Moors in Spain and of the Jews in India. In the case of the Moors, and of Muhammad/Boabdil in particular, Rushdie does not deviate from the historical record, which Westerners probably know best from Washington Irving's nostalgic sketches in *The Alhambra*. As for the Jewish communities in India, their origins are ancient and will probably never be known with certainty. However, the communities preserved certain legends of origin, and to these legends Rushdie adheres without embroidering, save for one superadded fiction: that the Zogoibys are descended from Sultan Muhammad (called by his subjects al-Zogoybi, the Unfortunate) via a Jewish mistress who sailed for India pregnant with his child. This story is specifically (though not unequivocally) bracketed as an invention by Moraes in his function as narrator.

It is against a background of recent history, in which Rushdie's own rather intellectualised play with varieties of identity was brushed aside by believers in a narrowly prescriptive notion of group identity, that we should understand the moment when Moraes, moving beyond a by now familiar Rushdian celebration of bastardy, mongrelhood and hybridity, rejects his 'anti-Almighty' father Abraham – a father ready to sacrifice him on the altar of his megalomaniac ambitions – and embraces a heritage that has hitherto meant nothing to him: 'I find that I am a Jew.' (pp. 336–7) For not only are Rushdie's Jews (the Jews of Cochin, the Jews of Spain) powerless, dwindling communities; but to claim, voluntarily, the identity of a Jew, after the Holocaust, is to assert, however symbolically, solidarity with persecuted minorities worldwide.

In a book in which ideas, characters and situations are invented with such prolific ease, one might wish that Rushdie had pushed the story of Moraes as rediscovered Jew further. 'Here I stand,' says Moraes/Luther, at the end of the journey of his life, 'I couldn't've done it differently.' (p. 3) What does it mean in real-life terms, in India or in the world, to take a stand on a symbolic Jewishness?

A final word. Five centuries after the campaigns of Ferdinand and Isabella swept Islam out of Iberia, the Muslims of south-eastern Europe faced genocidal onslaughts from their neighbours, Catholic and Orthodox. Though the word *Bosnia* is not so much as breathed (or sighed) in his book, it is inconceivable that the parallel did not cross Rushdie's mind as he wrote.

17 Aharon Appelfeld, *The Iron Tracks*

I

WHEN AHARON APPELFELD began writing in the early 1960s, the Holocaust did not count, in Israel, as a fitting subject for fiction. The prevailing public position was a Zionist one: that the assault on the Jews of the European Diaspora had been objectively predictable; that they had failed to escape it because of a certain passivity, a certain blindness on their part; that this passive set of mind would be eliminated, among survivors, by the new conditions of existence in Israel. Insofar as Israel was a new beginning, the Holocaust could have no relevance to its future.

Combined with this public silence was a feeling that there was something indecent in representing the Holocaust, that the subject ought to be, if not beyond the reach of language, at least out of bounds to anyone who had not lived through it.

The trial of Adolf Eichmann in 1961 can be seen in hindsight as having been a watershed. A generation of Israelis, educated under Zionism but now exposed to the European side of the story, realised that the Jewish victims of the Third Reich could not be blamed for their fate and excluded from the history of Jewry. Since then a gradual shift in thought has been taking place, towards giving the history of European Jewry its proper place in the narrative of Israel, and thus towards accepting a conception of Israeli identity more eclectic than that prescribed by Zionism in its pioneer phase.

As part of this national reorientation, the Holocaust has forced its way back into Hebrew literature. The work of David Grossman is particularly important here. In his novel *See Under: Love* (1986) Grossman drew upon the resources of international postmodernism to create a language in which whatever has been unsayable about the Holocaust could be, if not said, then at least adumbrated.

To this movement in Israeli fiction Appelfeld has been a somewhat peripheral figure. Although, with Amos Oz and A.B. Yehoshua, he belongs to the front rank of novelists of his generation, he remains the most European of Israeli writers, mapping, in one short book after another, a narrow fictional territory based on his own, and his family's, past. Of these books, one sub-series, including *Badenheim 1939* (1975), *The Age of Wonders* (1978), *The Retreat* (1982), and *To the Land of the Reeds* (1990), focuses on assimilated Jewish society on the eve of catastrophe. Another, including *For Every Sin* (1987), *Unto the Soul* (1994), and, most notably, *Tzili* (1983), tells stories of physical survival during the war and in its immediate aftermath. *The Immortal Bartfuss* (1983) and *The Iron Tracks* (1991) follow the fates of survivors of the war and the Displaced Persons camps.

Appelfeld has testified eloquently to the struggle he faced before he could write about his own war experiences. He was born in Czernowicz, in Bukovina, into a German-speaking family. When the Germans moved in, his mother was shot, his father sent to a labour camp. He himself spent the war years wandering the Romanian countryside with other children, hiding, pretending not to be a Jew. He arrived in Israel in 1946, at the age of fourteen. To begin a new life there seemed to require a deliberate effort of forgetting. '[One] learned how to live without memory the way one learns to live without a limb of one's body.' As for finding a form of 'artistic expression' for his people's suffering, this seemed merely insulting. 'The pain and suffering called either for silence or for wild outcries.'[1]

Appelfeld was able to re-enter his own past as a creative intelligence only when he took the step of re-imagining himself not as a clever young boy hiding from his pursuers but as a dull, inarticulate girl, Tzili. 'Had I remained true to the facts, no one would have believed me. But the moment I chose [Tzili] . . . I removed "the story of my life" from the mighty grip of memory and gave it over to the creative laboratory.'[2] Faith in the power of fiction to recover and restore the wounded self – 'to give the tortured person back his human form, which was snatched away from him' – has since then been at the core of Appelfeld's work.[3]

Despite his ostensible confidence in the healing powers of art (which would make of him a simpler, less self-doubting practitioner than his master Franz Kafka), the vision of the soul of the long-term Holocaust survivor that we get in Appelfeld's fiction remains bleak. Both Bartfuss in *The Immortal Bartfuss* and Siegelbaum in *The Iron Tracks* are men who have cannily used the confusion of the postwar years to launch themselves to material success, yet in their mature years find themselves living impoverished, affectless lives, driven by compulsions they do not understand.

Erwin Siegelbaum, in the latter book, is a creature of ritual, a trafficker in religious objects who since the end of the war has been travelling the iron tracks of the Austrian railway network, following a circular route. It begins each spring at Wirblbahn, site of the labour camp where he and his family were confined during the war – an 'accursed place', 'a wound that won't heal' – and takes in twenty-one more stops. Each stop evokes memories; following the circuit entails reliving his life.[4]

On his circuit Siegelbaum visits country fairs, buying up the surviving relics of Jewish religious life (goblets, menorahs, old books), which he sells to a collector who will eventually ship them on to Jerusalem. But his travels have a darker purpose too: he is on the trail of Nachtigel, onetime commandant of the Wirblbahn camp and murderer of his parents.

As a family, the Siegelbaums had followed a pattern of assimilation common among Central European Jews. Erwin's grandfather had been a rabbi in rural Bukovina, his father a dedicated Communist who even in the labour camp held to his new religion: 'In a few generations people will remember us and say, Jewish Communism was the true Communism.' (*The Iron Tracks*, p. 74)

Young Erwin (whose name is a Germanisation of Aharon) is brought up speaking not Yiddish but German and Ruthenian. He does not go to school, but instead shares his father's clandestine Party life. This involves winning converts among the Ruthenian working class by committing arson and sabotage against Jewish factory owners, treated by his father as 'the very source of evil'. His father's view of the Ruthenian peasantry, in contrast, is sentimental and uncritical. 'Their way of life [is] correct and organic, and were it not for the estate owners and the Jewish merchants, they would live in complete harmony with nature.' (pp. 63, 54)

When war breaks out in 1941, the Ruthenians turn against the Jews among them. Of the Siegelbaums, only fifteen-year-old Erwin survives. After the war he finds himself in a transit camp in Italy, among hundreds of thousands of other displaced persons. He becomes a smuggler, trading cigarettes, liquor and watches, and accumulates a modest personal fortune. Ignoring the Zionist call to emigrate to Palestine, he remains near the grave of his parents, following the path of the iron tracks, never settling down, taking on the mantle of the Wandering Jew.

II

Appelfeld has acknowledged a debt to Kafka, but Kafka read as a Jew who in the course of being assimilated lost the core of his being and ached to recover it.[5] His landscapes certainly have the pared-down, abstract quality of Kafka's. Nevertheless, *The Iron Tracks* is recognisably set in rural Austria.

The picture of Austrian life that emerges is as spiritually mean as anything produced by Thomas Bernhard, to whom Appelfeld is closer in tone and feeling than to his Israeli coevals. Appelfeld's Austria is a land of smouldering, resentful anti-Semitism. A convert to Christianity who has quietly preserved some Jewish observances pronounces her verdict on it: 'I should have left this accursed land . . . It should be wiped from the face of the earth, like Sodom and Gomorrah.' (p. 114)

Siegelbaum himself has no religious faith. But he does not live by faith: he lives by duty. His duty is to track down the killers from the camps. 'As long as they live, our lives are meaningless.' (p. 77) In his dedication to revenge he is the most sombre of all Appelfeld's protagonists.

Siegelbaum finds Nachtigel on a snowy country road, aged, toothless, sunk in depression. He shoots him in the back. But the success of his mission brings no release. 'I had done everything out of compulsion, clumsily, and always too late,' he reflects. Commended for the multitude of Jewish materials he has saved from destruction in the course of his labours ('The Jewish people won't forget your contribution'), he can respond only with raging anger. (pp. 218, 205)

III

A distinguishing feature of assimilated Jews of the generation which perished in the camps, says Appelfeld, was 'anti-Semitism directed at oneself'.[6] One invention of Christian anti-Semitism that has engraved itself deeply on history has been the myth of the Wandering Jew, roaming the face of the earth, unable to attain the peace of death. Erwin Siegelbaum, like other of Appelfeld's protagonists, has swallowed and internalised this myth.[7] Beneath his rage at the iron circuit to which he is bound we can detect a complex victimage: a sentence of self-hatred and self-punishment which, since it is handed down by an authority invisible to the sufferer, is understood not as a sentence but as a fate − a paradox worthy of the Kafka of 'In the Penal Colony'.

'The Jewish experience in the Second World War was not "historical",' Appelfeld has written. 'We came into contact with archaic mythical forces, a kind of dark subconscious the meaning of which we did not know, nor do we know it to this day.'[8] In his very ordinariness, Nachtigel embodies the paradox of the banality of evil on which Hannah Arendt put her finger. Facing Nachtigel, Siegelbaum confronts, in a sense, evil; but it is an evil whose essence it is to disappoint and frustrate its hunters. In this respect *The Iron Tracks* is a deeply pessimistic and even despairing book, the darkest that Appelfeld has written.

18   Amos Oz

I

IN AUTOBIOGRAPHIES OF childhood the first moral crisis often looms large – the moment when the child faces for the first time a choice between right and wrong action. It is a moment which, in retrospect, the autobiographer recognises as having had a formative effect.

One such moment is the theft of the ribbon in Book 2 of Jean-Jacques Rousseau's *Confessions*. The young Jean-Jacques steals a ribbon and, rather than speak up, allows a maidservant to be blamed for the theft and dismissed. He has chosen for ill, but his choice contributes to the nagging sense of guilt that makes him into the man he becomes and the author of, *inter alia*, the *Confessions*.

For the young William Wordsworth, the moment comes when he borrows a boat without permission and goes for a row on the lake. The whole natural world around him seems to the imaginative boy to join forces to reprove him: the universe, he is learning, is instinct with moral force.

For James Joyce's Stephen Dedalus, the moment comes when he is unjustly punished by a teacher, and must decide whether to complain to the headmaster or accept the cynical view of the rest of the boys that might is right.

In each case, the adult writer organises his story of his childhood around such critical episodes, identified as key moments in his moral growth.

Panther in the Basement (1994) tells a story Amos Oz has told several times before, as autobiography (in *Under This Blazing Light*, 1979) or as fiction. At its barest, the story is about an Israeli boy who has arrived at a crossroads in his moral development. Is he to continue to cherish the childish fantasies of violence which his environment encourages in him, or is he to advance to a new stage of life, learning to love as well as to hate, to accept that the people around him cannot simply be classed as friends or enemies?

The fact that this crossroads in his life coincides with a crossroads in the life of his nation – *Panther in the Basement* is set in Jerusalem in the last year of the British mandate, with war against the Arab states looming – gives the choice facing the young protagonist a political meaning (is Israel to continue on a path of violent self-assertion or to reach an accommodation based on give and take?) which Oz, to his credit, handles with the lightest of touches.

The predecessor of *Panther in the Basement* in Oz's fictional œuvre is *Soumchi* (1978), which draws upon similar plot elements: a young boy, Soumchi, consumed with fantasies of violence against the British occupier and dreaming of becoming an Underground fighter (but also, contradictorily, an explorer in darkest Africa); a meeting with a friendly British soldier, which leads to exchanges of language lessons; persecution by erstwhile friends, who claim that by fraternising with the enemy he has become a traitor to his people; and a first experience of falling in love, which puts a distance between him and his murderous dreams. So close are the similarities, in fact, that *Soumchi* can be read as a sketch, marred by one or two moments of sentimentality, for the later novella.

In *Panther in the Basement* the boy is nameless, known simply by the nickname given him because of his bookish habits: Proffy. The

Englishman who brings confusion to his life is an army pay clerk who, because of a clerical background, speaks some Hebrew, though of a comically Biblical variety. Oz's translator, Nicholas de Lange, catches its flavour by rendering it in sixteenth-century English. 'Whither dost thou hasten?' demands Sergeant Dunlop of Proffy, whom he has caught out of doors during the curfew. 'Please, kindly sir, let me go home,' replies Proffy in his best English ('the language of the enemy', he reminds himself sternly).[1]

Unattractive and lonely, Dunlop is attracted to the strange boy; Proffy – whose own father plays sarcastic distancing games with him – responds with guarded warmth. The two agree to meet and exchange Hebrew for English lessons, using the Bible as their textbook.

To himself Proffy rationalises these meetings as a cunning way of extracting military secrets from the enemy. For his part, Dunlop – in marked contrast to the teachers to whom Proffy is exposed at his Hebrew National school – selects biblical stories not about the victorious heroes of Israelite history but about weaker, more marginal figures. Dunlop thus becomes a moderating influence on the boy. He also takes on a mildly prophetic role. Once the British have left, he foresees, the Jews will defeat their Arab foes, after which 'perhaps it [is] the Creator's decree that [the Palestinians] should become a persecuted people, instead of the Jews'. He quotes from Scripture: 'Wonderful are the ways of the Lord: . . . the one he loves he chastizes, and the one he would uproot he loves.' (p. 85)

Their meetings, which take place over lemonade and crackers at the Orient Palace Café, are discovered by Proffy's friends; this leads to public humiliation (graffiti on the walls of his apartment block reading 'Proffy is a low-down traitor') and thus to the soul-searching about patriotism and treason that is at the core of the book.

Though the voice of Proffy's upbringing tells him that Dunlop is an outsider and an oppressor, his heart tells him that his generous response to the stranger is good. When he subjects the Englishman to petty insults like refusing to shake hands with him, he is left with a bad taste in his mouth. Brought before a tribunal consisting of fellow Underground members, he denies betraying any secrets. 'Loving the enemy, Proffy, is worse than betraying secrets,' (p. 69) replies Ben Hur, leader of the cell (in later life Ben Hur Tykocinski will become not a security policeman, a calling to which he seems eminently suited, but a Florida property tycoon; Proffy, on the other hand, will remain in Israel and write books). Only Proffy's mother is prepared to stand by him: 'Anyone who loves isn't a traitor,' she says. (p. 2)

But a mother's affirmation is not enough. It takes Yardena, Ben Hur's attractive nineteen-year-old sister, to confirm Proffy on the path along which his instincts are already pointing him. Sent over one evening to babysit him, Yardena cooks him a mouth-watering Mediterranean meal, effortlessly elicits from him his store of Underground secrets, teases him for talking in the clichés of 'The Voice of Fighting Zion', (p. 121) and delivers some home truths, including: 'Why don't you start being a professor instead of a spy or a general? . . . You're a word-child.' (p. 131)

Proffy does not truly hate the British. He would be satisfied if they admitted their mistake and withdrew from Palestine ('[At the time] I thought of the British as Europeans, intelligent and almost enviable,' Oz reminisces elsewhere. 'We had to teach them a lesson . . . and then – to conciliate them and win them over to our side').[2] This would enable him to meet Dunlop on a new footing, be a friend to him, perhaps even a son of a kind.

He turns to his parents for support. If our enemies acknowledge they have done us wrong, he asks, should we not forgive them? Their responses reflect the tension in the household. Yes, replies his mother – 'Not forgiving is like a poison.' (p. 72) Yes, replies his father – but only from a position of strength.

Proffy does not know which of the two to side with. Though his inclination is to follow his mother, the crucial problem for him as a boy-child – and this is common to both the autobiographical and the fictional variants of the story – is how to negotiate relations with his father, how to become a worthy son.[3]

Without admitting they were wrong, the British do indeed withdraw from Palestine, Dunlop the weak pretender-father among them. The Arab armies attack and are defeated; the United Nations recognises the new state of Israel. In the middle of night Proffy is woken by his father, who lies down beside him on the bed. In the grip of emotion, weeping, he tells Proffy the story of 'how . . . when he and mother lived next door to each other in a small town in Poland . . . the ruffians who lived in the same block abused them, and beat them savagely because Jews were all rich, idle, and crafty. And how once they stripped him naked in class . . . in front of the girls, in front of Mother, to make fun of his circumcision . . . "But from now there will be a Hebrew State." And suddenly he hugged me, not gently but almost violently.' (p. 145)

Never again, as long as the state of Israel exists, will the Jewish people stand defenceless before their enemies. Finding some way of reconciling this vow, here virtually imposed on him by his father, with the softer and sometimes traitorous urgings of the heart favoured by his mother, all the while bearing in mind Sergeant Dunlop's warning of how easily the persecuted becomes the persecutor, will be the task facing Oz's young hero in the years ahead.

II

The repeated reworking of the Proffy story suggests that the material holds deep meaning for Oz, rich potential for exploring both his own moral history and the history of Israel. Not only does understanding our past – making our past into a narrative – explain our present: our life, Oz seems to suggest, is in a sense the acting out of one or other story we chose as our own while we were yet a child. A story is thus a way of projecting ourself into the future; and likewise with nations and national myths. (The notion of history as the fulfilling of prophetic myth, is of course thoroughly at home in Judaic thought.)

In the very personage we call 'Amos Oz' there is a strong element, if not of the fictive, then of willed self-creation. Born Amos Klausner, son of a European-trained scholar of comparative literature, the author of these various rewritings of himself quit his father's home – according to his own testimony – shortly after his mother's suicide, changed his last name to Oz (in Hebrew the word means power or vigour), and at the age of fourteen joined a kibbutz, where, through a regime of work and study, he set about making himself.

As in the story of Proffy, Klausner the scholar-father with his Old World culture and ironic Diaspora mentality had wanted his son to become one of the 'new kind of Jew, improved, broad-shouldered, fighters and tillers of the soil . . . [who] when the time came . . . would stand up, bold and suntanned, and not let the enemy lead us like sheep to the slaughter again'. (p. 18)[4] The boy was sent to a school with strong National Religious leanings, where he was taught 'to long for [the] resurrection in blood and fire' of the ancient Jewish kingdoms.[5]

Jerusalem in the last years of the British mandate provided more than enough action to fuel this mesmerising vision of prophecy fulfilling itself. To the sensitive and suggestible child, the city became a panorama not only of romance and heroism, but also of hatred and violence. 'My Jerusalem childhood made me an expert in comparative fanaticism,' writes Oz retrospectively. One may venture to guess that it was his timely escape from the crucible of Jerusalem that spared Oz from the intolerance and intransigence which have marred the public face of Israel. In contrast to Jerusalem, Kibbutz Hulda, to which Oz retreated, stood for secularism and rationality, for the defeat of evil not by violent means but through the old Zionist ideal of 'labour, simple living, sharing and equality, a gradual improvement in human nature'.[6]

III

Soumchi is not the sole rehearsal of the Amos/Proffy story. Many of its elements are also to be found in the three long stories published in 1976 under the collective title *The Hill of Evil Counsel*. Again we are in the Jerusalem of the 1940s. Again we have the only son of immigrant parents trying to make sense of himself and his violent times. He dreams of engines of destruction (rockets carrying explosives extracted from bottles of nail varnish, a submarine built to travel through the lava beneath the earth's crust) that will bring about the defeat of the British in a flash; he hero-worships the Underground fighters; his parents' home is searched by British soldiers, who are a little awed by the evidence of high European culture; he has fantasies of dying under torture rather than revealing Underground secrets. Even the motif of the leopard lurking in the forest (or the panther hiding in the basement) is present: an emblem of primitive power and specifically of the Hebrew state on the eve of revealing itself.

Taken in conjunction with *Panther in the Basement*, these early stories, particularly the third of them, provide an intriguing insight into Oz's process of self-revision. The third story is given to an outsider to narrate: an older man, Dr Nussbaum, a neighbour of Uri's (as Proffy is known in this incarnation). Nussbaum is a version of Sergeant Dunlop, attracted to the gifted, intelligent boy trapped in his fantasies. 'He writes poems about the ten lost tribes, Hebrew cavalrymen, great conquests, and acts of vengeance. Doubtless some little teacher, some messianic madman, has captured the child's imagination with the usual Jerusalemite blend of apocalyptic visions and romantic fantasies.'[7]

From his conversations with Nussbaum it emerges just how inhumanly limited Uri's inner world has become. 'Nothing comes from words,' says Uri. 'I'm very sorry. Everything is war . . . That's how it is in history, in the Bible, in nature, and in real life, too. And love is all war. Friendship, too, even.' (p. 163)

The irony of the child to whom words are life-blood pleading to be treated as an adult, to have the secrets of the adult world and its 'Underground' revealed to him, vowing that he can be trusted with secrets, that not a word will pass his lips, even under torture, is terrible, particularly when the story is read in the light of the conclusion of *Panther in the Basement*, where Oz unveils (perhaps too gently and ruminatively) his ultimate question to himself: has he, Amos Oz, not betrayed the Uri and Proffy selves out of whom he was born (or out of whom he fashioned himself) by bringing the panther up out of the basement or the leopard out of the forest, by exposing their secrets to the light and treating them with the amusement, even the mockery, that time and distance inevitably bring? Who is the traitor, and who deserves to be trusted: Amos Oz, author, or the Uri who promises Nussbaum 'They won't get anything out of me'? ('Once more', records Nussbaum, 'the beautiful rage flashes in his green eyes and dies away.' p. 164) To betray oneself, one recalls, is an English idiom for revealing what one does not consciously want to reveal. *Panther in the Basement* is not a vastly ambitious book, but it does, with a light hand, stir some of the deepest questions about the ethics of autobiography.

19   Naguib Mahfouz, *The Harafish*

I

WHEN NAPOLEON BONAPARTE invaded Egypt in 1798, the slumbers of the Arab Near East were rudely broken. Egypt, followed by the rest of the region, was forced to reorient itself away from Turkey and towards Europe. A body of secular European ideas — those that had inspired the French Revolution — broke through the barriers that had separated Islam from the West.

Long before 1798 the Islamic world had been the object of Western interest, and had been fitted into the body of scholarship and myth that Edward Said has called Orientalism. Islam, on the other hand, knew (and cared to know) little about the West. It had nothing to show that could be called Occidentalism, no view of the West through the medium of Islamic arts and sciences.

In the century and a half that followed Napoleon, Islamic countries took on a range of Western concepts and institutions identified by them as essential to their modernisation. Much of the unsettledness of the region today issues from a failure fully to absorb and domesticate such essentially secular Western concepts as democracy, liberalism and socialism. The question the region faces is: can a culture become modern without internalising the genealogy of modernity, that is, without living through the epistemological revolution, in all its implications, out of which Western scientific knowledge grew? 'The new outlook [in the Islamic world] is modern in a way, but it is a *mutilated outlook*,' writes Daryush Shayegan. Modernity has been absorbed, but only in a 'truncated' way. Internally the Islamic world is still 'trailing behind modernity'.[1]

One of the art forms imported from the West by the Islamic world has been the novel. As a storytelling genre, the novel, particularly the realist novel, comes with heavy intellectual baggage. It concerns itself not with exemplary lives but with individual strivings and individual destiny. Towards tradition it is hostile: it values originality, self-founding. It imitates the mode of the scientific case-study or the law brief rather than the hearthside fairy tale. And it prides itself on a language bereft of ornament, on the steady, prosaic observation and recording of detail. It is just the kind of vehicle one would expect Europe's merchant bourgeoisie to invent in order to record and celebrate its own ideals and achievements.

The first Western-style novels in Arabic appeared a century ago. Since then the genre has flourished particularly in Egypt, whose civil society and sense of national identity have been more durable than in other countries of the Arab Near East. There the great middleman has been Naguib Mahfouz (born 1911). Though Mahfouz may receive less attention in Arab letters today than he did in the 1950s and 1960s, it was his example above all that spurred the advance of the novel in Arabic, from Morocco to Bahrain.[2]

II

Mahfouz is above all a novelist of Cairo, and specifically of medieval Cairo, an area of about one square kilometre in the heart of the huge Cairene megalopolis (present population: sixteen million). As a child, Mahfouz recalls, he stood at the window of the family home in the al-Gamaliyya quarter watching British soldiers trying to halt the street demonstrations of 1919 (the scene is replayed in *Palace Walk*). Though his family left al-Gamaliyya when he was twelve, its alleys, with their blend of social classes, have remained the centre of his fictional world. 'In the same alley', writes the Egyptian novelist Gamal al-Ghitani, 'one could easily find a mansion surrounded by a beautiful, spacious garden and right next to it the modest house of a merchant. In the vicinity there would be . . . a tenement for dozens of poor people.'[3] (Since the 1930s the quarter has been in decline, however, and the poverty of the alleys is now unrelieved.)

The novels of Mahfouz's realist phase, notably *Midaq Alley* (1947) and the Cairo trilogy (1956–7), use al-Gamaliyya as a setting with meticulous verisimilitude. By 1959, with *Children of Gebelawi*, this fidelity to the real has diminished and the alleys of the quarter have been allowed some of the fabulous quality of the streets of the Baghdad of *The Thousand and One Nights*.

Mahfouz's realist novels concentrate on city people. There is no trace of the peasantry or the countryside: his city dwellers seem not even to have country relatives. If the city is opposed to anything, it is to itself at an earlier stage of its growth, not to the village. Mahfouz deals particularly with people of limited means trying to keep their heads above water in hard times, doing their best to maintain middle-class standards of conduct and appearance.

The narrowness of focus that results has been criticised by Amitav Ghosh, among others. Ghosh sees the standards that Mahfouz's families set themselves as having less to do with Egyptian tradition than with Victorian respectability. But such a reading, with its implication that Mahfouz's heart lies with anxiously imitated (and soon to be outdated) Western models, misses what Mahfouz, in his darker moments, has to say about the ethic of respectability. *The Beginning and the End* (1949), for instance, a novel that follows the self-sacrificing efforts of a petit-bourgeois family trying to fund the climb of one of its sons into the Egyptian officer class, and the subsequent efforts of that son to hide his shameful social origins, is as bleak and relentless as anything penned by Dreiser.[4]

Mahfouz's reputation rests – and rightly so – on the solid achievement of the Cairo trilogy (*Palace Walk*, *Palace of Desire*, *Sugar Street*), which when it appeared was at once recognised as setting a new standard for the novel in Arabic.[5] The trilogy traces the vicissitudes of two generations of a middle-class Cairo family, from the revolution of 1919 to the Second World War. Its leisurely pages record the gradual emancipation of women, the decline of religious adherence among the middle class, and the increasing prestige of science and of Western cultural forms in general. Among a cast of vivid characters the grocer al-Sayyid Ahmad stands out: at home a forbidding tyrant over his wife and children, but on his evenings out a wit and *bon vivant*, an accomplished singer and generous lover of women of the *demi-monde*. His brilliant and adored son Kemal – coeval with Mahfouz himself – grows, in the course of the trilogy, into a troubled young nationalist intellectual.

In style and narrative method, the trilogy (completed by 1952 but not published for another four years) and its predecessor, *The Beginning and the End*, grow out of Mahfouz's methodical study of the Western novel. They follow the example of the soberer late masters of Western realism. At their best they rise above the scrupulous chronicling of family fortunes and the dissection of *mœurs* to an unwavering yet compassionate unveiling of the lies that people – particularly middle-class people – find it convenient to live by, with a sureness that reminds one of Tolstoy.

III

Like Salman Rushdie, Mahfouz has had a serious brush with Islamic religious authorities. The fact that he emerged unscathed testifies to greater political savvy on his part, to a readiness to make symbolic concessions where necessary. The occasion of conflict was the novel *Children of Gebelawi*, serialised in *Al-Ahram* in 1959 but never published in Egypt as a book (it first appeared in integral form in Beirut in 1967).

Children of Gebelawi, set like several of Mahfouz's other novels in a single Cairo alley, is a complex allegory that functions on both religious and political levels. As a religious allegory, it starts with the founding of a great estate by the godlike al-Gebelawi; it goes on to recount the betrayal of his trust by his younger son, Adham or Adam, the subsequent building of the alley, and the efforts of a series of four heroic leaders, the first three corresponding to Moses, Jesus and the Prophet Muhammad, the fourth a modern man, a scientist, to wrest back the destiny of the alley and the common folk who live there from the gangsters who have taken control. The political message of the book was spelled out by Mahfouz in a 1975 interview. The gangsters who run the alley correspond to Nasser's army officers: 'The question which . . . bothered me was: are we moving towards socialism or to a new kind of feudalism?'[6]

Not surprisingly, *Children of Gebelawi* was attacked for heresy. Out of respect for religious feelings, Mahfouz declined to contest the ruling of Al-Azhar, the highest Islamic institution in the country, proscribing the work: he argued that it would be unwise to alienate Al-Azhar over a relatively minor matter when its support might be needed against what he called 'the other medieval form of Islam', that is to say, the growing fundamentalist movement.[7]

This compromise seemed to have headed off confrontation with the religious authorities. In 1988, however, the award of the Nobel Prize brought renewed pressure for the book, now almost thirty years old, to be published in Egypt. When, shortly thereafter, the storm burst out over Rushdie, *Children of Gebelawi* was coupled in the media with *The Satanic Verses* and Mahfouz was pressed to make public statements on the position of the writer in Islamic societies. He spoke openly in favour of freedom of speech and condemned Khomeini's *fatwa* on Rushdie. Fundamentalists counterattacked, accusing him of 'blasphemy, apostasy, and Freemasonry', and a *fatwa* was pronounced on him by the mufti of a fundamentalist group: 'Mahfouz . . . is an apostate. Anyone who wrongs Islam is an apostate . . . If they do not repent, they must be killed.' There can be little doubt that behind this proscription lay resentment against Mahfouz's support for some form of coexistence with Israel.[8]

IV

The 1960s were dark times for Egypt. As Nasser's regime took on an increasingly repressive aspect, disillusionment set in, particularly among the country's intellectuals. Mahfouz expressed his own distress – somewhat obliquely – in novels such as *The Thief and the Dogs* (1961). *Adrift on the Nile* (1966), which used parody to attack the frivolity and escapism of Egyptian high society, aroused Nasser's particular ire; publication was allowed only after interventions on the author's behalf. After the military defeat of 1967 the environment grew distinctly uncomfortable for doubters and Mahfouz could no longer count on patrons like the then Minister of Culture, Tharwat Ukasha, to protect him. Nasser's death brought relief; in *Al-Karnak* (1974) – published, it must be said, only after Nasser's excesses had already been criticised by Anwar Sadat – Mahfouz documented some of the more gruesome practices of Nasser's secret police.[9]

Mahfouz has never been a full-time writer. Between 1934 and 1971 he was employed in the Civil Service, for part of that time as head of film and theatre censorship. After retiring in 1971, he joined the editorial staff of the prestigious newspaper *Al-Ahram*. In this role he recommended in 1975 that the Arab states should seek a way of coexisting with Israel. Subsequently he openly supported the Camp David accords. He was the first major Arab writer to take up such a stance; as a result his books were for a while banned in certain Arab countries. In his newspaper articles he also expressed his distaste for Sadat's economic policies, which led, in his view, to the poor becoming poorer and the rich richer.[10]

Despite this honourable if cautious record of independence, Mahfouz was criticised for falling behind the times. In the view of the Lebanese writer Elias Khoury, for instance, Mahfouz was failing to resolve the tension between his large project of chronicling the rise to power of the class he knew, the older petit-bourgeoisie, and the pressure – felt particularly after the 1967 war – to give voice to wider ethical and political concerns. Khoury suggests that Mahfouz's turn away from realism towards symbolism and allegory was a symptom, at a literary level, of loss of contact with the classes really at the centre of the social struggle in present-day Egypt.[11]

A comparable criticism has been made by feminist commentators. According to them, Mahfouz's retreat from the complex, socially significant women characters of his realist period, like Nefisa in *The Beginning and the End* – an unattractive woman ready to submit to poverty and spinsterhood for the sake of her brother's career but unable to overcome her need for sex, and therefore doomed to humiliating contacts with men who use her and then jeer at her – to the more stereotyped women of his later work is no more than a defensive reaction to a newly assertive feminist movement.[12]

To those who have criticised his turn to allegory and symbol,

Mahfouz has responded that, while in the 1950s he felt it appropriate to write in the manner of European realism, he thereafter lost interest in the individual as individual in a specific, concrete, historical milieu.[13] In his subsequent work he prefers to exploit a more concentrated, more poetic, but also less 'modern' fictional language than the European masters of his early years could provide.

V

By itself, the title of the sixteenth in Doubleday's admirable Mahfouz series, *The Harafish*, is enigmatic. The word *harafish* is Arabic, but has fallen out of use in the modern language. In medieval times it meant the *mobile vulgus*, the poor of society in their more volatile and threatening aspect. Thus the Arabic title *Malhamat al-harafish* could be – and has been – Englished as 'The Epos of the Rabble'[14] or 'The Epic of the Riffraff'. Yet neither 'rabble' nor 'riffraff' is fair to the *harafish* as we see them in the book: volatile, certainly, but fundamentally fair-minded and responsive to benevolent leadership. For her translation, Catherine Cobham retains the Arabic word, noting that Mahfouz uses it for 'the common people in a positive sense' (for which concept the English language, one may observe, lacks a specific yet down-to-earth word – why?).

The Harafish (first published in 1977) is set in one of the alleys of old Cairo. It deals with the life of the common people, but more specifically with the leaders of the gang – or 'clan' – that generation after generation runs the affairs of the alley. The first of these clan leaders is a humble carter named Ashur. After foreseeing in a dream a plague that is about to hit Cairo, Ashur retreats into the desert with his wife and child. When the plague is over he returns to the decimated city, takes over an abandoned mansion, and redistributes the wealth it contains to revive the economy of the alley. A spell in prison only boosts his reputation among the poor; as Ashur al-Nagi, Ashur the Survivor, he comes home to a hero's welcome, takes over as clan chief, and inaugurates a golden age, 'restraining the powerful, protecting the rights of the humble breadwinners, and creating an atmosphere of faith and piety'.[15]

Then one night Ashur mysteriously disappears. The merchants are delighted, but their relief is shortlived. In a series of battles with neighbouring clans, Ashur's son Shams al-Nagi confirms the pre-eminence of the al-Nagi clan; under its new leader the *harafish* continue to prosper and live in justice.

With the third al-Nagi, Sulayman, however, the dynasty starts to go into decline. Sulayman diverts to clan members protection money which had previously been distributed among the poor; the people suffer while the clan grows rich. As for Sulayman's sons, they fail to understand that prosperity – their own and that of the alley – depends on the power and prestige of the clan. They devote themselves to making money; the chieftainship leaves the al-Nagi family, and soon the clan has become more an exploiter than a protector of the common people. (As they veer between these two roles, the clans of Mahfouz's old Cairo are in essence little different from gangs in the ghettos of any great city today.)

For three more generations the downward slide of clan and alley continues. The *harafish* live in idleness and poverty, despairing that the days of Ashur will ever return. The chieftainship passes to Galal, a gloomy tyrant who uses bribery and extortion to build himself a huge, art-stuffed mansion, then hires a famous necromancer and devotes himself to attaining immortality. The covenant of Ashur has been betrayed; the clan system, mutter the *harafish* – who double as a kind of Greek chorus commenting on the doings of the powerful – has become 'one long-standing calamity'. (p. 335)

Famine strikes Cairo. The merchants hoard food; when the

harafish rebel, the clan strikes back, punishing the poor, protecting the wealthy. Against this tumultuous background a humble descendant of Ashur, Fath al-Bab, lights the spark that sets off an explosion of popular violence. The clan leader is vanquished and driven out and Fath al-Bab is installed as the new chieftain. He tries to end the predatory ways of the clan and return it to the road of service; but his followers murder him and the *harafish* sink back into their 'deep sleep'. (p. 393)

Meanwhile, in an obscure corner, a young man named Ashur, a distant relative of Fath al-Bab, is growing up. Meditating on his mythical namesake, on how he managed to reconcile power and virtue, he is vouchsafed a vision. He challenges the clan and in a rather unbelievable episode the *harafish* rally spontaneously to his banner. 'The *harafish*, the overwhelming majority of the populace, had suddenly joined forces and prevailed over the clubs and long sticks . . . The thread holding things in place had been broken. Anything was possible.' As their new leader, Ashur transforms the *harafish* 'from layabouts, pickpockets, and beggars into the greatest clan the alley had known'. He imposes heavy taxes on the rich, establishes a popular militia, creates jobs, founds schools. 'So began an epoch in the history of the clan which was distinguished by its strength and integrity.' (pp. 402–4)

A summary such as the above conveys little of the flavour of Mahfouz's book. *The Harafish* is not a novel but a sequence of linked tales. The tales do not have a common hero, though they can be said to have a common victim: the suffering people. For his narrative models Mahfouz has gone back to indigenous oral storytelling. In this sense the book is part of an enterprise in which Mahfouz is only one participant (perhaps taking his lead from such younger Egyptian writers as Gamal al-Ghitani): to redefine modern Arabic prose fiction, building upon its classical and folk antecedents, distancing it from the conventions of Western realism it had earlier embraced.

Western readers of *The Harafish* may have trouble with a huge cast of ephemeral characters with unfamiliar names and with the story's thoroughly traditional preoccupations with ancestry and inheritance. Halfway through, in the chapters on the 'bad' al-Nagi generations, readers may begin to lose track of (and perhaps cease to care) who married whom and begat whom. At such moments it is salutary to recall that oral cultures – or cultures with a strong oral substratum – train the faculty of memory in a way that cultures of writing – to say nothing of the new electronic culture – do not find necessary (writing was invented, after all, to cope with the impossibility of remembering everything).

The prose of *The Harafish* may seem formulaic, but there is no doubt that Mahfouz draws strength from the formulae. At the emotional highpoints of his earlier realist novels, particularly in his descriptions of falling in love – something that happens very often in his world, where boys and girls brimming with sexual vigour have few opportunities to meet, and must fall back on the lightning of the occasional charged glance, followed by weeks of erotic musing and fevered plotting – Mahfouz lapses too easily into what Galen Strawson calls 'the fioriture of classical literary Arabic' – the fluttering heart, the blood afire, etc.[16] In its storytelling context, however, the old language comes back to life with surprising crispness.

He . . . noticed her for the first time at the Feast of the Dead . . . She was slim, with sharp features, well-proportioned limbs, a smiling face, and she exuded life and femininity. He felt a surging desire to be joined to her. Their eyes met in mutual curiosity, responsive like fertile earth. The scorching air, the heavy sighs of grief, the fragrance of cut palm leaves, basil, and sweet pastries for the festival fused with their secret desires. He inclined toward her like a sunflower. The death all around spurred him on. (p. 145)

Though, by any computation, the chronology of *The Harafish* must take in several centuries, there is no evidence of changes in the outside world penetrating the closed-off existence of the alley. It is not so much a question of the alley sealing itself off from Egyptian history as of Mahfouz ignoring or wishing away the tyranny of historical time. Even in the days of the first Ashur, for instance, people are building houses with sheet-metal roofs and applying to the authorities for licences to sell alcohol; thirteen generations later nothing in the detail of their daily lives has changed and the agencies of the modern state, particularly the police, remain remote, alien, predatory forces.

The Harafish is built around the lives of a succession of strong-men, some of whom give in to private vices or the temptations of luxury, others of whom keep a vision of greatness before their eyes like a lodestar. The fortunes of clan and common people rise and fall with the fortunes of their leaders. What the clan seeks is a powerful general; what the people need is a protector, a man of justice. The elusive combination of strength and political far-sightedness on the one hand, and justice and compassion on the other, constitutes that quality of greatness which is the underlying theme of Mahfouz's book and makes it into a fable about Egypt's search for a just ruler.

Mahfouz's concern to link private virtue with civic justice, his interest in character and his indifference to systems, give his political thought a refreshingly simple if old-fashioned colour. It would be a mistake, however, to dismiss him, on the evidence of books like *The Harafish*, as stuck in the past. It is rather the case that as a social thinker the later Mahfouz became more interested in salvation than in history. There are two contending tones to be heard in *The Harafish*. One, poignant and elegiac, emerges in the second Ashur's meditations on a world in which the get-rich-quick methods of his businessman brother Fayiz seem to be rampant.

At night he still went to the monastery square, wrapped in darkness, guided by the stars . . . He sat down in al-Nagi's old spot and listened to the dancing rhythms. Didn't these men of God care about what happened to God's creatures? When would they open the gate or knock down the walls? He wanted to ask them . . . why egotists and criminals prospered, while the good and loving came to nothing. Why the *harafish* were in a deep sleep. (p. 392)

It is telling that while Fayiz is allowed to scoff at the conservative ways of the alley, he is given little chance to speak for his chosen life of 'brokerage' and 'speculation', that is to say, for the methods of modern capitalism: he is soon killed off, and we are told that his fortune has been based not on business at all but on the crime of murdering rich men and taking their money. (p. 377)

The other tone – less true, perhaps – is to be heard in the fairy-tale ending: in the ascendancy of Ashur, the eclipse of the bourgeois 'notables', the awakening of the *harafish*, and intimations that the day of revelation is at hand.

[Ashur] looked at the great door [of the monastery] in astonishment. Gently, steadily, it was opening. The shadowy figure of a dervish appeared, a breath of night embodied.

'Get the flutes and drums ready,' the figure whispered . . . 'Tomorrow the Great Sheikh will come out of his seclusion. He will walk down the alley bestowing his light and give each young man a bamboo club and a mulberry fruit. Get the flutes and drums ready . . .'

[Ashur] jumped to his feet, drunk on inspiration and power. Don't be sad, his heart told him. One day the door may open to those who seize life boldly, with the innocence of children and the ambition of angels. (p. 406)

The Harafish is not only, in the main, about men and their fortunes, but sets before itself a particularly male ideal. Nevertheless, it includes several piquant seduction scenes (Mahfouz's men are rarely a match for the wiles of women), while the most striking, and certainly the most lively, character in the book is Zahira, mother of Galal. Restless in the role of dutiful wife, mother and daughter-in-law, she uses the liberal divorce laws of Islam to rid herself of a succession of unsatisfactory husbands, only to be murdered by a *deus ex machina* ploy that leaves one wondering whether her author had not begun to grow anxious at the thought of where the trajectory of this furious, volatile and ambitious woman might take her.

With no Arabic, one should not pretend to judge the quality of the translation. Catherine Cobham's version reads both authoritatively and fluently. Certain colloquialisms – 'cover my back', 'son of a gun', 'getting stoned' – carry American connotations which sit uneasily with the faintly (and appropriately) archaic English of the rest. (pp. 9, 148, 202) 'Call girl' (p. 370) surely depends on the existence of telephones; and 'crusade' is perhaps the wrong word for the campaign for justice mounted by one of the better clan leaders. The text is punctuated with fragments of Persian poetry – songs wafting down the alley from a nearby Sufi monastery – which have been left untranslated. This decision seems to me contestable but probably correct: the *harafish* of yore would have understood the Persian no better than would Mahfouz's readers in Cairo today.

ONE YEAR THE image of Africa is of herds of giraffe sailing across boundless sunlit plains. The next year it is of stick-like starving children with ballooning bellies and great sad dark eyes. Another year it is of soldiers in tattered fatigues lobbing mortar shells into the bush in yet another incomprehensible war. Africa is still peripheral enough to the West for the West to be able to afford to see it in terms of a repertoire of images like these, purveyed by journalists to a public impatient of far-off complexities.

For centuries, in fact, it has been the fate of Africa to be used by the West as a kind of image bank from which emblems, sometimes of savagery, brutality and hopelessness, sometimes of innocence, simplicity and good nature, can be drawn at will. Even to well-disposed outsiders, Africa remains a place that one studies, to which one sends teachers and aid: Africans are not people from whom one learns. The richness of Africa's resources is acknowledged, but the resources referred to are natural, not human. What Africa has to offer is always raw: raw produce, raw ores, raw people, raw experience. What Africa gets in exchange is finished: systems of government, health clinics, computers.

Ali Mazrui is a political scientist from Kenya with a distinguished academic career behind him. He has written authoritatively on subjects important to post-colonial Africa, such as the notion of national identity, the role of the army in the State, the function of Third World intellectuals. In 1986 he put together a television series, commissioned by the British Broadcasting Corporation and other bodies and intended primarily for Western consumption, whose purpose was not only to correct Western images of Africa but to confront these images in the most direct way. This approach promised a degree of discomfort to the politically sensitive viewer. The National Endowment for the Humanities, which provided some of the funding, was upset enough when it previewed the series to withdraw its name from the credits, though in fact Mazrui treats the United States quite kindly by comparison with Britain and France. The series has been screened widely; it is used as a resource in many schools and colleges.

The dismay of the NEH administrators was not without cause. There is a certain self-righteousness, a certain relentlessly needling tone to Mazrui's presentation. On the other hand, perhaps it is time for the West to accept that almost any African intellectual, asked to speak about Africa, will speak about a continent abused, exploited and patronised by foreigners, an Africa still living in the aftershock of colonialism, bitter, angry and suspicious. If Africa is the most peripheral of the continents to the interests of the West (save Antarctica, perhaps), the West is not at all peripheral to Africa and has not been for centuries. What the West has thought of Africa has had a great deal to do with how Africans have lived their lives and died their deaths. This situation did not end when the British and French and Portuguese pulled out, or when the last colonies – the internal colonies run by the whites of southern Africa – fell. So Mazrui's *The Africans* may usefully be seen as another shot in the continuing anti-colonial war, a shot for which (in an irony Africans will appreciate) the colonialists have this time footed the bill.

One of the aspects of the series about which NEH expressed its displeasure is the absence of any voice to gainsay Mazrui's. Of the nine hours' worth of Africa we see, every minute is interpreted to us by a single commentator. Other Africans certainly get a chance to talk, but they talk only to exhibit how they talk in their everyday lives. They are simply characters in a story Mazrui is telling; they are not permitted to address the greater issues.

What might a counter-voice to Mazrui's say, if there were true dialogue in this production? The sequence on the Ivory Coast will provide a good example. Mazrui takes us on a tour of the new, modernistic capital city. No human face is to be seen: against a background of soft, eerie music, the camera tracks across empty streets from one stark building to another. The message: President Houphuet-Boigny has been overtaken by delusions of grandeur, he is squandering his nation's resources, his mind has been colonised by mechanical Western fantasies, what he has built is not an authentic African city but a façade, an illusion, even a nightmare.

It is easy enough to imagine an entirely different narrative, backed by different images – jets taking off and landing at Abidjan airport, a busy dockside, the bustle of commerce in the streets, well-fed, lively children saying their lessons, smiling workers assembling consumer goods, farmers hoeing their fields – while a smooth voice-over coaxes us along with facts and figures – rising GNP, rising literacy, declining infant mortality – all of which would 'prove' (is seeing not believing?) that the Ivory Coast is a haven of stability and prosperity on a continent elsewhere collapsing into chaos.

Which is the true story: the official one, or Mazrui's story that the Ivory Coast is a mere French outpost run by a black puppet and a clique of cronies for their personal aggrandisement? History – to which Mazrui, in his writings and in this film, will have made a contribution – will decide. All I point to here is that the Ivory Coast and Africa in general, including those countries like Tanzania and Zimbabwe of whose political direction Mazrui approves, will provide a veritable treasure hoard of images to support either political position. The camera has no ideology: it will lie on behalf of whoever points it and presses the button; it will lie even more persuasively when there is the right music in the background.

What we mean when we say that Africa is a continent of contrasts is in fact that Africa is particularly rich in contradictory images: images of joy, images of woe. Mazrui picks and chooses his images to suit his case. His case is that behind the smart neo-colonialist façade created by Africa's strongmen lies another Africa of potholed roads, derelict factories, empty schools, rundown clinics, decayed buildings, gutted cars, dead radios, dry taps; but that behind this moribund Africa there lies yet another Africa, the old Africa of sturdy, self-reliant peasants, respected elders, tight family ties, deeply ingrained myths and observances, out of which, one day, the true Africa of the future will be born.

This faith in old Africa marks Mazrui as receptive to the school of thought known once as Négritude and later as Black Consciousness, a school of thought that urges people of African descent to rediscover their ancestral origins and build upon their authentic African foundations, rather than give themselves to Western-style individualism and materialism. The Black Consciousness critique is directed not only at an exploitative outside world but at the prevailing order in Africa itself, starting at the top: at politicians who have lost touch with the forces of tradition and rely for support on a rootless, demoralised, urban *lumpen* populace; at ambitious military men in love with their Western toys of destruction; but also, further down the social scale, at hunters who have lost touch with the old feelings of reciprocity toward animals and who slaughter Africa's wild life for profit; at woodcutters to whom destroying the forest is no longer sacrilege; at women who ape Western standards of beauty.

In the strictest sense of the word, this is a conservative critique. It rests on a belief that, before the catastrophic impact of colonialism in the nineteenth century, African societies functioned well, relying, behind the institution of chieftainship, on a uniquely African system of checks and balances which the West has never taken the trouble to understand; and that the great task now facing Africa is, first, to weather the last shock-waves of the colonial onslaught, and then slowly to begin rebuilding on the foundations of the old heritage, until Africa is at last restored as the one truly humanistic society on earth. 'You are not a country, Africa, you are a glimpse of infinity,' says Mazrui; Africans are 'people of the day before yesterday, potentially people of the day after tomorrow'.

The position Mazrui takes here clearly lays him open to the charge that he romanticises old Africa, claiming for the continent a cultural unity that has no basis in reality ('Before slavery we were all one huge village called Africa,' he says) and espousing policies that will simply delay Africa's economic take-off even further. But Black Consciousness has a great deal to do with black pride; and it is a moot point whether Africa can be a serious participant in world affairs as long as African self-esteem remains low. To this extent the Black Consciousness project – of which I take Mazrui's *The Africans*, in its general thrust, to be representative – may in fact have a quite pragmatic purpose.

Black Consciousness rejects as a vicious caricature the picture of Africa in the old Tarzan movies: childish and superstitious jungle folk in the thrall of bloodthirsty chiefs and sly witchdoctors, people with no arts or crafts worth mentioning, ignorant of the simplest science. It justifiably calls this caricature part of a colonialist plot to show that colonialism liberated the natives from forces of benightedness. In Mazrui's series we see instead many of the technological and artistic achievements of precolonial Africa: iron-smelting and forging, architecture, masks and statuary. But the real emphasis falls on Africa's resilient social substructure, on the bonds which hold people together and have held them together through generations of adversity.

The case that Mazrui makes against mere imitation of the West, the case for a uniquely African road to the future, is an appealing one. It has appealed particularly to intellectuals in Africa and the African diaspora. But there are some hard questions it has to face. One is this: unless it imports Western technology on a large scale, and along with Western technology the problem-solving Western outlook, Western materialism and Western values, can Africa hope for anything but economic stagnation, which, coupled with a fast-rising birth rate, will mean that the future promises not a return to Eden but to a hell of disease and starvation?

Mazrui's answer is that Africa must import wisely, adapting Western techniques and values so that they become authentically African. As examples, he points to what Africa has done with Islam and to a lesser extent with Christianity. He does not face up to the likelihood that Western science and technology may unavoidably come in a package with rationalism, materialism, Western-style economics, the profit motive, the cult of the individual, the nuclear family and much else un-African.

Mazrui himself was brought up in the Islamic tradition. One of the facts he stresses (to the surprise of most Westerners, I would guess) is that Islam is Africa's principal religion. In the scenes he gives from Islamic societies, we see religion closely woven into the texture of daily life. In scenes of Christian worship, on the contrary, what we see seem to be European rather than African ceremonies, stiff and dour, performed by black men in European costume. We also see one abandoned, dilapidated Christian church after another. If Christianity is not to die out in Africa, warns Mazrui, it must identify with African aspirations, as churchmen in South Africa did in identifying with the liberation struggle, or as independent African sects have done in breaking free of European control and developing their own syncretic rituals.

Upsetting though the news may be to the West that Christianity in Africa is on the decline, it is news that ought to be heard. What may make the news doubly hard to stomach is that the messenger who brings it has little good to say about the entire mission enterprise. The West remembers its missionaries as, by and large, selfless men and women who did their quiet bit for brotherhood and light. To Mazrui, on the contrary, missionaries, whatever their personal qualities, simply acted as the propaganda wing of the colonial army of occupation, undermining the ancestral religions which held societies together, admonishing Africans to turn the other cheek whenever they were struck, providing the kind of rudimentary education that fitted African children for lives as clerks and underlings. From the film archives he unearths an old clip showing teenage African girls, clad from neck to knee in drab, shapeless smocks, dancing a Scottish reel. That, suggests Mazrui, was mission education: at its best absurd, at its worst viciously anti-African.

No doubt the image of the Victorian missionary in his black serge suit toiling under the African sun to turn his African charges into stiff, repressed imitation Westerners has a ludicrous side to it. But were the missionaries not achieving much that they and their political masters never intended? Those parents who decided to take what the mission schools had to offer saw their children advance fastest and furthest under the colonial system, while those with the independence of mind to remain on the outside often got left behind. Mazrui's sympathies clearly lie with the latter: he devotes a long sequence to the Ashanti of Ghana, who tenaciously resisted cultural penetration and as a result preserved their traditional forms of government to an unusual degree. But the Ashanti have as a result been marginalised in the politics of modern

Ghana; while the young men who received their first education in the mission schools went on to create the instruments (the political parties and trade unions) which expelled the colonialists.

There are moments when Mazrui comes close to rejecting an educational policy whose broad purpose would be to bring the young African into world culture (which, the distribution of power being what it is, is inescapably Western culture), endorsing instead the criterion that all education must be relevant to the problems of present-day Africa. There is even a moment when he seems to advocate for young people the kind of training in practical skills that, under the name Bantu Education, was foisted on to Africans – and rejected by Africans – in South Africa in the 1950s.

Though a great deal of Mazrui's time is devoted to the past, and to an exposé of what colonialism actually did to Africa, the question at the heart of the series is: what should Africa do *now*? What distinguishes Mazrui's answers from those of other commentators is the time perspective he grants himself. Africa will certainly have to adapt, he says, but we cannot even imagine what form the adaptations will take, so long and complex will the process be. Africans have a genius for adaptation, so we can be optimistic; but Africa must beware of taking any short cuts that will entail the loss of its essence; for Africa without its African essence will be no more than a lifeless, inauthentic parody of the West.

What is the essence of Africa? It is to be found, first, says Mazrui, in a certain anti-metaphysical body of thought and feeling that he calls 'the theology of nearness', in which gods, ancestors, living creatures and the great earth itself are all bound together in the same realm of being; and, second, in social structures based on the family ('We in Africa invented the family'). This essence will be betrayed if Africa gives in to the 'culture of violence' that its armies have picked up from the West, or if its soul is colonised by Western-style consumerism, or if the family itself breaks down under the pressures of urbanisation, loss of parental authority, easy morals, crime, drugs and alcohol, or perhaps even if African women allow themselves to be drawn away from their traditional role to become typists in the cities (though Mazrui acknowledges sexism to be 'a problem engulfing the whole of Africa', there is a degree of veiled sexism in his glorification of African woman as 'custodian of fire, protector of the fertility of the earth', that is, as the person who must fetch firewood and take care of the garden).

All in all, *The Africans* presents a picture of a turbulent, confused, but exciting Africa, facing material and spiritual problems compared with which the problems of the West pale into insignificance. Because of the range of its coverage and because of its trenchancy (what NEH might call its dogmatism), the picture captures and holds our attention.

What must be said as well, however, is that *The Africans* is clearly the brainchild of a social scientist, not a poet. There is an all-important facet of Africa that is entirely missing from it. I refer neither to what is called the romance of Africa (tall Masai leaning on their spears, staring into the distance), nor to the mystery of Africa, but to the experience of African personality. In nine hours of film I can recollect no moment of intimacy with any of the thousands of people who pass before our eyes. Starving children are seen by the camera simply as examples of starving children, market-sellers as examples of market-sellers, and so forth. The camera never lingers, never explores, seems utterly uninquisitive about the unique personal identity behind the exterior. It is as though the series were telling us that Africans have no souls, or that their souls are unimportant. The only African we truly meet is Ali Mazrui himself, and then only Mazrui the public man.

A final observation. From Africa came the music of the New World; and the music of the New World has, in the twentieth century, conquered the rest of the world. Why, in a series devoted to Africa, is the background music not African but European? Would the Mau-Mau ever have believed that one day a Kenyan would be telling their story to the accompaniment of Samuel Barber's *Adagio for Strings*?

21 The Poems of Thomas Pringle

THOMAS PRINGLE WAS born in 1789 into a family of Scottish farmers. An admirer of Burns and an enthusiastic participant in the Scottish literary revival, he tried but failed to find a niche for himself in the small Edinburgh literary world. When in 1819 the British government announced an aid scheme for emigrants to the Cape Colony, he, together with most of the Pringle family, enlisted; a year later they were settled on the Colony's inhospitable eastern frontier.

Dismayed by conditions on the frontier, Pringle did not remain a farmer for long. Through the intervention of patrons he found a position as librarian in the colonial administration in Cape Town, and there started the colony's first newspaper. His activities soon brought him into conflict with the authoritarian Governor, Sir Charles Somerset: at issue was his right to publish information embarrassing to the administration. Though he eventually won his case, he lost his job. In 1826 he returned to Britain. There, till his death in 1834, he was a prominent figure in the anti-slavery movement.

Pringle holds an honourable if minor place in South African history as proponent of a free press and as part of a pressure group in Britain which prodded a series of unwilling colonial administrations towards accepting the principle of broad legal rights for the

Crown's African subjects. He also has a minor reputation as a Scottish literary figure, the author of a body of sweetly flowing but rather facile nature poetry.

His main claim to fame, however, is as the founding father of English language poetry in South Africa. It is a claim based on his *Poems Illustrative of South Africa*, which was published in more or less final form in 1834 (versions had appeared earlier). Some of these poems – for instance, 'Afar in the Desert' – soon became popular anthology pieces.

Can this Scot who spent a bare six years in Africa be considered a South African poet? Yes, say Pringle's most recent editors, Ernest Pereira and Michael Chapman, and give their edition the bold title *African Poems of Thomas Pringle*.[1] The poems they reproduce consist of the forty-odd poems of *Poems Illustrative of South Africa*, plus miscellaneous verses composed in South Africa and some rhymes for children written as anti-slavery propaganda. But their case for an African identity for Pringle is not based solely on the African content of these poems. Pringle's poetry should be read, they argue, not in isolation but as part of a larger text including his prose writings (of which his *Narrative of a Residence in South Africa* [1834] is the most substantial) and even the historical text constituted by his life. 'It is our knowledge of Pringle and his situation,' they write, 'of the historical and physical setting, of the particular circumstances or events which inform and prompt his responses, that gives his poems significance.' (p. xxi) 'It is the consistency of his engagement with real concerns in this country [i.e., South Africa] that lends substance to his writing.' (p. xxiii)

> We are not suggesting that Pringle simply transcends his time, but that his poems offer loci of interest, experience and debate that continue to have currency in South African social and literary life. Instead of measuring his style against the

'invention' of his great Romantic contemporaries and finding him wanting, we may begin to see Pringle's shifts between the indigenous phrase and the Augustan poeticism, between the exile's lament and the local commitment, as part of his valid attempt to find his own voice in utterly strange surroundings. (p. xxiv)

It is clear, then, that Pereira and Chapman aim for more in their edition than merely to put back into print, in a handy, inexpensive form, a canonical poet – canonical at least in South African terms – whose work has not for a while been easily available. Their aim is to reclaim for Pringle a status as a writer commensurate with his historical status, and thereby to some extent to redress the balance of South African literary history in favour of historically particular writers of the liberal Left, like Pringle, as against mythically oriented writers of the Right, like Roy Campbell.

Pereira and Chapman conduct their case not only in a solid and capably argued introductory essay, but by means of an extensive editorial apparatus that reprints Pringle's explanatory notes to his poems as well as illuminating extracts from his *Narrative*. In addition, following Robert Wahl's researches of 1970, they supply accounts of the complex textual history of the poems and, in certain key cases, scrutinise Pringle's revisions.

The question remains, however, whether the category of 'African poems' has any substance. Editorially, the question presents itself in a different form: if we are not to have a *Collected Poems*, is the best alternative to separate the 'African' poems from the 'Scottish' poems, or should we not instead produce a *Selected Poems* comprising the best of Pringle's verse, whatever its provenance?

To some extent, the latter question is answered by the brute fact that the only body of readers Pringle can expect to engage nowadays is in South Africa; and these readers have no reason to be interested in his sub-Romantic Scottish versifying. For Pringle to come alive to anyone but a specialist he must, as his editors say, be read historically, against the background of early-nineteenth-century British colonial penetration of southern Africa.

Nevertheless, there is a certain danger in basing Pringle's claim to continuing relevance on his fidelity to 'real concerns' and 'actual people', as against what the editors rather tendentiously call 'myths and phantoms of the colonial psyche'. (pp. xxiii, xxiv) After the dedicatory verses to Walter Scott, the first and one of the most famous of Pringle's *Poems Illustrative of South Africa* is 'The Bechuana Boy'. This poem, as we learn from Pringle's notes and correspondence, draws on a real-life person, an orphan named Hinza Marossi who fell under Pringle's protection, returned with him to England and died there shortly afterwards. Hinza's life-story tells us a great deal about banditry, slavery and the destruction of communal life on and beyond the nominal frontiers of the Colony in the 1820s. Hinza is an 'actual person' in more than a trivial sense. But we derive his actuality more from Pringle's notes and letters than from the poem itself, which, aside from the frank liberties it takes with facts (Pringle acknowledges, for instance, that, while the boy of the poem wanders the desert with a tame springbok fawn, the real Hinza had no such pet), through its diction draws us away from the specificity of Africa towards a generalised landscape of the Romantic sublime dotted with the more celebrated African mammalian fauna. Here, for instance, is Hinza telling of how the slavers drove their captives across the Gariep [Orange] River:

> Hoarse-roaring, dark, the broad Gareep
> In turbid streams was sweeping fast,
> Huge sea-cows in its eddies deep
> Loud snorting as we passed;

> But that relentless robber clan
> Right through those waters wild and wan
> Drove on like sheep our wearied band:
> – Some never reached the farther strand. (p. 5)

This is not to deny that stories like Hinza's, reconceived in the poetic imagination, retold in ballad form, could evoke pathos and awaken outrage in their British readers and thereby enter history as forces for change. It is simply to say that, in turning story into poetry, Pringle rather uninventively assimilates his data under the categories provided for him by the dominant poetic models of his time and place. Hinza is indeed not a 'myth or phantom of the colonial psyche', but he does merge into a line of abused European children, and is in this sense a figure already prepared in the European imagination for discovery in Africa (his fawn, exotic equivalent of a lamb, is a giveaway, a merely literary emblem of pastoral innocence).

In other words, in converting experience into poetry Pringle, partly because this was the line of least resistance for his derivative talent but partly also because such was his intention, generalises from the African particular to the universal (in fact the European universal) in the best manner of the country-life poets of the generation before Wordsworth, whom he admired and copied – particularly James Thomson. It is certainly possible, using all the textual sources available to us, to read back into the poem some of its historical fullness; but we must recognise that to read Pringle thus is to some extent to read him against the grain, counter to his own poetic exertions. It is, literally, to miss the poetry, indifferent poetry though it is.

22   Daphne Rooke

I

DAPHNE ROOKE WAS born in 1914 in the then Transvaal province of South Africa. Her mother came from a prominent Afrikaans family; her father, who was English-speaking, died in the First World War. Educated in English-language schools, Daphne, née Pizzey, was also at home in Afrikaans language and culture; an uncle, Leon Maré, still occupies a minor niche in Afrikaans literary history. Through spending part of her childhood in Zululand, she became familiar with the Zulu language and Zulu customs; her novel *Wizards' Country*, set in the Zulu kingdom of the 1870s, is one of the more thoroughgoing efforts of empathic identification by a white writer with a black world-view, albeit an imagined one.

In 1946 Rooke won a contest for new writers, for which the prize was publication of her manuscript (ironically by an Afrikaans publishing house – until the 1970s English-language publishing in South Africa tended to wait rather timidly for London's lead). Retitled *A Grove of Fever Trees*, her novel came out in 1950 in the United States, and then in Britain. It was soon followed by *Mittee* (1951), which was widely translated and brought Rooke her first taste of fame and fortune. During the next fifteen years she produced a series of successful novels (*Ratoons*, 1953; *Wizards' Country*,

1957; *A Lover for Estelle*, 1961; *The Greyling*, 1962; *Diamond Jo*, 1965), as well as children's books. Though widely read, she was not regarded (and perhaps did not regard herself) as a serious writer: her romances of blood and passion set in bygone times or in incestuous settler communities – 'colonial Gothic', one critic called them – seemed to have little relevance to the great issues of the day.

Married in 1937 to an Australian, Irvin Rooke, Daphne Rooke left South Africa for Australia definitively in 1965. There she wrote *Boy on the Mountain* (1969), set in New Zealand, and *Margaretha de la Porte* (1974), set in nineteenth-century South Africa, as well as more children's fiction.

Since 1987, when *Mittee* was republished in South Africa, there has been a rebirth of interest in Rooke in her native land. To a large extent this interest has been generated by feminist readers of a body of literature, colonial and postcolonial, shaped to an unusual extent by women writers. The originating South African novelist was Olive Schreiner (1855–1920); the 1920s and 1930s were dominated by Pauline Smith (1882–1959) and Sarah Gertrude Millin (1889–1968); the pre-eminent figure since the 1950s has been Nadine Gordimer (born 1923); while the formative period spent by Doris Lessing (born 1919) in Southern Rhodesia and South Africa earns her a foothold in the tradition. The first question to ask, then, is whether Rooke belongs in the line of Schreiner, Smith, Gordimer and Lessing, writers engaged with moral and political issues of class, race and gender in South Africa, and with the deeper human problems of colonial and postcolonial southern Africa in general, or with Millin (say) and the exploitation for literary/commercial ends of the more spectacularly violent features of South African life, the more picturesque episodes of South African history.

II

'Sometimes she forgets I am a coloured girl and calls me Sister. I love her and I hate her.'[1]

The 'coloured girl' who speaks is Selina; the 'she' who sometimes calls her sister is her childhood playmate Mittee, to whom she is now bodyservant, confidante and sexual rival. In a more equal world would Mittee and Selina be true sisters, would there be love and no hatred between them? Sceptically one answers, no: the germ of sexual rivalry lies too deep. What makes Daphne Rooke's *Mittee* different, then, from any other story of two girls competing for the same man – a man who in this case happens to be worthy of neither of them?

The answer has to do with the racial caste system of colonial South Africa (*Mittee* is set in the old Transvaal, but the mores and prejudices of Paul Kruger's Republic, as Rooke presents them, are no different from those of the Cape Colony). Selina desires Mittee's beau, the villain Paul du Plessis, *because* Mittee (in her milk-and-water way) desires him, *because* Mittee is the object of Selina's obsessive imitation in all affairs, *because* to Selina her own desires are by definition inauthentic, the desires of 'a coloured girl'. The stratifications that set white and black in worlds apart, and leave 'a coloured girl' wandering in no girl's land between them, define the consciousness of Mittee and Selina and of everyone in their society – everyone except the missionary doctor Basil Castledene who, formed not in the colonies but in England, will eventually open Mittee's eyes to the error of her ways and take her away to civilisation. What makes Rooke's girl-rivals different, then, is that one of them, the disadvantaged one, acts as a sexual being not out of pride of the body, not to assert her own desire and desirability, but in order to enact the desires, and to have a far-off experience of the desirability, of the rival who obsesses her, yet whom she can no more *be* than the leopard can change its spots.

This is by no means the whole story, however. It is the story that Selina, as storyteller, allows to emerge. But we would not be attributing excessive subtlety to Daphne Rooke, behind Selina, to wonder whether there is not a degree of self-deception in Selina's story, perhaps even a degree of willed self-deception. For though Selina tells a story in which the desires of white girls are authentic and the desires of coloured girls mere pathetic imitations, the novel *Mittee* tells a story in which Selina is the passionate woman whom Paul, once he has had a taste of her, cannot leave alone, while Mittee, confined by propriety as much as by layer after layer of clothing, is barred from fulfilment, moving from the shock and disillusionment of the nuptial bed through a phase of embittered contraception to what one can only imagine as ethereal transports with Castledene. In other words, there is a second story looming behind the first, a story invisible to its teller, in which Selina, by virtue of her colour, is the child of nature to whom pleasure comes naturally, while Mittee remains a frustrated heir of civilisation and its contempt for the body.

It is to be doubted whether Rooke sees through, or even consciously recognises that she is here invoking, a myth of the black man – and even more the black woman – as a creature of nature in instinctive touch with his/her own desires, a myth which the greater colonial enterprise had no difficulty in incorporating into its stock of received ideas, particularly since its obverse side is that the black is slave to his or her own desires, incapable of those sublimations from which higher cultures grow. One is not even sure whether, at this stage of her career, Rooke questions the folklore that the merest touch of 'black blood' makes one *in essence* black, a child of nature, wild.

There are two related episodes in *Mittee* that are clearly intended by Rooke to reflect on the question of wildness and civilisation. In one episode a half-tamed baboon slips its chain and terrorises the women of the farm until Castledene arrives to calm it and lead it away. Because the farmers are away fighting the British, there is no one to protect their women; the baboon stands for the wildness that conquest has penned up but which may erupt as soon as the iron colonial grip is relaxed. (Shortly after this episode two black men do indeed exploit the absence of the farmers to go on a rampage. To her credit, Rooke does not indulge in the *ne plus ultra* of colonial horror-fantasies, the rape of a white woman, though she does come close to it. As for the offenders, the colonial grip soon reasserts itself: they are tracked down to the mission station and summarily castrated.)

But there is a second captive ape in the novel, a female with a 'tragic' face which sits on its pole, forever staring toward the mountains, where 'its tribe lived its thrilling life'. Under Castledene's tutelage, Mittee sets the animal free. 'It's the most wonderful thing I ever saw!' cries Mittee as it races away. (p. 157) Wonderful indeed; but, in the context of Rooke's parables of captivity, what does it mean? What is Mittee learning should be unchained, and what is the admiring Selina (also half in love with Castledene, though too overwhelmed with awe to do anything about it), telling the story over Mittee's shoulder, learning too? And what of ourselves, Rooke's readers: what are we being told?

I will not pursue the point because it is here, more or less, that Rooke loses control of her tale. And not only in *Mittee*: in other novels as well (most damagingly in *A Lover for Estelle*) she has recourse, when it takes a certain courage to face the issues she has stirred, to whisking her characters off into the wilds, away from civilisation and its nagging discontents, to face life-and-death adventures instead. It is this habit of evading the implications of her own fables, this rather easy way of bringing novels to an end, that most damagingly backs the charge that Rooke is a mere romancer, out of her depth with larger issues.

Thus far I have treated Selina as playing out the myth of the half-caste (the bastard, in even blunter old-style racist terminology) as a divided self, yearning to be white and civilised, drawn back willy-nilly to the darkness of nature by her never wholly submerged blackness. In South African literature, this is a myth exploited particularly by Sarah Gertrude Millin in her widely read novel *God's Step-Children* (1924). God's step-children are, in Millin's words (from a preface she wrote to a re-issue of the novel in 1951, the year in which *Mittee* appeared), 'the mixed breeds of South Africa, those . . . who *must* [my emphasis] always suffer'. 'Mixed blood' is, to Millin, the source of 'tragedy': *God's Step-Children* tracks, through generation after generation of a single family, the tragic workings of the taint of black blood in the lives of those unfortunate enough to bear it.

Millin inherited from European and American biology of the nineteenth century an entire pseudo-science of degeneration which associated race-mixing with the decline of civilisation. Political discourse in South Africa between the world wars is full of reference to this pseudo-science. While in the West the atrocious extremes to which the prescriptions of racial eugenics were carried under Hitler had the effect of driving the science of degeneration underground, and perhaps even of killing it, the shadow of the Nuremberg trials passed over South Africa too lightly to drive the lesson home: the laws of apartheid passed after 1948 depended heavily on it for their justification.

In line with conventional wisdom about people of mixed race, Rooke portrays Selina as a divided self. The question of what kind of self Selina's posterity will have is finessed by having her left sterile after an assault by a jealous lover. But, one must add, there is no hint that Selina bears the fatal, protogenetic flaw of degeneracy (her experiment with home-made brandy does not mark the beginning of a slide into alcoholism, for instance), and indeed her end is by no means tragic: sundered from her beloved Mittee, she nevertheless achieves modest happiness with the dutiful, easily pleased Fanie, while the tyrant Paul meets with a well-deserved nasty end.

III

Rooke returned to the triangle of the Mittee–Paul–Selina type twice more in her career, developing different aspects of it.

In 1962 she published *The Greyling*, an altogether more sombre book than *Mittee*, written in the shadow of the so-called Immorality Act. A young coloured woman who bears her white lover's child is murdered by him as he desperately tries to protect himself from exposure. The murderer's parents, conventional Afrikaners and supporters of the government, undergo a catharsis of pity and terror, adopt the child and leave the country.

Like Alan Paton's *Too Late the Phalarope* (1953), *The Greyling* records the devastation wrought by a law that sought to police the most intimate acts. (The South African censors struck back at once, banning the book.) It is Rooke's most overtly political novel, one in which she adopts, not without unease, the mode of naturalistic tragedy practised by Hardy and Dreiser. The tragedy she sees, however, is not Millin's tragedy of blood, in which misfortune proceeds inexorably from a taint in the blood, but the tragedy that results when a fragile and unequal sexual relationship is placed under threat of public censure and legal prosecution. The coloured woman in Rooke's story is friendless and socially isolated, the white boy has a streak of sadism (to say nothing of racism) in him; disaster is inevitable.

In 1974 Rooke re-explored the Mittee–Selina rivalry in a novel of failing power, *Margaretha de la Porte*. The wealthy heiress Margaretha has a Bushman servant and 'sister', a vulgar, irreverent shadow of herself, envied and punished for the satisfying and 'natural' sex life she seems capable of enjoying. After some highly implausible machinery has been brought in to justify the move, Margaretha, in an act of mercy, strangles her mortally wounded shadow-sister with her bare hands; the book ends with an unhappy Margaretha, thwarted as an artist, baffled in her desires, facing the whispered censure of her community.

Thus far I have treated the tensions with which Rooke deals, and which structure her books, as racial in nature. But the murderous Paul in *Mittee* and Maarten in *The Greyling* are not only whites exercising white power, they are men exercising male power in the crudest of ways. Rooke's novels are full of male violence. A farmer stifles his dying wife's newborn child, forcing his daughter to bring up her own illegitimate baby in its place (*Ratoons*). A German baron packs off his gifted but eccentric young bride to a bleak asylum to have the nonsense knocked out of her (*Margaretha de la Porte*). A teenage boy rapes and kills an insufficiently welcoming girl (*Boy on the Mountain*). An Indian husband rapes his eight-year-old bride (*Ratoons*). A miner rapes and casually disposes of a woman (*Diamond Jo*). An attractive, simple-minded boy turns out to be a murderous psychopath (*A Grove of Fever Trees*).

Male power in Rooke's world is not exercised at a remove, through money, for instance: women who look to men for love are as likely as not to meet violence and oppression instead. This is the disillusioning truth Mittee discovers when she marries Paul. It is a truth Selina has already learned, though it does not stop her from returning to Paul again and again.

What draws the half-caste woman and the sadistic man so obsessively together? To explain Paul's craving, Rooke seems to hark back to the folklore of the *luxe et volupté* of the mixed-blood mistress, combining savage abandon with European refinement of pleasure. Selina's own motivation is harder to understand or accept. Is she simply continuing to compete sexually with Mittee; is Paul to be understood as one of those dark, forceful men whom, in the world of romance, women find irresistible; or is Selina, as a creature of romance too, seeking in Paul's embrace her own romantic doom? The retrospective first-person narrative mode makes deeper motives such as these difficult (though not impossible) to explore. As is often the case when she is in a fix, however, Rooke dodges the problem by shifting into a higher rhetorical gear: 'Would I live again those nights of terror and passion? Each time I said to him, I will never come here again. But when the moon was high and nothing stirred on the veld but the night wind, I would leave my mat in Aunt Lena's house and run down the path to the great wild fig tree.' (pp. 116–17)

The somewhat asexual Mittee is not typical of Rooke's heroines. For the most part they are frankly physical beings, in quest not only of love but of glamour and of sexual experience too. Set in the context of the high-minded but rather prim South African liberal novel, Rooke's world of pissing and farting, of menstruation and masturbation and orgasm (for which her code-word is 'his/her moment') is a welcome relief. It is a world seen through the eyes of children: not of the presexual children of Schreiner's *African Farm* but of vigorous late teenagers, typified by Andrina in *Mittee*, who stalks about in a sexual fever-heat, laughs 'low and sweet' in the bushes, allows 'a long, slender leg, bent in ecstasy' to stick out – desiring beings not yet trapped in the net of proprieties and obligations which has turned their parents into such hypocrites. (p. 60) In this respect Rooke brings together two commonplaces of Romantic primitivism: that savages and children are Man in unfallen state, and that civilisation is the great enemy. (In an interview as late as 1956 she spoke of her fear that the Zulus would be spoiled by civilisation; *Wizards' Country*, over which she laboured for three years, is a lament for the passing of the old Zulu world.)

In fact, it can be argued that for Rooke the fundamental conflict is not between black and white, not between man and woman, but between young and old. The narrator-heroes and heroines of her books are all young. Even when they are looking back on their youth from a distance (as in *Mittee*), this distancing device is purely nominal: the narrating, experiencing sensibility is young, indeed juvenile. *Boy on the Mountain* breaks down the book-trade distinction between juvenile and adult fiction in a disturbing way, weaving a trail of drug addiction, violence, sex and death through a story of public schools and masculine sports, of youthful camaraderie and gauche courtship. The crude comedy of *Mittee* (circus animals lifting their tails and spraying the well-dressed public, old men swallowing lizards' eggs thinking they are pills, runaway carriages that upset their drivers into patches of thorns) appeals to a child's sense of humour. Selina's consciousness may be intended to be a divided consciousness, a bastard consciousness, or something even more complicated, but it is above all a juvenile consciousness, unrefined, unsocialised, crude, eager.

Crude and eager too are the young Afrikaner men who surround Mittee: great laughers and jokers and pinchers of bottoms and players of pranks. With a difference, however: Rooke has an eagle eye for the sadism indulged by a male culture of pranks, and for the sinister latitude allowed to prank-players in a country where a white skin assured invulnerability (the prank-players set an Arab's beard on fire and pass on, laughing at his anguish). In a telling comment on these same young men, now become fighters in a war against the British, she writes, 'Their eyes had grown watchful. Sometimes they spoke of the War; of the stealthy rides across the veld, of the blowing up of trains, as exciting as a vicious practical joke.' (p. 163) Practical jokes and sabotage: two sides of the same coin, the first a training ground for the second, turning boisterous boys into hard men.

IV

One of Rooke's more engaging features is a robust familiarity – or at least the appearance of such – with the wider world. She crashes boldly into such preserves of the male writer as public-school life, warfare, sport (even boxing!) and casual philandering. She seems to know all about the economics of sugar farming, the workings of land tenure, the tricks that traders use to cheat rural blacks. She handles colloquial Afrikaans, which she imitates in English to give the dialogue of books like *Mittee* a stylistic colouring, with a sure hand. (This practice explains such exclamations as 'All the world!' or 'Almighty!' which pepper the dialogue, as well as Mittee's odd-sounding and vulgar warning to Selina, 'Watch your mouth, you thunder, you lightning!' [p. 146] When Selina is spoken of, in her presence, as a 'creature', more of a racist jibe is intended than may be apparent: in Rooke's day *skepsel*, which 'creature' translates, was a common term of disparagement for a person of colour.) (p. 50)

On the other hand, Rooke's novels are no models of fictional composition. All too often she loses her narrative line in a welter of detail, in recountings of tangential events, parades of ephemeral characters with confusing names; she writes with her nose so close to the page that she loses sight of the larger picture.

Like other novelists of her era, she thought of the last decades of the nineteenth century – the scramble for diamonds and gold, the Zulu Wars, the Anglo-Boer War – as the high point of South African history, a time when adventure and excitement at last broke into the country's long provincial slumber. These decades supply the materials for her historical romances. For current tastes, there is a more sobering historical interest in *Ratoons*, set in her own day, a novel that traces the ramifying tensions in the micro-environment of a white farming community as it loses land to more enterprising Indian competitors and begins to clamour for protective legislation ('Group Areas').

Rooke's position on black–white conflict is broadly liberal. In *Mittee* she sides with the missionaries as protectors of black interests against the rapacity of white farmers. In *Wizards' Country* she records the less known aftermath of the pitched battles fought and lost by the Zulus against British armies: organised destruction of their homes and decimation of their herds by gangs of settlers. If her novels in general give a voice to the woman as underdog, and the child as double underdog, then *Mittee* in particular gives voice to the black woman child, trebly oppressed. (To cap it all, Selina is shunned by the Shangaans, her mother's people.)

Rooke's treatment of settler society – the society in which she grew up in Natal – varies between the genially satiric and the savagely accusatory. Some of the malicious exchanges of gossip in *Ratoons* are worthy of Patrick White's Sydney suburbs. If she avoids adult protagonists, it is perhaps because she cannot imagine an older person who has not been deformed by the boredom, moralism, philistinism and prejudice of colonial life.

Parents in Rooke's world are capable of the vilest oppressions. They extort emotional and sexual consolations from their children, they tell them the most fantastic lies (that they are feeble-minded, that they bear hereditary taints, that they are products of incestuous unions) and hint at the most fearful punishments (castration, sterilisation) to keep them at home and prevent them from knowing love. Mittee has had the good fortune to lose both parents at the age of two. She promptly discards the name they gave her (Maria) and becomes her own person, Mittee – a baby-name, as Castledene observes, and one she has difficulty outgrowing.

The generative energy for Rooke's fictional project comes from a shadowy family ur-romance whose outline is only dimly discernible at the surface level. It includes siblings locked in murderous rivalries, revered but treacherous fathers, engulfing, devouring mothers. The family in Rooke's imagination is the site of a war of all against all; those who escape alive refrain, perhaps wisely, from reproducing it.

23   Gordimer and Turgenev

I

IN AN ADDRESS given in 1975 Nadine Gordimer spoke about the pressures and demands upon South African writers created by racial polarisation, pressures and demands felt particularly keenly by black writers. On the one hand, she said, the black writer needed to preserve his freedom to express 'a deep, intense, private view', 'the truth as he [saw] it' (the masculine pronoun is Gordimer's). On the other hand, the people whose lot he shared, and who regarded him as their spokesman, expected him to subordinate his individual talent to political imperatives and write in 'the jargon of struggle'.[1]

Although the particular urgency of Gordimer's speech came, I believe, out of a feeling that she herself was being pulled in exactly these two directions, she chose to concentrate on the dilemma of the black writer. She urges him to maintain his freedom: only from a position of freedom, she says, will he be able to make his unique 'gift' to the liberation struggle. She invokes Jean-Paul Sartre: 'The writer is someone who is faithful to a political and social body but never stops contesting it.'[2]

As her prime example of a writer who throughout his life was faithful to the cause of social reform, yet continually criticised and contested the strategies of fellow progressives, Gordimer points to the Russian Ivan Turgenev and to his novel *Fathers and Sons* (1862). As a consequence of presenting his hero, Bazarov, in his full, all-too-human complexity, Turgenev had to face the anger and contempt of the young Russian radicals, who had hitherto considered him their champion but now felt he had stabbed them in the back. Though disappointed by their response, Turgenev did not budge. As an artist, he said, he had to follow the truth. 'In the given case, life, according to my ideas, happened to be like that, and what I wanted above all was to be sincere and truthful.' And elsewhere: 'Only those who can do no better submit to a given [i.e. laid-down] theme or carry out a programme.'[3]

The 1975 speech was the last occasion when Gordimer explicitly held up a European writer as a model to black writers. Four years later she would entirely revise her position. In South Africa there were two cultures, she would now say, a white culture and a black culture. The time was past when white culture could impose its standards as universal. 'For the black artist at this stage of his development relevance is the supreme criterion. It is that by which his work will be judged by his own people, and they are the supreme authority.' No matter how well intentioned the white writer may be, 'the order of his experience as a white [differs] completely from the order of black experience.' He – and here she clearly included herself — is therefore in no position to offer advice or proffer models.[4]

Although Gordimer did not persist for long in this mode of radical cultural hermeticism, her reservations about imposing or even offering European models remained. 'Whites must learn to listen,' she writes in 1982, in words she has heard from the poet Mongane Serote.[5] There are many senses in which Gordimer from 1976 onward spends her time listening or listening to. One sense is that she scrupulously no longer tells black writers whom to read and imitate.

Yet in the 1984 essay 'The Essential Gesture' Gordimer returns to nineteenth-century Russia. Is there some way, she asks, in which the black South African writer can reconcile the demands of his community with the demands of artistic truth? In answer she calls upon Vissarion Belinsky: 'Do not worry about the incarnation of ideas. If you are a poet, your works . . . will be both moral and national if you follow your inspiration freely.'[6]

In itself this advice is vapid, as Gordimer must have recognised. Why then quote it? The clue seems to me to lie in the endorsement Gordimer attaches to it: its author, Belinsky, was 'the great mentor of Russian revolutionary writers of the nineteenth century'.[7]

Gordimer is right, or almost right. Belinsky was a critic and editor who by clarity of intelligence, integrity of purpose and a certain fearlessness of utterance, left a mark on two generations of Russian writers: the generation of Herzen (born 1812) and Turgenev (born 1818), and the generation of Chernyshevsky (born 1828) and Dobrolyubov (born 1836).

On Turgenev, Belinsky's influence ran particularly deep. Turgenev met Belinsky in 1843, when he was twenty-five and Belinsky thirty-two; Belinsky became a respected friend – some would say a father figure.[8] Gordimer's word 'mentor' is not inaccurate. Under Belinsky's influence, in such early works as 'The Landowner' and *A Sportsman's Sketches*, Turgenev launched a scathing attack on the landowning class, balancing it with an affectionate and even sentimental account of the peasantry. *Fathers and Sons* was dedicated to Belinsky's memory. In his *Literary Reminiscences*, published in 1868, twenty years after Belinsky's death, Turgenev was still concerned enough with the balance of power between the two of them to attempt to align Belinsky with him (as a moderate, Westernising liberal), whereas earlier in his career he had been the one to be aligned with Belinsky (as a radical).[9]

Yet finally Gordimer's characterisation of Belinksy creates a false impression. Herzen and Turgenev are not revolutionary writers; Chernyshevsky and Dobrolyubov may have expressed revolutionary, or at least radical, views, but as writers they are mediocre. To put the point in another way: it is more to Belinsky's credit that his political-aesthetic credo of social responsibility plus social realism was respected by Turgenev than that it was carried into practice by Chernyshevsky. As an historical figure, Turgenev is a bigger fish than Chernyshevsky, indeed than Belinsky. If Gordimer chooses in 1984 to hold up the name of Belinsky rather than of Turgenev, it is, I think, because Belinsky can plausibly be presented as a proto-revolutionary, while Turgenev cannot.[10] The move from Turgenev − or what Turgenev stood for − to Belinsky and what Belinsky stood for was the adjustment, the concession she felt she needed to make before she could return to nineteenth-century Russian literature and plead its relevance to South Africa under late apartheid.[11]

One of the paradoxes of the four critical forays by Gordimer I have referred to, coming from the years when African writers were beginning to turn their backs on Western models, is that she continually returns for guidance, for signposting, to Europe: to those influential left-wing critics who helped to orient her when she was still finding her way as a writer-intellectual; and to nineteenth-century Russia, where writers − not always of their own volition − found themselves in the vanguard of social change, suffering censorship, imprisonment and exile for what they wrote (here we should remember that even the patrician Turgenev, after his 1852 obituary on Gogol, was arrested and sentenced to internal exile on his estate).

Writing is a lonely business, writing in opposition to the

community one is born into even lonelier. It is understandable that Gordimer, as an oppositional South African writer, should have sought for and annexed historical precedents and antecedents wherever she could find them.

As for why she should have worked herself into a position of on the one hand listening to, accepting, even approving the repudiation of Europe by black fellow-writers (thesis), while on the other hand asserting her own allegiance to a powerful European literary-political tradition (antithesis), and yet (synthesis) claiming an overriding commonality of purpose with her black colleagues, all one can say is that the reasons are complicated. They have a great deal to do, one suspects, with the two halves of the imaginary audience to whom Gordimer, at least at that time, was addressing herself: inside South Africa, to a radical intelligentsia, mainly black; outside South Africa, to a liberal intelligentsia, mainly white; each (as she was acutely aware) listening with one ear to what she was saying to them, with the other ear to what she was saying to the other half.

How Gordimer manages her split audience is a fascinating subject in its own right, but is not my concern here. Instead I return to Turgenev: to the real Turgenev and to Gordimer's Turgenev, to Turgenev's Russia and Gordimer's South Africa. What does it mean to map Turgenev's Russia on to Gordimer's South Africa? Does it illuminate the South Africa of the embattled years of apartheid if we map the failure of the last czars, from Alexander II to Nicholas II, to phase out feudalism and Westernise the country, while at the same time holding revolution at bay, on to the failed efforts of the Vorster and Botha administrations to deracialise politics, modernise the economy and bring a black middle class into the electorate, while at the same time holding revolution at bay? Does either 1905 or 1917 (depending on one's vision of the future) correspond usefully to the South African settlement of 1990? In contemplating these questions, one might prudently bear it in mind that what people outside Russia know about nineteenth-century Russia comes largely from Russian novelists (Turgenev prominent among them), just as much of what people outside South Africa know about modern South Africa comes from South African writers, Gordimer prominent among them.

II

Ivan Turgenev is best known, to readers worldwide and, on the evidence of her essays, to Gordimer as well, as the author of *Fathers and Sons* (1862). This novel, which brought it home to the Russian public that a phase in Russian history had ended and a new one, however ill understood, was about to begin, was immediately surrounded with controversy. *Fathers and Sons* was a talking-point everywhere in Russia, among not only the intelligentsia but the entire literate population. The author received anonymous threats. He was on the one hand congratulated (sometimes by people he loathed) and on the other denounced.[12] Isaiah Berlin writes: 'No one in the entire history of Russian literature, perhaps of literature in general, has been so ferociously and continually attacked, both from the Right and from the Left.'[13]

Turgenev was taken aback by the intensity of these responses. To his credit, however, he did not overplay the part of the naïve innocent. From when he embarked on the book he was aware that he was entering dangerous territory, and he measured the risks carefully. One colleague after another was asked to read the manuscript; he modified it repeatedly, on the basis of sometimes conflicting advice.[14]

What Turgenev could not foresee was that the debate about the right to insurrection, played out between the fictional characters

Bazarov and Pavel Petrovich Kirsanov in the fictional year 1859, the year in which the novel is set, would take on a new complexion when read and actualised in the context of Russia after May 1862, when demonstrations and arson had broken out in St Petersburg, ushering in a wave of radical violence and terrorism.[15] The question of whether Turgenev was for or against Bazarov was now unavoidably translated into the question of whether Turgenev was for or against revolution, or, at a slightly more sophisticated level, into the question of what Bazarov stood for.

In other words, *Fathers and Sons* was overtaken by history almost as soon as it appeared. Against his own wishes, Turgenev was interjected into the contemporary political scene as the disseminator of a specific if cryptic political message. The protestations of the author himself (in private letters and later in his memoirs) that the message, if message there were, could be deciphered only according to the conventions and procedures of literary criticism were understandably brushed aside. A stand-off developed, with Turgenev insisting that Bazarov was a character in a fictional action from which he could not be abstracted, and opinion around him insisting that Bazarov was the actualisation of a political figure, 'the Nihilist'.

To complicate matters, Turgenev, in reflecting on his authorial intentions, was not consistent. Part of the time he claimed that he was behind Bazarov in all respects except in Bazarov's attitude toward art, implying that he approved of his politics.[16] He also claimed for Bazarov a revolutionary or at least insurrectionary lineage: 'I wanted to create [in Bazarov] a strange sort of counterpart to Pugachev.'[17] At other times, however, he claimed that Bazarov simply grew, according to a process that only artists would appreciate, a process in which the conscious will is subordinated to the imperatives of the work itself.[18]

At some higher level of synthesis, these two claims may not be incompatible. Turgenev himself, however, never articulated a position that would subsume both. Alexander Herzen's comment is apt: 'Turgenev was more of an artist in his novel than people think, and for this reason lost his way, and, in my opinion, did very well. He wanted to go to one room, but ended up in another and a better one.'[19]

It is in large measure out of this record of resistance on Turgenev's part – first, to pressures from the Left to write a novel with a hero who would be positive, revolutionary, effectual (unlike Rudin in *Rudin*), and Russian (unlike Insarov in *On the Eve*), then later to pressures from the Right to betray his novel by publicly interpreting it as an attack on the young radicals – that the legend grew of Turgenev the artist, faithful only to the inner voice of his artistic conscience, and in that sense above politics.

How far can the claim be sustained that Turgenev was above politics? More pointedly, what aspect does the politics of being above politics take on in *Fathers and Sons*?

As a young man, Turgenev studied philosophy in Germany. His mind was not notably abstract, but insofar as he had an articulated philosophy of art, it came to him from German idealist philosophy. When he made pronouncements about art and literature, they tended to be couched in idealist terms: art is disinterested; the great artist is a seer or prophet, aloof from the everyday world.[20]

Whether Turgenev's practice as a novelist exemplifies his theory is another question. His various self-presentations as an artist drawn unwillingly into a political role are similarly to be read with a degree of caution. The works by which he is remembered are, after all, embedded in the great social and political issues of his day; furthermore, over his not always consistent protests, they were read by his public not as freestanding artworks but, in Richard Freeborn's words, as 'fragmented reflections of, and personal comments upon, the development of Russian society and the ideological attitudes of the intelligentsia during the forties, fifties and sixties'.[21]

Here *Fathers and Sons* is very much the key book. It is difficult, perhaps impossible, to understand the growth of the myth of Turgenev as a hero of writing without considering Bazarov in his successive stages: Bazarov as a character in a novel, Bazarov as a figure constructed in the popular imagination, and Bazarov reworked in what I will call the Bazarov paratext.

Bazarov is one in a series of Turgenev heroes, men of real gifts, energies and sensitivities which they can find no way to use in the Russia of their day, rural Russia in particular. (They are matched or paired with a series of Turgenev heroines, girls of passion and intelligence who can equally find no way of living into woman-hood without reducing themselves to doll size.) The fate of these heroes, as they cast about for actions commensurate with their potential, is both tragic and comic – in Turgenev's term, Quixotic.

The fact that their lives end futilely or absurdly implies an indictment on Turgenev's part of the stagnancy and repressiveness of Russian life; he here continues a critique of Russian back-wardness that goes back to Chaadayev.

Bazarov is the most driven and therefore the most poignant of this line of heroes. He is seen by Turgenev with a mixture of Cervantean amusement and Aristotelian pity and terror. Specifically, Bazarov is made to fall in love so that he may learn that the passions are not under the control of the utilitarian calculus of pleasure and unpleasure; and he is made to die, full of the bitterest regret, fighting to the last, so that he may learn what it means to be merely an animal, merely part of nature, which is ironically the lesson he tried to teach the benighted Kirsanovs at the beginning of the book.[22]

In the process of loving and dying, Bazarov is taught what life is really about; his own modern, up-to-date, radical-utilitarian reduction of humanity is put in place by a greater, older, starker, more classical reduction. His 'I revolt!', which in the beginning imagines that its object is merely the political and philosophical structures which constrain the self, is revealed (to him) to be only one instance of the futile 'I revolt!' of living beings against their mortality.

There is a double tragedy in the fate of a Bazarov: universal in the grief it evokes that such a gifted and passionate being should have to die so young; Russian in that a certain chain of causality, a chain whose abstract links are Russian backwardness, Russian social stagnation, Russian political repressiveness, leads to a country doctor cutting himself with an infected scalpel. This doubleness of the tragedy – on the one hand universal and apolitical, on the other denunciatory and socio-political – makes the 'message' of *Fathers and Sons* hard to encapsulate, and contributes to the myth of Turgenev as the even-handed, Olympian artist.

But we cannot collapse Turgenev's novel into the striking figure of Bazarov alone. A reading that begins and ends with Bazarov will simply repeat the inadequacies of the readings of 1862. Bazarov is part of an action, an evolving structure of relationships. This action starts with two young men, two sons, cockily deriding the backwardness of the generation of the fathers, and promising (or threatening) to overturn the world of the fathers. It ends with one of them, son of a country doctor, dying in the occupation of country doctor, and the other about to step into the shoes of his father on the ancestral estate. Thus fate in *Fathers and Sons* enters the action not only as mortality on the one hand or the inertia of rural life on the other, but also as family tradition, as the slow but inevitable metamorphosis of sons into fathers.

This generational version of destiny – with its master-metaphor the evolution of rebellious son into complacent father – is profoundly anti-utopian; as Kathryn Feuer points out, it is the aspect of Turgenev's thought to which Chernyshevsky responds most urgently when, in *What Is To Be Done?*, he tries to persuade his readers that the biological, economic and dynastic bonds between the generations (to say nothing of bonds of affection) can be replaced with a range of affective relations between peers. The success of *What Is To Be Done?* in recruiting young people to the revolutionary cause surely lay in its implicit claim that comradeship is enough for human beings, that the bonds between the generations – between fathers and sons, mothers and daughters – can easily be snapped.[23]

III

It is inconceivable that the *Fathers and Sons* I have been describing, a *Fathers and Sons* read with an ear to what it actually says about fathers and sons, could after 1976, the year of the uprising that began in the high schools of Soweto, be advanced to young, politically aware, black South African intellectuals as a model to be imitated.

Why then should Gordimer ever have considered Turgenev relevant to South African experience and instructive to the South African writer? To answer this question we need to place Turgenev and readings of Turgenev, including Gordimer's reading, in the broadest historical context.

The failure of the revolutions of 1848, over much of Europe, and the harsh repressions that followed, meant the eclipse, in Russia, of optimism about a steady evolution toward a Western-style liberal democracy. The generation of the intelligentsia that came to maturity in the 1860s was humbler in its social origins than the patrician liberals of the 1840s, more radical in its politics, impatient with the mumbo-jumbo of individual rights, utilitarian in its attitude toward the arts. Bazarov is the type of this generation; in the realm of fiction, he is its finest flower.

Among old-fashioned Russian liberals, writes Isaiah Berlin, there began to grow up, after 1848, a justifiable sense of unease.

Made more painful by periods of repression and horror, [this] became a chronic condition – a long, unceasing malaise . . . [Their] dilemma . . . became insoluble. They wished to destroy the regime which seemed to them wholly evil. They believed in reason, secularism, the rights of the individual, freedom of speech, of association, of opinion, the liberty of groups and races and nations, greater social and economic equality, above all in the rule of justice. They admired the selfless dedication, the purity of motive, the martyrdom of those, no matter how extremist, who offered their lives for the violent overthrow of the status quo. But they feared that the losses entailed by terrorist or Jacobin methods might be irreparable, and greater than any possible gains; they were horrified by the fanaticism and barbarism of the extreme Left, by its contempt for the only culture that they knew, by its blind faith in what seemed to them Utopian fantasies, whether anarchist or populist or Marxist . . . Caught between two armies, denounced by both, they repeated their mild and rational words without much genuine hope of being heard by either side . . . Many suffered from complex forms of guilt: they sympathized more deeply with the goals upon their Left; but, spurned by the radicals, they tended to question . . . the validity of their own positions . . . Despite all its shortcomings, the Left still seemed to them to stand for a more human faith than the frozen, bureaucratic, heartless Right, if only because it was always better to be with the persecuted than with the persecutors.[24]

If the plight of Berlin's Russian liberals seems to echo the plight of liberal white South Africans in the 1960s and 1970s, that is only partly because the South Africa of those times eerily reiterated the Russia of Nicholas I. The other reason for the echo is that Isaiah Berlin, as a liberal, left-leaning intellectual caught in the vice of the Cold War, between revolution and repression, is here in effect writing himself into the Russian nineteenth century, in order to claim an historical lineage and draw strength from it. In so doing he points a way in which comparably lonely South African liberals, caught up in a provincial sideshow of the Cold War in which parodies or perversions of Cold War dogmas seemed to confront each other, could see themselves in a kind of prospective retrospect as the great-grandchildren of the Russian liberal progressives, the class whose stand now, in the 1990s, seems to have been vindicated by history, the class that might have saved Russia and brought it into the modern world had they not been too pitifully few.

In particular, in describing the complex and highly ambivalent feelings of Russian liberals toward Russian radicals, Berlin captures much of Nadine Gordimer's attitude toward South African Leftist radicals, at least prior to 1975 or 1976: siding instinctively with them while reserving her position on the cleansing power of violence, sympathising with their ardour and dedication while resisting their indifference towards what they saw as the museum of the past, yet all the while doubting her own right to reserve her position, or even to have any position at all.

A complex set of overlays, then; and not simplified by the fact that to both Berlin and Gordimer the key text of nineteenth-century Russian liberalism is *Fathers and Sons*, which, otherwise than in 1862, arrives packaged with an authorial paratext in certain ways more powerfully present behind Gordimer's pages on Turgenev than is the novel itself. By the paratext I mean the various letters, memoirs and prefaces in which Turgenev defended himself against charges from the Left that his novel was an attack on Leftist radicals, in the process producing an authorial reading which saves him from these charges by the strategy of in certain senses removing him from responsibility, presenting him as servant and voice of what he calls the truth.

IV

If Gordimer has any theory of the novel (and one can be a perfectly good writer without having a theory of writing), it is one put together from, on the one hand, certain Marxist critics prominent in the 1950s (Lukács, Ernst Fischer, Sartre, with Camus as a counterweight); and on the other the doctrines of the aestheticist, anti-naturalist wing of European realism and early Modernism: Flaubert, Henry James, Conrad.

Since Gordimer's practice is only rarely the playing out of a theoretical programme, it is not important that it is hard to reconcile these two bodies of theory. What she extracts from her masters is more a theory of the artist than a theory of the novel: a theory of the special calling of the artist, of his/her special gifts and the special responsibilities these entail. For this theory of the artist, the paratext to Turgenev's *Fathers and Sons* is a key document.

Gordimer has throughout her career held to the belief that the artist has a special calling, a talent which it is death to hide, and that his art tells a truth transcending the truth of history. Though this position has become increasingly old-fashioned, Gordimer has, to her credit, remained tenaciously faithful to it. At the same time, however, she has been concerned to give her work a social justification, and thus to support her claim to a place inside history, a history which she herself has to some extent been successful in shaping, as, in her fictional œuvre, she has written the struggle of Africa against Europe upon the consciousness of the West.[25]

To substantiate her sense of her own writing as a form of

political action, she has at times invoked a Romantic Marxism according to which false or bourgeois art, the art of the dis-integrated consciousness with no vision of the future, is opposed by true art – that is to say, the art of the true artist: an art that emerges from a dialectic between artist and people (or, as she later calls it, a dialectic between relevance and commitment); an art whose goal it is to transform society and reunite what has been put asunder.[26]

In certain periods of history – in South Africa in its revolution-ary phase, for instance – the artist may thus have his subject dictated to him by the people without needing to feel any 'loss of artistic freedom'. Between artist and people there ought to exist at such times a 'dynamic of collective conscience' to which the artist should be sensitive.[27]

It is not necessary to follow further the twists and turns of Gordimer's thinking as, in a series of forays into a philosophical discourse over which her control is at best uncertain and which she anyhow, and avowedly, does not trust, she seeks to reconcile fidelity to a transcendental vocation with fidelity to the people and to history. My purpose has been to point out how Turgenev's *Fathers and Sons*, and the texts surrounding it, were taken up by Gordimer, and later abandoned, in her engagement with her times.

In the reading I have given her, Gordimer in 1975 saw in the plight of Turgenev – the liberal progressive who was overtaken, in his middle years, by the march of a revolution to which he gave, however reluctantly and ambivalently and intermittently, his emotional assent while at the same time expressing his horror at its methods, but who preserved a sacred space in his novels where he did not lie to himself, and defended the right to existence of such sacred spaces – an example, *mutatis mutandis*, of and to herself, an example, furthermore, from which she, in her lone (as she conceived of it) and embattled position in South Africa, could draw sustenance and even honour.[28]

After 1976 the ground shifted. In the new, charged atmosphere, Turgenev was set aside (too politically cautious? too comfortable in his exile?). The question of whether European models were still viable in Africa was subsumed under a more complex, more personal, more urgent question: how to continue to manage a double discourse in which she could claim for the artist the role of both lone Shelleyan visionary and voice of the people, without being driven to accept a hierarchy of high art and popular art, one standard for herself and like-minded Eurocentric writers, another for black African writers. To judge from the essays collected in *Writing and Being* (1995), the answer has not yet been found.[29]

24   The Autobiography of Doris Lessing

I

PRESENTED WITH SNAPSHOTS of the Tayler family on their farm in Rhodesia and asked to pick out the artist or artist-to-be among them, one might at a pinch settle on the father, rather stiff and military but clearly not unintelligent. Certainly not on the daughter, pleasant-looking enough but ordinary as a loaf of bread. Yet the daughter had it in her not only to escape the future staring her in the face – marriage to a decent young fellow followed by a life of managing servants and having babies – but to become one of the major novelists of her time.

Alfred Cook Tayler, Doris's sad-eyed father, having lost a leg in the trenches of the First World War, married the nurse tending him and quit a native country whose manifold hypocrisies he could no longer bear. His wife, already in her mid-thirties, gave up her career to have a family. Their first child Doris – later Doris Wisdom, then Doris Lessing – was born in Persia in 1919.

Following ideas about child-rearing fashionable at the time, Emily Maude Tayler imposed on her children a rigid schedule of feeding times and bowel movements, reproducing upon them her own upbringing at the hands of an unloving stepmother. Doris responded with deep anger against a mother who on principle refused to feed her when she cried, who made it clear that she preferred her son to her daughter, and who chatted openly to guests about 'how the little girl in particular (she was so difficult, so naughty!) made her life a total misery'. No child could have stood up to such an 'assault on [her] very existence'. 'For years I lived in a state of accusation against [her], at first hot, then cold and hard.'[1]

Since her mother would not love her, she turned to her father. 'The smell of maleness, tobacco, sweat . . . enveloped her in safety.' But there was a darker side to his love. The stump of his amputated leg poked out at her from his dressing gown, an obscenity with a life of its own. There was also the tickling game, 'when Daddy captures his little daughter and her face is forced down into his lap or crotch, into the unwashed smell . . . His great hands go to work on my ribs. My screams, helpless, hysterical, desperate.' For years afterwards she had dreams in which she struggled while brutal male faces loomed over her. 'I wonder how many women who submit to physical suffering at the hands of their men were taught by "games", by "tickling".' (pp. 28, 31)

After Persia the Taylers moved to Rhodesia – a colony officially founded only thirty-five years earlier – drawn by the lure of quick fortunes to be made in maize farming. But their thousand-acre farm ('It would not have occurred to [my parents] that the land belonged to the blacks') was not large enough to be economically viable. Though her mother adapted well, her father lacked the doggedness needed for farming; they were always in debt. (p. 74)

For the two children, however, growing up in the back country was a wonderful formative experience. From their parents they learned about geology and natural history; bedtime stories fed their imagination. Books were ordered from London, and devoured. (Books were cheap enough in the 1920s for a struggling colonial family to buy them in quantities; no Zimbabwean child of today, and certainly no rural child, could afford such a wealth of reading matter.) By the age of twelve Doris knew

> how to set a hen, look after chickens and rabbits, worm dogs and cats, pan for gold, take samples from reefs, cook, sew, use the milk separator and churn butter, go down a mine shaft in a bucket, make cream cheese and ginger beer, paint stencilled patterns on materials, make papier mâché, walk on stilts . . . drive the car, shoot pigeons and guineafowl for the pot, preserve eggs – and a lot else.

'That is real happiness, a child's happiness: being enabled to do and make, above all to know you are contributing to the family, you are valuable and valued.' (p. 103)

Later Lessing would indict settler society for its 'coldness [and] stinginess of the heart' toward blacks (p. 113); the charge would be fleshed out in *The Grass Is Singing* (1950), an astonishingly accomplished debut, though perhaps too wedded to romantic stereotypes of the African for present-day tastes, as well as in *African Stories* (1964). Yet Rhodesia was not a wholly bad social environment in which to grow up. Aside from the restorative power of the natural world (about which Lessing is unabashedly Wordsworthian), there reigned among the children of the settlers a strongly egalitarian spirit that helped her escape the class obsessions of her parents. And among the 10,000 whites in Salisbury, the capital, she would in time discover a sizeable contingent of refugees from Europe, most of them Left-leaning, many of them Jewish, who would exert a decisive intellectual and political influence on her.

Meanwhile, to the confusing signals which her parents sent out, Doris responded with behaviour typical of the unloved child calling for love. She stole, lied, cut up her mother's clothes, set fires; she wove fantasies that the Taylers were not her real parents.

At the age of seven, 'a frightened and miserable little girl', (p. 90) she was packed off to a convent boarding school where the nuns – themselves the unwanted daughters of German peasants – frightened their charges with hellfire stories. There she spent four wretched years. After a further stretch in an all-girls high school in Salisbury, with weekly letters from her mother reproving her for the money she was costing them, she dropped out of the education system definitively. She was thirteen.

Yet she had never been a poor student. On the contrary, if only to please her mother, she made sure she always came first in class. She was popular with the other girls, inhabiting a false self she calls 'Tigger' (after the A. A. Milne character), 'fat and bouncy . . . brash, jokey, clumsy, and always ready to be a good sport, that is, to laugh at herself, apologize, clown, confess inability'. When later she gravitated into Communist circles, she was known as 'Comrade Tigger'. She repudiated the nickname once she left Rhodesia in 1949; but, refusing to go away, the Tigger self mutated into what Lessing calls the Hostess self, 'bright, helpful, receptive, attentive', and disturbingly reminiscent of her mother. (pp. 386, 89, 20)

Is this a clue to the title of the first volume of her autobiography: *Under My Skin*? In isolation the title gestures in conventional fashion toward self-revelation. But an epigraph reminds us of its context in Cole Porter: 'I've got you deep in the heart of me / So deep in my heart you're really part of me . . .' The hidden addressee of the book, the 'you' deep in Lessing's heart, under her skin, emerges all too plausibly as her mother, dead since 1957.

Averse to any display of emotion, her mother had found a way of expressing tenderness toward her children by persuading them they were ill and then nursing them to health. Back at home, Doris played along, using illness as an excuse to spend days in bed reading. But she could not find the privacy she craved. When she began to menstruate, her mother trumpeted the news to the males of the household. When she tried to diet, her mother piled her plate. Her fourteenth year was spent fighting for her life against a mother who, as she had tried to control her infant bowel movements, now seemed to be asserting ownership over her body.

To escape, Doris took a job as a nursemaid. Guided by her employer, she began to read books on politics and sociology, while nightly the same employer's brother-in-law crept into her bed and ineptly toyed with her. Characteristically, she does not pretend she was a passive victim. She '[fought] the virginity of [her] placid suitor . . . in a fever of erotic longing'. 'It is my belief', she writes, that some girls – among whom she clearly includes herself – 'ought to be put to bed, at the age of fourteen' with an older man as a form of 'apprentice love'. (p. 185)

II

Lessing's precocious pre-school reading had included Scott, Stevenson, Kipling, Lamb's versions of Shakespeare, Dickens. (In her time, she notes tartly, children were not 'patronised', but on the contrary encouraged to try things that were beyond them. p. 83) Now she began to read contemporary fiction, D. H. Lawrence in particular, as well as the great Russians. By the age of eighteen she had written two apprentice novels herself. She was also selling stories to South African magazines. She had, in fact, slipped into being a writer.

Of the three best-known women writers to emerge from southern Africa – Olive Schreiner, Nadine Gordimer and Lessing (who, though reluctant to accept the label 'African writer', freely acknowledges that her sensibility was formed in and by Africa) – none completed high school. All were substantially self-educated, all became formidable intellectuals. This says something about the fierceness with which isolated adolescents on the margins of empire hungered for a life they felt cut off from, the life of the mind – far more fiercely, it turned out, than most of their metropolitan cousins. It also says something about how desultory the pressure was on girls to proceed all the way through the educational mill, domesticity being their ultimate lot.

Intermittent visits to her parents' farm only confirmed to Lessing that she had done well to escape when she did. Her mother was beginning to conform to the worst of colonial stereotypes, complaining about the servants in a 'scolding, insistent, nagging voice full of dislike', while her father slowly wasted away from diabetes, a 'self-pitying, peevish, dream-sodden old man talking, talking about his war'. When eventually he died, she had an urge to scratch out the words 'Heart failure' under *Cause of Death* on the death certificate and write instead, 'First World War'. (pp. 157, 326, 372)

Becalmed in what felt more and more like a backwater (this period of her life would be evoked in *Landlocked* [1965]), she wrote and rewrote *The Grass Is Singing*. 'I was waiting for my future, my real life, to begin.' (p. 418)

III

Lessing's first marriage, at the age of nineteen, was to a man much older than herself – a marriage involving not the real woman but the Tigger self, the 'jolly young matron'. (p. 207) Not yet ready for motherhood, she gave birth to a son, then neglected him. The child responded with anger and bewilderment uncannily like that of the young Doris.

A second child followed. She was drinking more and more, having affairs, treating her husband badly (much of this material went into *A Proper Marriage* [1954], the second of the Martha Quest novels and the most directly autobiographical). The situation was clearly untenable. Vowing to herself that her children would one day inherit 'a beautiful and perfect world where there would be no race hatred, injustice, and so forth', she gave them into the care of relatives and began to make plans to leave the country. She bore within her, she felt, the same 'secret doom' that had ruined her parents' lives and would ruin her children's too if she stayed with them. 'I was absolutely sincere,' she records dryly. 'There isn't much to be said for sincerity, in itself.' (pp. 262–3)

In the wake of the battle of Stalingrad, with the glory it brought to Russian arms, Lessing was converted to Communism. In her account of her Communist years a certain defensiveness is still detectable. In truth, she writes, 'I was never committed with all of myself'. By the time the Cold War broke out and she and her comrades suddenly became pariahs to white Rhodesian society, she was already beginning to have doubts. By 1954 she was no longer a Communist, though for years she felt 'residual tugs of loyalty'. (pp. 284, 397)

Recruits tended to be people with unhappy childhoods behind them, looking for a substitute family; their own children they shrugged off as unwanted nuisances. As an enthusiastic newcomer (and as a woman), Lessing was assigned the task of peddling *The Guardian*, organ of the South African Communist Party, in the poorer areas of Salisbury. Of all her Party activities, this may in fact have been the most useful to her as a writer: it enabled her to meet working-class people and see something of working-class life (*A Ripple from the Storm* [1958] gives a fuller and livelier account than we get here).

The activities of the Salisbury Communists, their loves and hates, take up much of the first three Martha Quest novels. Lessing justifies the extended treatment she gives – in both autobiography and novels – to this politically insignificant clique on the grounds that it exhibited on a small scale 'the same group dynamics that made and unmade the Communist Party of the Soviet Union'. (p. 292)

One consequence of joining the Communists was that Doris met Gottfried Lessing, whom she married in 1943. Gottfried came from a prosperous Russian family of assimilated German Jewish descent, turned back into Germans by the 1917 revolution and then back into Jews by the Nuremberg laws. He was also, in his wife's words, 'the embodiment of cold, cutting, Marxist logic', a 'cold, silent man' of whom everyone was afraid. (pp. 288, 301)

Gottfried does not figure directly in the Martha Quest novels because he was still alive when she wrote them (he ended his career as East German ambassador to Uganda, where he perished during the coup against Idi Amin). Lessing does her best to explain and humanise this unappealing man, with whom she describes her sexual life as 'sad'. What he really needed, she writes, was a woman kind enough to 'treat her man as a baby, even for a few hours of the dark'. (pp. 303, 318)

Gottfried encouraged her writing, though he did not approve of what she wrote. 'What I liked most about myself, what I held fast to, he liked least.' She had married him to save him from internment as an enemy alien; to strengthen his application for British citizenship she remained in an 'unhappy but kindly marriage' until 1948, long after it should have ended. (pp. 293, 358)

IV

Lessing has never been a great stylist – she writes too fast and prunes too lightly for that. The first three Martha Quest novels, or at least long stretches of them, go bent under the burden not only of prosaic language but of an uninventive conception of novelistic form. The problem is compounded by Lessing's passive heroine, dissatisfied with life but unable to take control of her destiny in any meaningful way. But if these novels have not lasted well, they at least attest to ambition on a large scale: the ambition of writing a

Bildungsroman in which the development of an individual will be followed within an entire social and historical context.

Lessing was not blind to her basic problem, namely that the nineteenth-century models she used were exhausted. After the third volume she interrupted the series, breaking entirely new ground with the formally adventurous *Golden Notebook*. *Landlocked*, with which the series resumes after a seven-year gap, reflects in its stylistic experiments not only Martha's impatience with a life without a future but Lessing's own impatience with her medium; while *The Four-Gated City* (1969), with which the series closes, points forward towards *Briefing for a Descent into Hell* (1971) (which Lessing called 'inner-space fiction'), *Memoirs of a Survivor* (1974), and the speculative fiction of the Canopus in Argos series, rather than backward to the early books. What Lessing was looking for, and to a degree found, was a more inward, more fully contemporary conception not only of character but of the self and of the self's experience of time (including historical time). Once this had been arrived at, the nineteenth-century trappings fell away of themselves.

Since the publication of *The Golden Notebook* in 1962, Lessing has had an uneasy relationship with the women's movement – which claimed the book as a founding document – and a positively hostile relationship with the academy, which claimed her book as a prototypical postmodern novel. Between herself and her most enthusiastic feminist disciples she has maintained a wary distance; literary critics she has dismissed as fleas on the backs of writers. She has in turn been attacked by feminists (among them Adrienne Rich) for failing to conceive an autonomous feminist politics, and by the academy for trying to control the interpretation of her books rather than allowing them to spin off into textual space.

In her autobiography she does not hesitate to let fly at 'correct' political attitudes, which she sees as little different from what in the heyday of the Party was called 'the line'. Thus – despite her father's tickling game – she labels the late twentieth-century concern with the sexual abuse of children an 'hysterical mass movement'. She condemns 'the avaricious or vindictive divorce terms so often demanded by feminists'. Ever since adolescence, she records, she has been more interested in the 'amazing possibilities' of the vagina than in the 'secondary and inferior pleasure' of the clitoris. 'If I had been told that clitoral and vaginal orgasms would within a few decades become ideological enemies . . . I'd have thought it a joke.' As for the social construction of gender, she recalls the 'ruthlessness' with which she stole her first husband from another woman, a 'basic female ruthlessness . . . [that] comes from a much older time than Christianity or any other softener of savage moralities. *It is my right.* When I've seen this creature emerge in myself, or in other women, I have felt awe.' (pp. 313, 25, 404, 266, 206)

On Western breast-beating about the colonial past, she comments, '[It cannot] be said too often that it is a mistake to exclaim over past wrong-thinking before at least wondering how our present thinking will seem to posterity.' (p. 50) A Nigerian writer found one of her stories good enough to plagiarise and publish under his own name, she recalls: so much for the politically correct line that whites should not write about black experience. Her own fiction explores male experience, including male sexual experience, without reserve.

As someone whose life has had a substantial public and political component, Lessing confesses a certain respect for people who *don't* write memoirs, who 'have chosen to keep their mouths shut'. Why then her own autobiography? Her answer is candid: 'Self-defence.' At least five biographers are already at work on her. 'You try and claim your own life by writing an autobiography.' (pp. 11, 14-15)

But one suspects larger reasons too. Besides the epigraph from

Cole Porter, her book bears another from Idries Shah, whose writings on Sufism have been important to Lessing since the 1960s. Shah links individual fate to the fate of society by arguing that no society can be reformed until its members can individually identify the forces and institutions that dictate and have dictated the course of their lives. Self-exploration and social progress thus go in tandem.

The two epigraphs come together and cohere in Lessing's thinking in a surprising way. Through the music to which her generation danced, music of the Cole Porter variety, she says, there pulsed a deep rhythm promising sex and salvation. When this subliminal promise of the Zeitgeist was not fulfilled, a whole generation, including herself, reacted as if cheated of its birthright. 'I feel I have been part of some mass illusion or delusion' – the illusion that everyone is entitled to happiness. (p. 16) (In contrast, she suggests, the deep rhythm of today's cacophonous popular music sends people out to torture, kill and maim.)

As a child born in the aftermath of the First World War, Lessing is convinced that, through her parents, she too vibrated to the *basso ostinato* of that disastrous epoch. 'I wonder now how many of the children brought up in families crippled by war had the same poison running in their veins from before they could even speak.' (p. 10)

The idea that the ship of history is driven by currents deeper than consciousness – an idea of which her deep-rhythm hypothesis is a slightly batty example – keeps coming back in Lessing's autobiography. In fact, the turn away from a Marxist, materialist conception of history had already been hinted at symbolically in *A Ripple from the Storm*, in which Martha dreams of a huge saurian, fossilised yet still alive, staring dolefully at her from an earth pit, an archaic power that will not die. One of the problems with the present autobiographical project – a problem of which she is well aware – is that fiction has better resources for dealing with unconscious forces than discursive self-analysis. Her own previous most successful explorations of the historically embedded psyche have been in such works as *The Golden Notebook* and the visionary symbolic-allegorical narrative *Memoirs of a Survivor* (in which, incidentally, she attempts to reposition herself as mother of a daughter rather than daughter of a mother). It is as novelist rather than as memoirist, therefore, that, three-quarters of the way through the present project, she pronounces her succinct verdict on it: 'There is no doubt that fiction makes a better job of the truth.' (p. 314)

The best parts of the first volume are about her early childhood. To most of us, early experience comes as such a shock that we repress the memory of it – an amnesia, Lessing suggests, that may be a necessary protective mechanism for the species. Her own powerful (and powerfully rendered) first memories revolve with distaste around the ugliness and loudness and smelliness of the world she has been born into – the 'loose bulging breasts . . . [and] whiskers of hair under arms' of adults in a swimming pool in Persia, the 'cold stuffy metallic stink . . . of lice' in a Russian train. (pp. 19, 40)

Much effort has clearly gone into the first five chapters. In their clarity of recall (or of imaginative construction – it makes no difference) and cleanness of articulation, they belong among the great pieces of writing about childhood:

It is as if the thatch is whispering. All at once I understand, my ears fill with the sound of the frogs and toads down in the vlei. It is raining. The sound is the dry thatch filling with water, swelling, and the frogs are exulting with the rain. Because I understand, everything falls into its proper place about me, the thatch of the roof soaking up its wet from the sky, the frogs sounding as loud as if they are down the hill, but they are a couple of miles off, the soft fall of the rain on the earth and the leaves, and the lightning, still far away. And then, confirming the order of the night, there is a sudden bang of thunder. I lie back, content, under the net, listening, and slowly sink back into a sleep full of the sounds of rain. (p. 63)

Passages like this celebrate special moments, Wordsworthian 'spots of time', in which the child is intensely open to experience and also aware of heightened openness, aware that the moment is privileged. As Lessing observes, if we give time its due phenomenological weight, then most of our life is over by the time we are ten.

There are also fine passages later in the book where Lessing candidly re-inhabits her youthful narcissism. She pedals her bicycle 'with long brown smooth legs she is conscious of as if a lover were stroking them'. 'I pulled up my dress and looked at myself as far up as my panties and was filled with pride of body. There is no exultation like it, the moment when a girl knows that *this* is her body, *these* her fine smooth shapely limbs.' (pp. 260, 173) There are also leisurely recollections of pregnancy, childbirth (trouble-free) and nursing, including reports on her babies' feeding habits and stools.

The first volume is dominated by the figure of Lessing's mother, who has also figured, either openly or in disguise, in much of what she has written during the course of a career now into its fifth decade. In this latest round, Lessing does her best to be fair to her opponent. For a page or two she goes so far as to hand over the narration to her – a half-hearted experiment soon abandoned. 'There was never a woman who enjoyed parties and good times more than she did, enjoyed being popular and a hostess and a good sort, the mother of two pretty, well-behaved, well-brought up, clean children,' she writes. (The hidden barb here, the barb Lessing cannot resist, is the code-word 'clean', which in the Tayler household referred to potty-training.) The trunks that accompanied them from Teheran to their mud-walled home in Rhodesia held silver tea-trays, watercolours, Persian carpets, scarves, hats, evening dresses – finery that her mother would never have a chance to show off. On the farm this 'handsome, well-dressed, dryly humorous woman, efficient, practical, and full of energy', found no outlet adequate to her ambitions. (p. 402) Her affections were transferred from her husband to her son as soon as he was born; he remained bound to her till he went off to boarding school, where, somehow, he learned to say No to her demands. 'Now I see her as a tragic figure,' Lessing writes; during her lifetime, 'I saw her . . . as tragic certainly, but was not able to be kind.' (pp. 33, 402, 15)

Yet despite a determined attempt to see her parents as ordinary human beings rather than as looming figures in the mind, the first volume repeats the pattern of blaming the mother familiar from earlier writings, and looks ahead to the return of the mother and a re-run of the mother–daughter quarrel in the second volume. There is something depressing in the spectacle of a woman in her seventies still wrestling with an unsubjugated ghost from the past. On the other hand, there is no denying the grandeur of the spectacle when the protagonist is as mordantly honest and as passionately desirous of salvation as Lessing.

V

Volume Two takes up the story with Doris arriving in London in 1949, a 'forthright, frank young woman', as she saw herself, blessedly free – thanks to her colonial upbringing – of the endemic English hypocrisy. She brought with her her young son and the completed manuscript of *The Grass Is Singing*.[2]

The novel soon found a publisher, and her career as a writer was launched. Through the 1950s, until the commercial success of *The Golden Notebook* (1962), her books sold steadily if not spectacularly. She did not need to go out to work. From them she earned about twenty pounds a week, she calculated – a working man's wage.

The move to England – or, in the parlance of Rhodesian settler society, 'home' – proved permanent. Telling the story of those early days, she tries to recreate something of the texture of life in a country still suffering the aftermath of the war. Though her social circle tended to consist of left-wing artists and intellectuals, she allows fair space to the ordinary Londoners she met. But, as she frankly concedes, *In Pursuit of the English*, the memoir she published in 1960, gives a more vivid and more engaged sense of the times than she is able to provide here.

Repeatedly she remarks on the remoteness of Britain of the 1950s from the prosperous Britain of today; young people cannot understand, she says, how poor their country used to be. *People cannot be made to understand*: is that the fault of these heedless young folk, one might ask, or of the writer who at this moment quails before the task of overcoming their historical amnesia?

Despite the grimness of life in the 1950s, those are times for which Lessing clearly feels some nostalgia. She misses, for instance, the commitment and sense of purpose she found in the ritual ban-the-bomb marches, with the opportunities they provided for easy contacts across class lines.

Involvement in the disarmament movement led her to pay a visit to Bertrand Russell and his secretary Ralph Schoenman. The memory of how the elderly philosopher was duped and manipulated by the younger man makes her determined not to be captured in her old age and turned into a 'wise woman' figurehead by feminist groups. (p. 302)

Looking back, she misses the excitement of a literary world in which publishing demanded a real enthusiasm for new writing and a readiness to take chances. By contrast, she condemns today's publishing industry for its cynicism and philistinism, as well as for the pressure it puts on writers to promote their own work. She deplores the obsession of the public with the writer's private life, and the humiliations that writers have to undergo in interviews with ignorant and indifferent interlocutors.

Now, as then, she detects in the British psyche 'a smallness, a tameness, a deep, instinctive, perennial refusal to admit danger, or even the unfamiliar: a reluctance to understand extreme experience'. In literature this manifests itself in an enduring preference for 'small, circumscribed novels, preferably about the nuances of class or social behaviour'. (pp. 96, 126)

The divisions of *Walking in the Shade* are based on the succession of apartments and houses Lessing lived in, always in search of an environment where she could get on with her writing in peace and at the same time bring up her child. She records two or three major love affairs, with men ever reluctant to take on the role of father to the boy. Her mother turns up again, demanding to live with her. She hardens her heart and refuses. Her mother returns to Rhodesia and dies there. Lessing is consumed with guilt, sympathising intensely with the old woman in her loneliness, yet creeping back regressively, despite herself, into the hard, selfish, self-protective shell she had grown as a child: 'No, I won't. *Leave me alone.*' (p. 223)

VI

Walking in the Shade is short on dates, but it would appear that sometime in the early 1950s Lessing gave in to pressure from her circle (pressure which she now ascribes to mere envy) that she do more than merely write books and articles, and formally joined the

British Communist Party. If a single question dominates the book, it is the question of how she and so many other intelligent, socially concerned, peace-loving people could, in effect, have given themselves as tools to the Communist Party of the Soviet Union; and of how, even when they had lost faith in the USSR itself, they did not lose faith in the religion of world revolution.

In exploring her own motives, Lessing recognises that her first, depressing experience of the inflexible British class system played a part (although technically an outsider to the system, in practice she found she was excluded from the working class by her accent). And of course she believed in the anti-colonial struggle, the brotherhood of man and all the other stated ideals of Communism. But finally she has to see her motive for joining the Party as irrational: at a trans-individual level she was participating in 'some kind of social psychosis or mass self-hypnosis', while at a personal level she was being controlled by 'a deeply buried thing . . . riding me like a nightmare', a 'continuation of early childhood feelings' that she cannot get to the bottom of. (pp. 58, 89)

From the very obscurity of this explanation, it emerges that to the present day Lessing does not understand why she did what she did. Insofar as the puzzle she is trying to solve is at the heart of this second volume, the ultimate goal of the autobiographical enterprise itself, namely, to get to the truth of oneself by going back over the ground of the past, by telling the story of one's life afresh, still evades her here.

This is by no means the first time Lessing has explored the mystery of the self and the destiny it elects. There is a strong autobiographical strain in her fiction, particularly the Martha Quest novels and *The Golden Notebook*, which cover the same decade of her life as *Walking in the Shade*. Did Lessing believe, when in the early 1990s she embarked on the autobiography, that it could yield deeper truths about herself than her fictions of thirty years before?

The answer is, very likely, no. Lessing has always been aware that the energies liberated in poetic creation take one deeper than rational analysis ever can. Something has changed, however, since she wrote the novels based on her Communist phase, namely, the terms of the enquiry itself. Time has passed; starting with the revelations of the 1956 Party Congress, the buried history of the USSR has year by year been emerging from the ice. Specifically, it has become more and more clear that Hitler was 'a mere infant in crime' compared with his exemplar Joseph Stalin, who was 'a thousand times worse' (Lessing's words). (p. 262)

Communism calls to the nobler impulses of the human heart, yet in its nature there is something that 'breeds lies, makes people lie and twist facts, imposes deception'. Why should that be so? Lessing cannot say. 'These are deeper waters than I know how to plumb.' (p. 65) What she does know is that she gave her allegiance to the Party. The Party chose her to visit Russia as a member of what was supposed to be a representative delegation of British intellectuals, and she went. Out of dedication to the greater cause, she did not afterwards publish the truth about what she saw in Russia, even though she (now) records that at least one ordinary Russian was prepared to risk his life to tell the delegation that what they were being shown was a lie. She was no mere rank-and-file member: she served on the committee of a Party Writers' Group. ('Accustomed as I am to being in a false position – sometimes I think it was a curse laid on me in my cradle – this was the falsest,' she writes forty years later.) She even wrote fiction according to the Party's prescription – for instance, the often anthologised story 'Hunger' ('I am ashamed of it,' she writes now). (pp. 95, 78)

Stalin was a thousand times worse than Hitler. If intellectuals like Martin Heidegger and Paul de Man have deserved to be investigated and denounced for the support they gave to Nazism, what do those intellectuals deserve who supported Stalin and the Stalinist system, who chose to believe Soviet lies against the evidence of their own eyes? This is the huge question that exercises Lessing's moral conscience, coupled with a second and equally troubling question: why does no one care any longer?

Though Lessing must be admired for broaching these unfashionable questions, it cannot be said that she gives either of them a satisfying answer. In an odd way, her exploration of her past as a Party member parallels her exploration of her past as a daughter. In both cases, looking back, she can see that she behaved badly, even culpably. Furthermore, at some obscure level, at the time, she knew she was behaving badly. But, with the best will in the world, she cannot get to the bottom of why she did what she did, beyond concluding that she was in the grip of a compulsion, a compulsion that was not unique to her but afflicted hundreds of thousands of others. It was, as she puts it in the first volume, part of the Zeitgeist.

VII

'You'd think my life was all politics and personalities, though really most of the time I was alone in my flat, working.' (p. 249) Lessing does indeed spend a lot of time on politics and as much time on personalities from the literary and theatrical worlds whose paths crossed hers, many of them of no great interest any longer. Her second volume is in most respects a memoir, and a memoir of a rather casual, scattered, life-and-opinions kind; aside from her treatment of her Communist past, it lacks the thoroughgoing self-exploration, and the concomitant anguish of tone, that marks the first volume.[3]

As for her political life, the story Lessing tells here is not to be read as an apology – in the climate of the 1990s, it would be far too politically correct a step to take, and Lessing has nothing but scorn for correctness, whose genealogy she (correctly) traces back to the Party and the Party line. Nevertheless, she does describe her wilful blindness to the truth as 'unforgivable', and does affirm that she tells her story so that her readers may learn not to do likewise. (p. 262) It is clearly a history she has wanted to set down in full before she dies. However one may qualify the term, it does, in the end, constitute a confession.

25 The Memoirs of Breyten Breytenbach

I

BREYTEN BREYTENBACH FIRST came to public attention when, from Paris, where he worked as a painter and poet, he sought permission from the South African authorities to bring his Vietnamese-born wife home on a visit, and was informed that as a couple they would not be welcome. The embarrassment of this *cause célèbre* persuaded the authorities, in 1973, to relent and issue limited visas. In Cape Town Breytenbach addressed a packed audience at a literary symposium. 'We [Afrikaners]', he said, 'are a bastard people with a bastard language. Our nature is one of bastardy. It is good and beautiful thus . . . [But] like all bastards – uncertain of their identity – we began to adhere to the concept of *purity*. That is apartheid. *Apartheid is the law of the bastard*.'[1]

A record of that visit appeared, first in the Netherlands, then in the English-speaking world, in *A Season in Paradise*, a memoir interspersed with poems, reminiscences and reflections on the South African situation; it included the text of the address.

In 1975 Breytenbach was back, but in a new role: on a clandestine mission to recruit saboteurs on behalf of the African National Congress. He was soon picked up by the security police, and spent seven years in jail. Returning to France, he publicly cut the ties with his people: 'I do not consider myself to be an Afrikaner.'[2] Nevertheless, during the 1980s he paid further private visits, under police supervision. A 1991 visit gave rise to *Return to Paradise*, the narrative of a journey through the 'reformed' South Africa of F.W. de Klerk. As he explained, the book was meant to be read together with *A Season in Paradise* and his prison memoir *The True Confessions of an Albino Terrorist* as an autobiographical triptych.

The titles of the *Paradise* books cast an ironical glance at Rimbaud's *Une Saison en enfer*. 'This region of damnation', Breytenbach calls South Africa in *Return to Paradise*. 'I am looking at the future and it chills me to the bone.' The revolution has been betrayed; cliques of middle-aged men are bargaining for their slice of the cake while on the ground their followers fight on mindlessly. The new order on the point of emerging – 'more broadly based hegemony but [the] same mechanisms and same sadness' – is not what he fought for. If his own 'whimpers for an impossible revolution' are utopian, it remains the right of the poet to imagine a future beyond the dreams of politicians, to have his prophetic say in the future. He even has the right to bite the hand that has fed him.[3]

At a more down-to-earth level, the story of the 1991 visit includes poetry readings in noisy halls where the audience does not understand the language and comes only to inspect the oddity named Breytenbach; perplexed reactions from old comrades-in-arms ('But aren't you *ever* happy? Now that we've won, can't you *rejoice?*'); incomprehension and hostility when he asserts that his role in the future will be, as in the past, 'to be against the norm, orthodoxy, the canon, hegemony, politics, the State, power'. These are sentiments which do not go down well in a country that has, as he observes dryly, slid straight from pre-humanity to post-humanity. (pp. 160, 196, 158)

He uses the book to lash out, in anguish and bitterness, in all directions: against white liberals, against the South African Communist Party and 'more-doctrinaire-than-thou' bourgeois Leftists, against former associates like Wole Soyinka and Jesse Jackson, and particularly, for their treatment of him when he was in jail, against the ANC itself:

> Not only did the ANC withhold assistance from my dependants, not only did they disavow me, but the London clique of bitter exiles intervened to stop any manifestation of international or local support for my cause. They blackballed and maligned me, abetted by well-meaning 'old friends' inside the country. Even Amnesty International was prevailed upon not to 'adopt' me as a prisoner of conscience. (p. 123)

The plague that Breytenbach pronounces upon all parties – a condemnation in which, despite the pungency of the language, there is something wild and out of control – makes up the less interesting half of the book. Its best pages address a more intimate and more fundamental concern: what it means to him to be rooted in a landscape, to be African-born. For though he has spent almost all his adult life in Europe, Breytenbach does not feel himself to be a European:

> To be an African is not a choice, it is a condition . . . To be [an African] is not through lack of being integrated in Europe . . . neither is it from regret of the crimes perpetrated by 'my people' . . . No, it is simply the only opening I have for making use of all my senses and capabilities . . . The [African] earth was the first to speak. I have been pronounced once and for all. (p. 75)

What he means by saying that Africa allows him to use his senses and his capabilities fully is revealed in page after magical page as he responds to the sights and sounds of 'the primordial continent'. As a writer, Breytenbach has the gift of being able to descend effortlessly into the Africa of the poetic unconscious and return with the rhythm and the words, the words in the rhythm, that give life. He is aware of the gift. It is not an individual matter, he insists, but is inherited from his ancestors, 'forefathers with the deep eyes of injured baboons', whose lives were spent in intimate relation with their native landscape, so that when he speaks that landscape he is speaking in their voice as much as his own. (pp. 4, 27)

It is this very traditional, very African realisation – that his deepest creative being is not his own but belongs to an ancestral consciousness – that gives rise to some of the pain and confusion recorded in *Return to Paradise*. For though Breytenbach may recognise how marginal he has become in what is nowadays on all sides, with varying degrees of irony, called 'the new South Africa', and may even enjoy dramatising himself as the one without a self, the bastard, the 'nomadic nobody', or, in his favourite postmodern figure, the face in the mirror, a textual shadow without substance, he knows that ultimately he owes his strength to his native earth and his ancestors. (p. 74) Thus the most moving passages in the book tell of visiting his father's deathbed, renewing friendships, making peace with his brothers, taking his wife to the old places of Africa.

II

Dog Heart, Breytenbach's 1999 memoir, confines itself to a tiny area of South Africa, a region of the Western Cape province dubbed by him 'Heartland', and within it to the town of Montagu, not far from his birthplace, where, as he records, he and his wife buy and restore a house for their own use. The economy of this area is based on viticulture and fruit farming; but in recent years Montagu itself (population 23,000), a town of some charm blessed with hot springs and a spectacular setting, has become a haven for retired people, artists and craft-workers. Demographically it is unrepresentative of the country as a whole. Whereas two-thirds of the national population is black (we will brave the minefield of racial terminology in a moment), the people of Breytenbach's Montagu are overwhelmingly brown or white; though nationwide Afrikaans is the mother tongue of only one person in seven, in Montagu it predominates; and, in a country whose population is skewed towards youth (nearly half of it is under the age of twenty-one), Montagu is a town of ageing people: the young have migrated to the cities in search of work.

Crude though they may be, these statistics should alert us against taking *Dog Heart* for what it is not and does not pretend to be: a report on the state of the South African nation in the 1990s. Breytenbach's Heartland is not a microcosm of South Africa; *Dog Heart* has little to say about politics or black–white relations on a national scale. What it does report on, with intimate attention, is power relations between white and brown in the countryside.

Who are Breytenbach's so-called brown people? The seeming innocence of the appellation conceals problems not only of anthropology (culture, genetics) and history (who holds the power to call whom what, and how was that power won?), but of a conceptual nature too: what does it mean to be neither black nor white, to be defined in negative terms, as, in effect, a person without qualities?

For that is how brown (or coloured or Coloured – with a C̲ the term still carries apartheid echoes; with a c̲ it is more or less neutral) people were defined under apartheid legislation. The category *Coloured* was meant to pick out the descendants of unions between people (usually men) of European (so-called Caucasian) descent and people (usually women) of indigenous African (usually Khoi – the term 'Hottentot' is no longer polite) or Asian (usually Indonesian slave) birth. But in practice it captured many others besides, of genetically diverse origins: people of 'pure' Khoi – or indeed of 'pure' 'African' descent – whom circumstance had led to adopt a European or European-derived name and language and lifestyle; people who through endogamy had retained a 'purely' Asian, Islamic identity; 'Europeans' who for one reason or another had dropped through the net of 'whiteness' and were leading 'mixed' lives.

Though apartheid legislation assumed a system of classification watertight enough to allocate each individual South African to one of four categories (white, Coloured, African, Indian), the basis of the system was ultimately tautological: a white was defined as a person of white appearance whom the white community accepted as white, and so forth.

The most conceptually sophisticated resistance to classification came from 'coloured' quarters: if there was no 'Coloured' community prepared to concede that it had pre-existed its creation by apartheid, then, logically, there could be no community criterion of 'Colouredness'. Throughout the apartheid years the status 'Coloured' was, across almost the entire range of people whom it implicated, accepted, so to speak, under protest, as an identity forced upon them. Insofar as there is or was a 'Coloured' community, it was a community created by the common fate of being forced to behave, in the face of authority, as 'Coloured'.

It is this history of contestation that Breytenbach calls up when he writes of 'brown' people: a history of two or three million South Africans of highly diverse ethnic and social origins first compelled to conceive of themselves as a community, even (in one of the loftier predictions of apartheid historiography) as 'a nation in the making';

then, in 1994, entering into a dispensation in which, while the old race laws were abolished, racial distinctions had nevertheless to be kept alive to make possible the social-engineering measures known in English as 'affirmative action' and in Afrikaans, more bluntly, as 'putting right'. 'First not white enough, then not black enough,' they complained, not without reason.

The issue of whether there is or ought to be a category between black and white is not unique to South Africa. The rights of ethnic or cultural minorities in the multi-ethnic nation state constitute a critical issue worldwide; debate is rife in Latin America and other corners of the postcolonial world on the politics of *mestizo* identity. In South Africa this ferment has prompted people excluded from the 'natural' identities of black and white to explore cultural identities for themselves entirely divorced from the set of options offered by apartheid – identities that link them to a precolonial past and even to a history older than that of 'black' South Africans. Archaeological researches push the date of the migration of 'black' Africans, speakers of Bantu languages, into the territory of the present South Africa further and further back in time, but no one proposes they have been there as long as the primeval hunter-gatherers of the dry south-west, the mythical heartland of Breytenbach's 'brown' people.

III

Being called, in 1973, 'a bastard people with a bastard language' jolted even those Afrikaners sympathetic to Breytenbach. But in the years that have passed since then, *bastardy* – or, more politely, *hybridity* – has become a fashionable term in cultural history and cultural politics. Revisionist historians are busy rewriting the story of the Southern African colonial frontier as a zone of barter and exchange where old cultural baggage was shed and new baggage taken aboard, and where new identities – even new racial identities – were tried on like clothing. For adventurously minded Afrikaners, laying claim to a dark ancestor now holds considerable cachet (Breytenbach himself is not immune to such self-fashioning).

Thus, half a century after the National Party came to power vowing to preserve at whatever cost the Christian Aryan identity of the Afrikaner, the wheel has come full circle: the intellectual vanguard of the Afrikaans-speaking sector, nervous of the name 'Afrikaner' so long as it carries its old historical freight of racial exclusivity, yet unable to offer a better one, proposes that it represents instead an embryonic, genetically hybrid, culturally syncretic, religiously diverse, non-exclusive, as yet unnamed group ('people' remains too loaded a term) defined (loosely) by attachment to a language – Afrikaans – of mixed provenance (Dutch, Khoi, Malay) but rooted in the African continent.

Breytenbach makes a large historical claim for his Heartland region: that during the time when it was part of the colonial frontier it bred a restless, nomadic, mongrel type of Afrikaner, without the social pretensions of farmers from the neighbouring, more settled Boland region, where the economy had been built on slave labour – a being, in fact, not unlike the alternative Afrikaner just described.

It is a claim that will probably not stand up to scholarly scrutiny, but it does enable Breytenbach to advance his revisionist version of the Afrikaner pioneer. Whereas in the establishment version these pioneers were white-skinned farmers who, Bible in one hand and gun in the other, trekked into the interior of Africa to found republics where they would govern themselves free of British interference, in Breytenbach's version they become people of inextricably mixed genetic origin who followed their herds and flocks into the interior because they had learned a wandering lifestyle from the Khoi pastoralists. And (Breytenbach's argument goes) the sooner the modern Afrikaner discards the illusion of himself as the bearer of light in the African darkness, and accepts himself as merely one of Africa's nomads – that is to say, as a rootless and unsettled being, with no claim of proprietorship over the earth – the better his chance of survival.

But bastardy, Breytenbach warns, is not an easy fate. It entails a continual making and unmaking of the self; it is necessarily dogged by a sense of loss. '[Yet] it is good to travel to become poor.'[4] Thus Breytenbach links the two themes of his ethical philosophy: bastardy and nomadism. Just as the bastard sheds his self and enters into unpredictable mixture with the other, so the nomad uproots himself from the old, comfortable dwelling place to follow the animals, or the smells of the wind, or the figures of his imagination, into an uncertain future.

It is against such a background that one must read the gruesome reports in *Dog Heart* of attacks on whites in the countryside of the new South Africa. These stories make disturbing reading not only because of the psychopathic violence of the attacks themselves, but because they are being repeated at all. For the circulation of horror stories is the very mechanism that drives white paranoia about being chased off the land and ultimately into the sea. Why does Breytenbach lend himself to the process?

His response is that rural violence is by no means a new phenomenon. From the old days he resurrects stories of men like Koos Sas and Gert April and Dirk Ligter, 'Hottentots' or 'Bushmen' who flitted like ghosts from farm to farm sowing death and destruction before at last being tracked down and killed. In the folk memory of brown people, he suggests, these men are not criminal bandits but 'resistance fighters'. (p. 136) In other words, farm murders, and crimes in general against whites – even the crime directed against the Breytenbachs when their home in Montagu is broken into and vandalised – are indeed part of a larger historical plot which has everything to do with the arrogation of the land by whites in colonial times.

The land, says Breytenbach, belongs to no one, and the correct relation to the land is the nomad's: live on it, live off it, move on; find ways of loving it without becoming bound to it. This is the lesson he teaches his French-born daughter, a child clearly drawn to the wildness and freedom of the country, as he takes her around the sacred sites of memory. Do not become too attached, he warns. 'We are painted in the colours of disappearance here . . . We are only visiting . . . It must die away.' (p. 145)

The elegiac tone that suffuses much of *Dog Heart* and distinguishes it from the previous memoirs comes in part from Breytenbach's sense of growing old and needing to begin to make farewells, in part from a Buddhist outlook in which worldly attachments retard the progress of the soul (this is the religious side of his ethics of nomadism), but also in part from a sense that the world into which he was born cannot survive. *Dog Heart* is the first of his prose works in which Breytenbach allows himself to articulate what emerges with intense feeling in the more private world of his poetry: that he comes out of a rural way of life which, despite being based on a colonial dispensation with all its manifold injustices, had become autochthonously African to a remarkable extent; and that in the same moment that the head condemns this way of life and judges it must perish, the heart must mourn its passing. (In this respect Breytenbach is suddenly and strikingly reminiscent of William Faulkner.)

In the tentative and ambivalent reconciliation that has taken place between Breytenbach and Afrikaners of the old breed, it is the Afrikaners who have had to make the greater shift. In losing political power, including control over the public media, the people from whom Breytenbach dissociated himself in 1983 have lost their power to dictate what an Afrikaner has to be, namely, a 'white' of North-European descent, an ethnic nationalist, a Calvinist, a patriarchalist. *Dog Heart* speaks for a counter-current in which a fragments of groups in disarray begin to define themselves, and perhaps even to assert themselves, in a new way, cohering this time not around a political philosophy but around a shared language larger and wiser than the sum of its speakers, and a shared history, bitter and divided though that history may be.

IV

Sharing a language, a history, a feel for the land, a history, perhaps even blood, with 'my people', (p. 60) the people of his Heartland, Breytenbach exchanges words with men and women of all states and conditions. Some of these exchanges disconcert him. The (brown) men who renovate his house treat him (the most celebrated poet in their language!) as a foreigner. Accompanying his brother – who stands as an independent candidate in the 1994 elections – on his canvassing rounds, he hears at first hand the level of brown prejudice against blacks. (His informants may of course be playing games with him: they are as much – or as little – Afrikaner as he, and of the Afrikaner, 'stupid but sly', he himself writes, 'my morning prattle and my night tattle are cut from the cloth which suits my interlocutor.') (p. 175)

At the dark heart of the memoir lies an event that Breytenbach alludes to several times but never explains. It would appear that at the age of seven he had a choking fit and stopped breathing, that in a sense he died and was reborn as a second Breyten (his very name, he points out, is like an echo; one of his poetic identities is Lazarus). 'When I look into the mirror I know that the child born here is dead. It has been devoured by the dog.' (p. 1) So returning to the land of the dog is in a sense a search for the grave of the dead child, the child dead within him.

In the town museum – where the bust of D.F. Malan, Prime Minister of South Africa from 1948 to 1954, has been discreetly relegated to a storeroom – Breytenbach comes upon a photograph of his great-grandmother Rachel Susanna Keet (d. 1915). From the archives he learns that as a midwife she brought most of the children of Montagu, brown and white, into the world; that she lived unconventionally, adopting and raising a brown child who was not her own. He and his wife search for Rachel Susanna's grave but cannot find it. So they take over one of the old unmarked graves in the graveyard, adopting it, so to speak, in her name. The book ends on this emblematic note, with Breytenbach marking out, in the name of his dead ancestor rather than of his living child, the most humble of family stakes in Africa.

V

Citizen of France, most untranslatable of Afrikaans poets, Breytenbach has published this account of his re-exploration of his African roots in English, a language of which his mastery is by now almost complete. In this respect he follows his countryman André Brink and a host of other writers (including black African writers) from small language communities.

The reason for his step is, one would guess, practical: the market for books in Afrikaans is small and dwindling. Breytenbach certainly does not resort to English as a gesture of fellowship with English-speaking South African whites, for whom he has never had much time. Nevertheless, it is odd to be faced with a book in English that is so much a celebration of the folksy earthiness of Afrikaans nomenclature, that follows with such attention the nuances of Afrikaans social dialect, and that entertains without reserve the notion that there is a sensibility attuned to the South African natural world which is uniquely fostered by the Afrikaans language.

There is a wider body of what I would call sentimental orthodoxy that Breytenbach seems to accept without much reserve. Much of this orthodoxy relates to what present-day cultural politics calls 'first peoples' and South African folk idiom 'the old people': the San and the Khoi. In two widely read and influential books, *The Lost World of the Kalahari* (1958) and *The Heart of the Hunter* (1961), Laurens van der Post presented the San ('Bushmen') as the original Africans, bearers of archaic wisdom, on the brink of extinction in a world for which their gentle culture rendered them tragically unfit. Breytenbach records moving twilight utterances of nineteenth-century San, while sometimes lapsing into Van der Post-like romanticising as well ('small sinewy men [with] an inbred knowledge of the drift of clouds and the lay of mountains'). (p. 84) But his main aim is to suggest that the old San and Khoi myths live on today in unconscious re-enactments: a woman who bites off her rapist's penis, for instance, is repeating the trick of the Khoi mantis-god. Passages of *Dog Heart* carry a whiff of hand-me-down Latin American magic realism. The case for an unarticulated psychic continuity between old and new brown people is similarly unpersuasive, while the recounting of the myths has an obligatory air about it, as if they are being copied over from other books.

Breytenbach's current political beliefs are spelled out in the essays collected in *The Memory of Birds in Times of Revolution* (1996). Insofar as he is still a political animal, his programme can be summed up as 'fighting for revolution against politics'.[5] In *Dog Heart*, however, his politics is implied rather than explained. Quarrels and antipathies emerge in the form of casual sideswipes: at white liberals, at the Communist Party colony within the ANC, at the Coloured middle class which has found a home for itself in the old National Party (rebaptised the New National Party and still, after the 1999 elections, holding on to power in places like

Montagu), at the 'dogs of God' (Desmond Tutu and Alex Boraine) of the Truth and Reconciliation Commission, at the new artistic and academic establishment with its stifling political correctness. A brief brush with Nelson Mandela is recounted, from which Mandela emerges in none too favourable a light. Thus Breytenbach keeps the promise he made in *Return to Paradise*: to be a maverick, 'against the norm'.

Like Breytenbach's other memoirs, *Dog Heart* is loose, almost miscellaneous, in its structure. Part journal, part essay on autobiography, part book of the dead, part what one might call speculative history, it also contains searching meditations on the elusiveness of memory and passages of virtuoso writing – a description of a thunderstorm, for instance – breathtaking in the immediacy of their evocation of Africa.

26   South African Liberals: Alan Paton, Helen Suzman

I

ALAN PATON MADE his reputation with *Cry, the Beloved Country*, published in 1948 at the very beginning of the National Party's forty-five year spell of power. It was not only Paton's first novel but his first book. It appeared when he was already in his middle years; it became a bestseller and brought him financial independence and fame. But in retrospect that sudden fame seems a mixed blessing. For from being an obscure public servant Paton was turned, not wholly unwillingly, into a sage and oracle on South African affairs. It was a role within which he remained to a certain extent trapped for the rest of his life. Its effects can be seen not only in the increasingly *ex cathedra* tone of his pronouncements, and in a tendency to think, speak, and write in brief, easy-to-chew paragraphs, but also in a general failure to break new ground and develop as an artist.

Paton was born in 1903, in the then province of Natal. After a decade as a high school teacher, he took over the principalship of Diepkloof Reformatory for African juvenile delinquents, where he did away with forced labour and introduced vocational education, transforming what had been a prison into a school. When he left Diepkloof in 1946, it was with the intention of studying penology abroad before returning to a career in the prisons service. But in Sweden something unplanned happened. Under the influence of what he later called 'a powerful emotion' he began to write a story based on his Diepkloof experiences.[1] Three months later *Cry, the Beloved Country* was completed.

In the remaining forty years of his life (he died in 1988), Paton wrote a great deal: two more novels (*Too Late the Phalarope* [1953] and *Ah But Your Land is Beautiful* [1981], the latter an embarrassingly poor piece of work), stories, memoirs, biographies, a two-volume autobiography and a sizeable body of journalism. But he remained a one-book man. His later fiction, in particular, is vitiated by a sentimentality that *Cry, the Beloved Country* escapes only by the sheer power of its sentiment. Like Olive Schreiner's *Story of an African Farm*, his novel gives the impression of having been written at the dictation of an overmastering daimon. In both cases the writers spent the rest of their lives fruitlessly trying to recover that first fine rapture.

Not all readers of *Cry, the Beloved Country* may remember where the strange title comes from. Here is the relevant passage:

> Cry, the beloved country, for the unborn child that is the inheritor of our fear. Let him not love the earth too deeply . . . For fear will rob him of all if he gives too much.[2]

Though overtly the novel takes up a confident liberal stance, calling for greater idealism and commitment to Christian and democratic values, the experience it deals with beneath the surface is, as Paton's best critic, Tony Morphet, suggests, more troubling. The 'powerful emotion' out of which Paton's novel emerged was fear for himself and his humanity, fear for the future of South Africa and its people. Fear was the emotion that had held Paton in its grip in the hotel rooms in Sweden and England and the United States where he did his writing; and the book that emerged, with its anxious ending, cannot be said to have settled his fear.[3]

Back in South Africa, Paton did not confine himself to writing. His most practical and most immediately effective act was to found, in 1953, the Liberal Party, a non-racial political party that survived in the face of continual official harassment for thirteen years, until it was legislated out of existence.

Though a committed Christian, Paton confessed that the 'deepest fellowship of [his] life' was felt not in the Church but in the Liberal Party. Liberalism, to him, was not only a political philosophy but a creed embracing 'a generosity of spirit, a tolerance of others, an attempt to comprehend otherness, a commitment to the rule of law, a high ideal of the worth and dignity of man, a repugnance for authoritarianism, and a love of freedom'.[4] In view of the forces of sectarianism, racism and nationalism ranged against it, this was, as Morphet rightly says, 'a politics of innocence'. (p. 8) Yet, though it never commanded the allegiance of more than a small minority of the white electorate, the Liberal Party did keep alive a certain spark of non-racial idealism as the fortress of apartheid began to be erected on all sides.

After the forced dissolution of the Party, Paton became a more lonely figure on the South African scene. He shared the common and perhaps blessed inability of liberals to sympathise with or indeed even understand how deep sectional passions can run. He had always feared and disliked Afrikaner nationalism; and one senses in him little welcome for black nationalism. He continued to hope, with less and less conviction, that fellow citizens of British descent would emerge from their slumber and exert themselves on behalf of such old-fashioned British values as respect for the rule of law (something, by and large, they never did).

He was little attracted by the prospect of a unitary, centrally administered state such as the African National Congress envisaged.

Though he conceded that a unitary state would be 'right and inevitable' if that was what the majority of South Africans wanted, and though a unitary state had in fact been part of the platform of the Liberal Party, he felt more and more that the price to pay for it would be too high: 'grief and desolation' on a huge scale. He therefore pleaded the case for a federal constitution based on universal suffrage, with effective power devolved to regions and communities. He pinned his hopes for the future on Chief Mangosuthu Buthelezi, whom he called 'one of the most powerful figures on [our] political stage, fluent, extremely knowledgeable, impossible to buy', and on the kind of accommodation with whites that Buthelezi seemed to stand for. (*SBC*, p. 104)

When it came to the question of what kinds of pressure Western states should exert to end apartheid, Paton took a cautious stance. In 1979 he counselled then US Secretary of State Cyrus Vance to exert pressure on the South African government, but to do so 'with the greatest skill and wisdom' lest the government, concluding it had everything to lose and nothing to gain by co-operating, decided to go its own way, taking the country to destruction. But he was utterly opposed to economic sanctions. 'I hereby solemnly declare', he wrote, 'that I will never, by any act or word of mine, give any support to any campaign that will put men out of jobs.' No goal could be grand enough to justify turning South Africa into 'a starving nation'. On the other hand, he did call in 1985 for 'the greatest moral and pragmatic pressure' to be brought to bear on the South African regime in the interests of its 're-education'. (*SBC*, pp. 220, 6, 9)

On the issue of sanctions Paton had more than one exchange with Archbishop Desmond Tutu. 'I don't understand how your Christian conscience allows you to advocate disinvestment,' he wrote in an open letter: 'I do not understand how you can put a man out of work for a high moral principle.' In the same letter he congratulated Tutu on winning the Nobel Peace Prize, then added, 'I have never won a prize like that. I am afraid my skin is not the right colour.' The comment is petty and does not reflect well on Paton. Yet at a human level it is understandable: little honoured in his own country, Paton was jealous of the standing he enjoyed in the outside world and unhappy when the invitations stopped flowing in his later years. (*SBC*, pp. 180, 179)

Though it may seem from his public statements that Paton moved to the right as he grew older, it would be more accurate to say that he stood still while the entire South African opposition, both black and white, moved left. His politics, in which a Christian-inspired commitment to non-violence coexisted not entirely easily with implacable detestation of apartheid and hawkish anti-Communism, never really changed. In the 1950s he had been denounced as a liberal from the Right; in the 1980s the Left freely used 'liberal', as well as 'humanist', as terms of abuse. Through it all he remained a liberal and proud of it. As a political force, old-style liberalism had missed the boat, he knew. But in the creed itself he saw nothing dishonourable. If blacks sneered at liberals, he said, it was not because liberals had ever been hypocritical or cowardly but simply because they had proved themselves powerless.

Nevertheless, Paton was plainly shocked by the scale of violence that erupted in black townships in 1985–6. His rather wistfully expressed hope, a hope against hope, that a booming economy and a gradual mellowing of the Afrikaner would allow a black middle class to come into being and make revolution unnecessary, was shattered; he called 1985 'the unhappiest year of my life'. All around him he saw attitudes hardening. President P.W. Botha, whom he had at one time considered an improvement on his predecessors and with whom he had exchanged what he calls 'firm but courteous letters', veered between dictatorial rages and dogged inaction. Afrikaner nationalism, once 'an arrogant and relentless juggernaut', Paton wrote, had now become 'a shambling giant who doesn't know where he is going'. (*SBC*, p. 292)

Here and there in *Save the Beloved Country* one encounters comparably pithy and perceptive observations. Of the 'half-emancipated' Afrikaner of the 1980s Paton writes: 'He wants to be more just, but he wants to remain the boss. It just cannot be done.' On the black leaders Nelson Mandela, Robert Sobukwe, Z.K. Matthews, Albert Luthuli: 'One cannot say that the [ruling] National Party destroyed their lives, because, in fact, it made them immortal.' On the death of Steve Biko: it was not so much the brutality of the police that was disturbing, but the nonchalance with which the government treated an historic calamity. 'The death of Mr Biko . . . will be remembered when . . . the Anglo-Boer War has been forgotten.' (pp. 183, 170)

But overall *Save the Beloved Country* is a thin and disappointing book. It is made up, for the most part, of short pieces originally written for newspapers, which are reproduced verbatim. Many of these pieces are about wholly ephemeral political infighting. Nevertheless, these Lilliputian and eminently forgettable squabbles are laboriously footnoted. Translations from the Afrikaans are often stilted and sometimes misleading.

The brevity of the pieces (few are more than five pages long, some only a few hundred words) does not allow Paton to develop his ideas. Among topics he mentions that he would have liked to expand on had he had the time (why did he not have the time?) are the inward effects of living in exile, and the damage to the moral lives of the South African security police caused by their work of torture. These are interesting and substantial questions, points of intersection between the human and the political: one would have welcomed the insights of Paton the novelist.

One would have welcomed, too, his insights into Hendrik Verwoerd, Prime Minister of South Africa in the 1960s, a man who cherished a particular animosity for Paton and was personally responsible for the undoing of all Paton's work at Diepkloof Reformatory. What does Paton think, in retrospect, of Verwoerd? Surprisingly, the question Paton chooses to take up is whether Verwoerd was a great man. His conclusion (unsurprisingly) is that Verwoerd was not great, that 'it was the very fervour of his loyalty to a narrow creed that prevented him from attaining greatness'. I would have thought it more important to ask the question of whether a man whose works were so unremittingly evil in their effects could escape being evil himself. (*SBC*, p. 21)

Paton's rather baffling treatment of Verwoerd provides a clue to his strength as well as his weakness as a judge of men. His weakness is a certain lack of curiosity about people in themselves. His strength is that he does not rush to judgement. Paton believed in what he believed in, but believed in it with less than white-hot singleness of conviction. There were always, to Paton, two sides to a question. If Paton was not a great man, he was at least greater than Verwoerd in his less-than-fervid loyalty to a broader and more human creed.

In his foreword, Paton observes that in the twenty years (1967–87) covered by *Save the Beloved Country* he had written about little but South Africa, and asks himself whether this will make the book 'boring and monotonous'. The answer he gives his own question is, no: South Africa is not just another country, it is a theatre for an age-old struggle between good and evil, a microcosm of the world.

The correct answer to his question is, sadly, yes. As a whole the book is indeed boring and monotonous, not because it is limited to South Africa but because of the quality of Paton's writing and thinking. The names of many significant actors on the South African stage crop up, but Paton has little that is new or penetrating to say about them. One begins to suspect that in the course of the years he lost interest in other people: in what they were in themselves, in what they thought. As in his novels, in which characters tend to be ethical rather than psychological beings, there is a certain blankness in these essays about what makes people tick. Neither his friends nor his foes are brought to life by his words.

As for the writing itself, one soon grows tired of Paton's Churchillian mannerisms ('There are those who ask, what good has [protest] done? It has done a lot of good. It enables us to say, South Africa is a land of fear, but it is a land of courage also'). As a novelist, Paton had no particular gift for narrative. His novels are statically constructed, depending for their effect on character and emotion and, in the case of *Cry, the Beloved Country*, the intensity of the driving passion. In his late writings there is even less opportunity for the novelist's art, and they are the worse for it. Perhaps the most memorable piece in *Save the Beloved Country* is a report on a trip Paton made in 1978 to a small country town to attend the funeral of Robert Sobukwe; and this piece draws its strength not only from the strong emotions of grief and outrage that the funeral evokes in him, but from being cast as a narrative. There are certain authors whose every scrap of writing, no matter how occasional, it is important to save. Paton is, alas, not of that stature.

II

Helen Suzman was born in South Africa, the daughter of parents who at the turn of the century had emigrated from Lithuania to a then British colony whose burgeoning economy and liberal administration promised a future of prosperity and security. They belonged to a wave of Jewish immigrants whose children and grandchildren, duly anglicized by their education, were to become the backbone of South Africa's liberal intelligentsia, playing leading roles in commerce, the professions and the arts, as well as in progressive politics.

Helen Suzman herself entered politics at the ground floor as a party worker for the United Party of Jan Christiaan Smuts. In 1952 she was put forward as a candidate for a prosperous Johannesburg constituency and won. From then until 1989, when she retired, she represented the same suburban white voters, though in 1959 she left the increasingly sclerotic, backward-looking United Party to become a founder member of a liberal-democratic party which, under the name of the Democratic Party, still existed at the turn of the century, claiming the support of some ten per cent of the South African electorate.

Suzman had become a party worker in the wake of the electoral shock of 1948, when Smuts, who had taken South Africa through the Second World War as part of the Allied camp, was defeated by the forces of Afrikaner nationalism. The victory of the Afrikaner Right, with its deep grudge against the British and British culture, its retrogressive race policies and its barely submerged anti-Semitism, alarmed the Suzmans (Helen had married at an early age) enough to make them think of emigrating. But, as she candidly admits in her memoir *In No Uncertain Terms*, the 'sunny comforts' of the country, including 'excellent domestic help, who attended to all the chores I hated', proved too seductive.[5]

The all-white Parliament of 1952 in which Suzman took her seat, dominated by middle-aged Afrikaner men, was not an environment, one would have thought, in which a young Jewish woman from an academic background would have felt comfortable. From its mother parliament in Westminster the South African lower house had inherited conventions of debate that permitted the heckling of speakers with often puerile gibes and interjections. Of the taunts thrown at Suzman across the floor, many of them anti-Semitic or sexist, one is worth pausing over: 'Neo-Communist, sickly humanist!' hissed one antagonist every time she spoke. (p. 113) It is a measure of the insularity of Calvinist

Afrikanerdom of the time that the term 'humanist' could have been intended as an insult.

In fact, Suzman flourished in Parliament. Among her opponents, she records, there were some who regarded her 'with amazed fascination. [They] had large, docile wives brought up in Calvinist fashion to be respectful to their parents and to their husbands. Here was this small, cheeky female with a sharp tongue which she used without regard to rank and gender. Some were shocked, but a few were amused and one or two actually liked me.' (p. 114)

It would be hard to overstate what Helen Suzman achieved during her thirty-six years in Parliament, for thirteen of them as the sole representative of her party. Operating within a near-totalitarian political system, she cannily exploited a structural weakness of that system – parliamentary privilege – to bring into the open abuses of power which, by means of bans on public speech and restrictions on reporting, the government would otherwise successfully have kept hidden. Backed by sympathetic liberal newspapers, she conducted campaigns from Parliament against the use of torture by the police and against the practice of 'forced removals' – the shifting of black communities from one part of the country to another in the interest of ethnic homogeneity. Of these removals she warned, 'A vast problem . . . is going to have to be solved by our children, because the conditions which are being set in the urban areas of South Africa for the African people are going to lead to the most terrible conditions of crime and delinquency.' (p. 79) In the crime-ridden South Africa of the 1990s, these words, spoken in 1969, came to have a prophetic ring.

Suzman made use of her right as a Member of Parliament to visit prisons to hear the grievances of prisoners and urge improvements in prison conditions. She visited Robben Island, where Nelson Mandela and other leaders of resistance movements were held, and complained vocally (and to good effect) about the wretched conditions there. Breyten Breytenbach, himself incarcerated during the 1970s, wrote, 'The prisoners, both political and common law, consider her as Our Lady of the Prisons. She is indeed a living myth among the people inhabiting the world of shadows.' (p. 146)

During the darkest years of State repression, the years of the notorious and aptly-named Terrorism Act, which allowed the security police to detain suspects indefinitely without charging them or bringing them to trial and made even the publication of their names an offence, Suzman was subjected to an orchestrated campaign of vilification in the House, a campaign clearly intended to break her nerve. Her mail was also intercepted (a defector later revealed her security police file number: W/V 24596, W/V standing for *wit vrou*, white woman). (p. 191)

Suzman is at pains to spell out the ideals that sustained her through these years and informed her activities on behalf of the oppressed. She acted for the sake of 'individual liberty, civil rights and the rule of law', 'to keep alive . . . democratic values'. 'My job in Parliament . . . was to provide an outlet, a means of expression, for all those people who were not prepared to conform to the bizarre practices known of as "the South African way of life".' 'I certainly was used by people who had political views and aims very different from my own, ranging from those who supported the banned Communist Party to extreme black nationalists. But . . . as long as [the government] locked people up without trial, I had no option.' (pp. 132, 3, 73) She was indeed a freedom fighter: a fighter for the principle of freedom rather than on the side of any specific group.

From her long parliamentary career, Suzman has emerged with unrivalled authority to comment on the series of autocratic Afrikaner leaders who built and steered the juggernaut of apartheid. Hendrik Verwoerd, ideologue of separate freedoms for separate races and mastermind behind the deliberately impoverished education system for blacks, was, she writes, 'a fanatic', 'the only man who has scared me stiff'. He and his immediate successors, John Balthazar Vorster and P.W. Botha, were 'as nasty a trio as you could encounter in your worst nightmares'. Between Botha and herself there was no love lost. 'An irascible bully', she calls him, 'spiteful [and] retributive'. F.W. de Klerk was, by contrast, 'a pragmatic, intelligent man'. (pp. 42, 65, 198, 238, 267)

That, unfortunately, is pretty much as far as the moral analysis goes. If one had expected an insider's insight into how pious, respectable, family men could decade after decade have hardened their hearts to the daily suffering they were causing, one will be disappointed. Suzman is no Hannah Arendt. She detects the callousness, the numbing of the moral faculty, that characterised the legislators of apartheid – she even reminds us that Verwoerd had written a doctoral thesis on the blunting of the emotions – but she does not explore any further the attrition of their human sympathies. She recognises the nihilism at the core of apartheid, an essentially uncreative system never intended to achieve more than postpone the inevitable. She quotes a telling remark by a cynically frank Nationalist politician: 'We can hold the situation for my generation and for my children's generation, and after that, who cares?' (p. 106) But she has nothing new to say about the amorality of a group of men who, too selfish and too limited to confront creatively the demands of postcolonial Africa, chose instead to bequeath the problem to their grandchildren.

There are other opportunities not taken up in Suzman's memoir. In 1966 Verwoerd was assassinated in the House of Assembly before her eyes. She spends three pages on the episode, but they are devoted mainly to a malicious insult flung at her by P.W. Botha in the heat of the moment, and to her subsequent efforts to extract an apology. There is no attempt to bring the events to life, and no reflection on the assassin, one of the more intriguing minor actors in South African history, a man with no political agenda, a drifter struggling with phantasmatic demons of his own.

In such episodes as her first visit to Pretoria Central Prison or the funeral of Robert Sobukwe (attended by Paton as well), one again feels the opportunity beckoning for Suzman to let the pen flow, to tell the story properly and make it live; but the challenge – that of becoming a *writer* rather than just a recorder – is declined. There is in the end a tired and incurious quality to Suzman's memoir. It has the air of a recital given so many times before that it has become affectless.

Suzman is by no means shy about quoting testimonials. The text is studded with tributes to her, from Albert Luthuli, Alan Paton, Robert Kennedy, Winnie Mandela, Gatsha Buthelezi, and many others. She is palpably upset when Andrew Young, US Ambassador to the United Nations, remarks of her that he 'can deal with cold hatred but . . . can't stand paternal liberalism', and she describes at length her efforts to get Young to change his opinion of her ('Simple justice was ever my motivation, not "paternal liberalism",' she protests). (p. 181)

High-minded liberalism in fact turned Suzman into an increasingly lonely figure by the mid-1980s, both inside and outside South Africa. She found this to her cost when she spoke against Western economic sanctions against South Africa and was shouted down on previously hospitable American campuses. Her argument – a perfectly reasonable one, on the face of it – was that sanctions would hit black workers before they hit white bosses; but the argument cut no ice when black leaders at home, including the respected Desmond Tutu, were of the sanctions party. 'We liberals were becoming a truly endangered species,' she writes, 'for many years under attack from the right, we were now attacked by the left as well, especially by bitter exiles.' (p. 162)

The truth is, the marginalisation of liberals like Suzman had begun even earlier. After the 1976 Soweto uprising she found that young blacks wanted no truck with her; even white students dismissed her as irrelevant. The middle ground had begun to shrink; soon there would be nowhere left for her to stand. It was only after the country had been saved by the 1990 settlement that she could be restored to her place as a beacon of personal courage and integrity.

27   Noël Mostert and the Eastern Cape Frontier

IN 1797 A YOUNG Englishman, John Barrow, made a 500-mile tour from Cape Town at the south-west tip of Africa to the eastern frontier of the Cape Colony on an assignment to report to the British Crown on the territory it had acquired, sight unseen, from the Dutch. A man of the European Enlightenment, an eager-minded amateur scientist, naturalist and geographer, Barrow visited the *kraal* of the twenty-year-old Xhosa chief Ngqika and was much taken with what he saw. 'No nation on earth . . . produces so fine a race of men,' he wrote. Raised on the simplest of diets, living vigorous outdoor lives, unashamedly naked, free of the vices of civilisation, the Xhosa were the very embodiment of the noble savage; whereas the Dutch colonists, after generations of isolation from Europe, seemed only to have degenerated. Given the benefits of science, Barrow saw every prospect that the Xhosa would become an ornament to the Crown, as long as their land could be protected from the encroachments of the colonists.

The Cape Colony had been annexed for reasons that had every-thing to do with geopolitics and nothing to do with the colony itself. Once the threat of Napoleon was past, Britain saw no need to maintain more than a naval base at or near Cape Town to guard the sea route to the east. Drawing in the boundaries of the Colony in this way, however, would be tantamount to abandoning its indigenous peoples to the mercies of the Dutch colonists; and this public opinion in Britain would not allow. The boundaries were therefore maintained; but in a self-defeating move the military garrison was reduced to a level at which policing of the frontier could not be properly carried out.

The Enlightenment, as represented by Barrow, was one of two great currents of thought to reach southern Africa with the British. The other was evangelism. Born out of the anti-slavery movement, drawing upon the energies of nonconformist Protestant fervour and the ethical convictions of humanitarian philanthropism, the missionary movement turned to southern Africa as its main theatre of operations after the West African climate turned out to be more than the missionary constitution could handle.

The missionaries who came to the Cape Colony scored considerable successes with the demoralised remnants of the Khoi peoples, but the Xhosa were another story. 'Secure in their culture, in the wholeness of their society . . . loyal to the shadows of their ancestors,' writes Noël Mostert in *Frontiers*, a history of a hundred years of conflict on the Colony's eastern border, the Xhosa 'regarded [Christianity] from a position of severe, disciplined cultural reserve'.[1] The missionaries made no converts worth speaking of. In some cases their impact was the opposite of what they had expected. Prophets along biblical lines arose among the Xhosa. One, Makanna, spread the word that there were two gods, a god of the whites and a god of the blacks. The black god should be worshipped not as the cunning missionaries taught, but by dancing and making love 'so that the black people would multiply and fill the earth'. (p. 473)

Nevertheless, as the evangelical movement grew in strength in Britain, more and more mission stations were opened on the frontier, and in the name of Christianity a broad assault was launched on traditional Xhosa culture. As time passed and the vision of mass conversions faded, the ambitions of the missionaries became narrower but more intense: the Xhosa must give up their more outrageous practices; they must become monogamous, wear clothes, deport themselves more soberly, own and care for property. Evangelism mutated into a campaign to impose Victorian moral standards on the natives, but also – and some of the missionaries were frank about this – to bring the natives into the colonial economy. Within mere decades, missionaries found themselves working in concert with the colonial government, acting as its eyes and ears and sometimes its voice. As in England, where evangelical Christianity had helped to turn the restless masses against radical agitators, so, Mostert argues, the missionaries in the Colony became a political force.

In his account of contacts between missionaries and pagans, Mostert is clearly on the pagan side. The picture he gives of traditional Xhosa culture is, if not idealised, certainly rosy. Though not a particularly pacific people, the Xhosa, in his account, were too committed to an ideal of *ubuntu*, humanness, to conduct warfare in the merciless manner of the Zulu or the British. Their system of chiefly rule was democratic, in the sense that the chief had to earn the respect of the people whose loyalty he inherited. Their culture was based on what Mostert calls polygamy, but is more accurately called polygyny (men might take several wives; women might not take several husbands). Mostert gives a vigorous defence of this institution as a stabilising force, as he does of the free and frank sexual mores of the Xhosa in general.

He has a harder job defending the practice of scapegoating: diviners would be ordered to 'smell out' the person responsible for some piece of ill fortune, and the 'witch' would then be cruelly put to death. In his defence of scapegoating, Mostert elides questions of right and wrong by taking a functionalist approach: scapegoating was a mechanism for maintaining social 'balances', for eliminating 'any who diverge[d] widely from the social norm'. (p. 205)

Mostert defends scapegoating not because he likes it but because it was the feature of Xhosa culture most abhorred by the missionaries. The same missionaries who sought to root out witch-hunting among the Xhosa, he points out, failed to acknowledge that not long before witches had been lynched in Europe. Given Mostert's general outlook – secular humanist with a dash of romantic primitivism – it is perhaps inevitable that he should regard as faintly ridiculous the project of travelling thousands of miles to save the souls of people one has never laid eyes on. To him the missionaries are no more than the front-line troops in a campaign of cultural imperialism hard to distinguish from economic and military imperialism. He concentrates his ridicule on the endeavours of zealots 'hatted, clad in their long black coats and leggings, choked in their cravats, steaming and suffering in the heat', to clothe the Xhosa like themselves. (p. 597)

Among the few individual missionaries who gain his approval are Johannes van der Kemp and James Read, both of whom went native in respect of sexual mores, while remaining vociferous (and much-vilified) advocates for the human rights of their charges.

As Barrow had observed in the course of his travels, the Dutch frontiersmen had lost touch with Europe to the extent of becoming indistinguishable from Africans: most were illiterate, counted their wealth in cattle, migrated from place to place according to the seasons. They had families on a large scale, often with black wives and concubines, and their descendants spread far and wide. In the course of time some of them, their genetic inheritance by now utterly scrambled – they called themselves, without shame, 'Bastards' though they still spoke Dutch – migrated beyond the northern border of the Colony and established themselves among the warring tribes of what would later become the Orange Free State and the Transvaal. Mostert calls these 'the real pioneers', in contrast to the Voortrekkers, the pioneers sanctified in official

Afrikaner historiography, whom he sees as informed by a particularly bigoted, exclusive strain of Calvinism. (p. 416) One of his larger objectives is to rehabilitate 'the alternative course of frontier history', the bastard history that has been written out of the story of South Africa. (pp. 610–12) Among his unlikely heroes is therefore the frontiersman Coenraad Buys, patriarch and pater-familias on a giant scale, whose mixed-blood progeny, so numerous that they came to be called the Buys Nation, settled the far northern Transvaal long before the Voortrekkers.

In the wake of the Napoleonic Wars Britain faced unemployment and concomitant social upheaval. Trying to kill two birds with one stone – export surplus population and cut the expense of maintaining a large garrison in the Cape Colony – the authorities offered free land on the eastern Cape frontier to suitable British settlers. Some 4,000 volunteers sailed for Africa, among them the Scottish poet Thomas Pringle, who was shocked to discover what company he was keeping, describing his fellow passengers as 'for the most part . . . low in morals or desperate in circumstances . . . idle, insolent, and drunken, and mutinously disposed towards their masters and superiors'. (p. 529) It was hoped that these specimens of British humanity would in time form a human buffer against mutual Boer and Xhosa encroachments.

Few of the new arrivals knew anything of farming, however; nor had they been told of the explosive situation on the frontier. Quitting their farms, they took to the towns. Grahamstown, once no more than a military outpost, flourished as the focus of settler power; by the 1840s voices would be raised demanding that the seat of colonial government be moved there from Cape Town.

Though Grahamstown is today no more than a provincial town, it remains the cradle of British culture in South Africa. As such it lays claim to embodying a link between white English-speaking South Africans and the liberal traditions (real or imagined) of their land of ancestry. Mostert shows just how illusory this link is. 'There was a quality of racial hatred in [Grahamstown] of a virulence that equalled, and probably surpassed, anything previously experienced in South Africa,' he writes. (p. 776) From the *Grahamstown Journal* emerged a stream of lies and propaganda against the Xhosa and their sympathisers intended to advance at any cost the material interests of the British-descended community; this propaganda would later be directed toward undermining the colour-blind franchise of the Cape Colony itself.

Why should Grahamstown have been such a centre of reaction? Partly because it was vulnerable to Xhosa attack and therefore in a state of war scare (it was nearly sacked in 1819). But Mostert advances an additional and more provocative explanation. Whereas the frontier Boers had accommodated themselves to their Xhosa neighbours to the extent of becoming in effect just another frontier tribe, albeit a bellicose one, the British settlers remained locked into the ideology of social self-advancement that had brought them to the Colony in the first place: the Colony was a place where they would be able to get ahead socially as they had not been able to in Britain. What they brought along with them – furnishings, books, heirlooms – constituted social capital. When their homes were razed in frontier wars, the loss of their possessions was felt as a crippling assault upon their social identity, as it was not by the Boers. Hence their rage; hence, ultimately, the hostility between white and black that characterises the Eastern Cape down to the present day.

Since 1778 the Xhosa had fought a series of increasingly bloody wars with colonists on the frontier. The causes of conflict were manifold: population growth, Xhosa cattle-rustling, settler greed for Xhosa land, the inconsistency and duplicity of official policy, the mischief-making of the colonists' propaganda organs. All of these contributed to what Mostert justly calls 'the most tragically disastrous and tarnished involvement between Britain and a sovereign black people in Africa in the nineteenth century', an involvement whose 'shadows continue to move with unappeased restlessness within the haunted house that is modern South Africa'. (p. xxviii) With the benefit of hindsight one can see the turning point in race relations to have been the moment when Sir Benjamin D'Urban, governor of the Colony, publicly characterised the Xhosa as 'irreclaimable savages', thereby placing them outside the pale and justifying total war against them (one is reminded of the judgement pronounced by Kurtz in Conrad's *Heart of Darkness*: 'Exterminate the brutes!').

In 1850 there began what was to be the most terrible of these wars, 'a war of race, perhaps the first of its kind'. (p. 1077) Mostert quotes from missionary diaries to attest the active, personal hatred by now felt by the Xhosa for whites. It was a war in which the British killed men, women and children without distinction, while the Xhosa tortured prisoners to death and mutilated corpses. Mostert devotes some two hundred harrowing pages to a re-creation of this war as it was experienced on both sides.

The British military establishment of the day was dominated by its commander-in-chief, the Duke of Wellington, a military thinker whose outlook had frozen with Waterloo. Till his death in 1852 Wellington resisted every pressure toward innovation. Fighting a bush war in Africa, British soldiers still marched in formation, wearing scarlet uniforms, burdened with heavy equipment. They were mown down by massed Xhosa rifle fire or stabbed with spears from under dense cover. Nevertheless, nothing was learned; battle tactics remained unchanged. (The chickens at last came home to roost, for Britain, in 1854, when the antiquated thinking and incompetence of the General Staff was laid bare by the ghastly sufferings of the Crimea.)

Governor of the Cape at the time was Sir Harry Smith, victor at the Battle of Aliwal in India and one of Wellington's darlings. Arriving at the frontier, one of Smith's first acts had been to force a Xhosa chief named Maqoma to prostrate himself. With his knee on Maqoma's neck, Smith announced, 'This is to teach you that I have come to teach Kaffirland that I am chief and master here, and this is the way I shall treat the enemies of the Queen of England.' As commander in the field, Smith almost managed to lose the war. But in the end, facing superior force, the Xhosa chiefs had to sue for terms.

A few years later the defeated Xhosa received, through the medium of a fifteen-year-old girl named Nongqawuse, good tidings in the form of instructions from the afterworld: they were to kill all their cattle, cease to cultivate their fields, scatter their food stores. A day of reckoning would follow: a new sun would rise, the British would be swallowed into the sea, there would be a grand resurrection of the ancestors; then would follow an earthquake, after which new herds of cattle, immortal, would emerge from under the earth and new corn stand in the fields.

Public opinion split in two between believers in Nongqawuse's prophecy and unbelievers. From the hilltops believers stood gazing eastward to sea for the ships that would bring the ancestors – incarnated as Russians – to defeat the English. Mostert records the emotion-laden reminiscences of people who spent 18 February 1857 waiting for the rising of the sun in the west. In vain: the new sun did not appear, nor did new cattle and new corn rise from the earth. Rage and reprisals against the unbelievers – whose unbelief was held to have led to the non-arrival of the millennium – took place all over the land. Tens of thousands starved to death; the integrity of Xhosa culture was shattered.

This act of irrational self-destruction can be explained only as a despairing reaction to a series of demoralising military defeats and to unrelenting pressure on the traditional institutions of the Xhosa.

Whether or not Mostert is right in claiming that the colonial authorities, and in particular Governor Sir George Grey, who has until the present enjoyed somewhat of a reputation as an enlightened man, foresaw the disastrous sequel, yet found reasons not to intervene, the fact is that the British stood to gain much. Without raising a finger, they could watch what their armies had failed to accomplish being brought about before their eyes.

As for Nongqawuse – whose role in the episode may well have been no more than that of a tool in the hands of an uncle who, having fallen under Christian influence, cherished ambitions of becoming a 'gospel man' himself – she lived out her life ostracized by her people. Mostert includes a photograph of her from the period, looking glum.

The cattle-killing may have marked the end of Xhosa military power, but it was by no means the end of the Xhosa. With the hold of tradition broken, individual Xhosa were released to sink or swim in the colonial economy. Many sank, some swam. The decades that followed saw the rise of a class of black farmers who farmed new crop types, using new techniques learned from the missionaries and competing successfully with white farmers. From Lovedale, the missionary institute for advanced education, began to emerge a new Xhosa elite, 'Christian, articulate, model Victorian gentlemen in their conservatism, respectability and sobriety'. (p. 1257) Westernised by force as the Zulu never were, the Xhosa were to provide black South Africans with political leaders for the new age they were entering, including most of the founding fathers of the African National Congress, established in 1912.

In the middle of the nineteenth century the Cape Colony had the most liberal constitution in the British Empire, in respect to the franchise more generous than the constitutions of some European states. It enshrined a vision, inherited from the Enlightenment, of a non-racial society of free individuals. But it was too much to hope that in 1910, when it finally gave over responsibility for an unendingly troublesome colony, Britain would insist that the constitution of the newly formed Union of South Africa be based on the Cape model. Exhausted by the Boer War, intent on withdrawal at all costs, Britain did what the enfranchised blacks and the liberals of the Cape feared most: abandoned them to their countrymen, Boer and Briton, washing its hands of the whole mess. 'The political tragedy of the twentieth century in South Africa was born in Westminster,' writes Mostert. 'It is impossible to avoid looking back wishfully . . . The Cape Colony *was* unique . . . Its value as the quintessential example and ideal for an emerging Africa at mid-century, and for most of the rest of the world . . . would have been inestimable.' (pp. 1273, 1275)

'I am of the Cape,' writes Mostert, presenting his credentials in the fashion now obligatory among historians. With its 'benignly occult' qualities, the Cape (by which he here means Cape Town and its immediate hinterland) is 'a spiritual birthright from which there is no departure'. (pp. 120, 121) It soon becomes clear that he shares a tendency, not uncommon in the Cape, to regard the region as both geographically and ideologically set apart from the passions and cruelties of a wider South Africa. (How he would square this with the fact that, in respect of murder and rape, Cape Town has long been the most violent city in Africa, I do not know.) His sympathies are clearly liberal, idealistic, and secular, though coloured by a somewhat mystical nostalgia for his lost African childhood.

As an historian he is consciously old-fashioned. His book contains no graphs or tables. He is well aware that the story of frontier conflict he tells can be retold as the working out in human affairs of variations in rainfall and the spread and retreat of cattle-fever bacilli. He acknowledges the importance of these material determinants. Nevertheless, to him history is primarily the story of men in conflict; his interest is not in economic forces but in (male) personalities. His principal documentary research has been carried out in an area he admits to be 'unfashionable': missionary records. (p. 1288) He visits overgrown battlefields and reports the melancholy effect they have on him. When he enters the narration in *propria persona*, it is not as part of an ironic postmodernist ploy. Sometimes, indeed, he reads like one of the more magisterial, all-knowing Victorian novelists – Thackeray, for instance.

This does not mean to say that he is an amateur. He has plainly read and taken his cue from the first volume (1969) of the *Oxford History of South Africa*, edited by Monica Wilson and Leonard Thompson, the first of the new, revisionist histories of colonial South Africa. His preliminary chapters on the history of precolonial Africa, the spread of Bantu-speaking peoples, early European voyages of exploration around the Cape, the first years of the settlement at the Cape, and life on the Cape frontier, are fully informed by contemporary historical scholarship, as are all his chapters on the Xhosa. His work on the missionaries breaks new ground.

His prose sometimes reminds one of Laurens van der Post at his most romantic. There are purple passages on the African continent and the 'occult' forces informing its landscape. (p. xxii) Some of his rhapsodies descend to hokum: in the indigenous languages of South Africa 'the cadences of the wild, of water and earth, rock and grass, roll onomatopoetically along the tongue'. (p. 35) There is a tendency to grandiose hyperbole (the Xhosa cattle-killing was 'probably the greatest self-inflicted immolation of a people in all history') and a degree of unconscious patronising (the Bushmen are 'delightful people'). (pp. 1187, 27) Too often the momentum of the narrative falters and the reader becomes bogged down in the jostlings of minor chiefs, correspondence between military commanders, petty intrigues, political shadow-boxing. *Frontiers* would be a better book if it were two hundred pages shorter.

Mostert treads carefully and for the most part wisely through the minefield of South African ethnic and racial terminology, in which an apparently neutral term like 'settler' or 'native' can be taken as the bitterest of insults. He is right to point out that, as black people began to be absorbed into a national economy, it made less sense to call them Xhosa, Zulu, etc., and more sense to call them simply Africans. Thus to nominate a person as 'a Xhosa' in a South Africa just emerging from decades of enforced ethnic categorisations and to make this the *primary* definition of his/her identity implies at best an old-fashioned ethnicist outlook, at worst the dogmatism of apartheid; even the more cautious locution 'a Xhosa-speaker' may be taken as an evasive euphemism.

Frontiers is a masterfully conceived book from which one can learn a great deal about why the South African past casts such a dark shadow over the present. It will certainly correct the notion that what happened on the eastern Cape frontier between 1780 and 1870 was no more than a series of bush skirmishes, that the battles that formed modern South Africa were fought solely between Boer and Zulu, Briton and Zulu, Boer and Briton. It will also contain no comfort for the reader who believes that, as far as race-hatred is concerned, the British in South Africa have clean hands.

28   Photographs of South Africa

PHOTOGRAPHY CAME TO South Africa in the 1840s, not long after its invention. Equipment of the first generation was cumbersome but not expensive, processing tedious but easy to learn: soon there were studios in most large towns, while itinerant photographers were criss-crossing the remoter parts. The invention of roll-film and cheap hand-held cameras in the 1880s made picture taking accessible to non-professionals. By the turn of the century, hundreds of thousands of images, perhaps millions, had been recorded on glass or celluloid.

Taking 1910 as her cut-off point, Mona de Beer has sifted through some 30,000 photographs in South African archives and collections to make a selection of 370, which she reproduces in a handsome book entitled *A Vision of the Past*.[1]

At the most obvious level, what these pictures have in common, particularly the earlier ones, and what distinguishes them from social-record photographs of our own time, is their stillness. Because the chemical emulsions in use reacted to light only slowly, shutter speeds had to be slow; because shutter speeds were slow, subjects in motion could not be photographed. In the case of human subjects the standard instruction was therefore, 'Keep still for the camera!' In the interval between this command and the click of the shutter, the subject had nothing to do but compose himself, becoming a self-for-the-camera whose trace, formed by the lens, given substance by chemical processes, would re-emerge into the world as a photograph.

The nineteenth-century people whose pictures we see are therefore strikingly conscious of themselves as objects of the gaze of the lens and strikingly composed before that gaze. In their formality, in the lack of any alternative to being posed, these subjects suffer a degree of constriction, but also – paradoxically – enjoy a degree of ease not open to present-day subjects, faced with mystifying commands to 'Be natural!' 'Relax – be yourself!'

The men in these pictures – or at least the white colonials – seem to compose themselves around self-ideals, or ideal selves, of the manly and the dapper. The women are harder to read. Perhaps the most that can be said is that one does not detect in them the narcissism of the looked-at woman of a hundred years later. I doubt that this is to be explained by unfamiliarity with the camera. Rather, the explanation may lie in the absence of iconic models of how to look while being looked at – models which abound today. In any event, the effect is that, in the cases of both men and women, the sexual appeal of the photographs is hard to read.

This is by no means to say that these subjects were innocent of aesthetic paradigms. On the contrary, singly or in groups they fall into poses characteristic of European figure painting – poses derived almost certainly not directly, from paintings themselves, but at third or fourth hand via the routine practices of studio photographers.

Even in pictures whose emphasis is on an activity – blacksmithing, haymaking – rather than on whoever is performing the activity, motion has to be interrupted till the shutter clicks and as a result the pictures take on an illustrative and even emblematic quality. Sometimes the effect can be eerie, as in a picture of women in *kappie* sunbonnets 'playing cricket' (so the caption says), or one in which a party 'playing tennis' on chalked-out but unfenced courts in the bare veld of Rouxville turn to the camera holding their rackets much as a king in a pack of cards holds his sceptre of office.

Little of the portraiture reproduced is of artistic value. On the other hand, outdoor scenes, particularly those which mix social levels, allow the more enterprising photographers opportunities that are sometimes well taken. The courtiers and shepherds of the European picturesque are interestingly translated, for instance, in an anonymous photograph of a well-dressed walking party waiting to be ferried across the Riviersonderend by an old boatman. Photographs in this genre from the Gribble studio in Paarl are particularly impressive.

Mona de Beer and her collaborator Brian Johnson Barker seem to be untroubled by any doubts as to their ability to read facial expressions from a bygone age. That is to say, they seem not to question the existence of a transhistorical and even transcultural code of looks reflecting universal inner feelings. In this they can call for a certain amount of support from modern human ethology as well as from those eighteenth-century philosophers of sentiment who argue that an inborn faculty of sympathy allows feelings to be transmitted from one breast to another without the mediation of a semiotic system.

Whether or not looks have the power to communicate feelings transparently, however, the captions in this collection raise questions. How many readers, I wonder, and specifically how many black South African readers, would join the compilers in interpreting the look on the face of the girl selling brooms (p. 140) as 'wistful'. And, while granting to the compilers that anyone about to be body-searched for illicit diamonds may feel anxious and/or resentful and/or angry, would any set of readers scrutinising the photograph of the seven naked men (p. 161) agree on which of the men are anxious, which resentful and which angry?

This is by no means to argue that all faces from the past must be as inscrutable as the faces of Martians. In the faces of British prisoners of war (p. 191), for instance, one can see the unmistakable lineaments of their great-grandsons, the football hooligans of the 1980s. It is merely to say that in this case the compilers claim a competence in cultural fine reading that their captions do not bear out.

The captioning is undoubtedly the weakest feature of the book. Running to 50–100 words per photograph, the captions often contain useful factual information, such as, for example, that bars across upper-storey windows were not to keep burglars out but to keep children in, or that old-style bicycle brakes exerted pressure not on the rim but on the tyre. But too often the tone of the captions is syrupy or patronising. Of a group of young girls at play: 'If this is a birthday it must surely be for the little girl . . . looking at the camera. What a real child she looks – happy, sweet-natured and quite capable of mischief.' Of farm workers at a dance: 'Their dance floor may be a dusty patch of veld, and the style of one or two a trifle vigorous, but these are people enjoying themselves.'

The compilers have made a brave and not inconsiderable attempt to give a selection that is socially representative: pictures of rich and poor, black and white, Christian and Muslim and Jew. But – unavoidably, given the uses to which photography was put in nineteenth-century South Africa – the overwhelming majority of the images from which they have selected, and the majority of the images they reproduce, are of the faces and the clothed bodies of middle-class white people and of the objects and occasions deemed important by these people. So while the endpapers of the book consist of a breathtaking group photograph of hundreds of men, black and white, looking back at the camera from the slopes of a dump at the New Primrose Gold Mine, disproportionate coverage is given to unremarkable pictures of family gatherings and sports teams and dressed-up children – to what the compilers call 'social history that embraces the ordinary man'.

Social history because not *history*. The compilers make it clear that they are not putting together an illustrated history of South Africa along the lines of the *Reader's Digest Illustrated History*. So instead of battles we have picnics, instead of famous men, ordinary folks. Fair enough. But where, in practice, does social history end and history proper begin? If the lepers confined to Robben Island are in the book because they belong to social history, are the Xhosa chiefs also confined to Robben Island not in the book because they belong to history? Does a dead baby in its little coffin (in the book) fall into social history, while trenches full of dead soldiers (not in the book) fall into history? The principle – that ordinary people doing ordinary things don't deserve to be forgotten – is a good one, but the inference – that there is a space that can be abstracted from history and called the space of social history – seems to me hard to sustain, and, insofar as it results in a book that constitutes a (broadly speaking) happy and peaceful representation of a time and place that were (equally broadly speaking) sad and filled with strife, pernicious.

It would be grossly unfair to assert that *A Vision of the Past* does anything quite so simple as celebrate Victorian South Africa. Nevertheless, the book is in many respects of a piece with an era that spent a lot of time and energy celebrating itself. The book certainly does not set out to subvert the comfortable image of itself that the era put out.

Should a compilation of this kind set out to subvert its subject? Behind this question lies the question of what historiography – including social historiography – is all about. Is it enough to reproduce an era's representation of itself without at the very least indicating the boundaries the era drew around that self-representation – without, in other words, indicating what was censored from the public image?

The Empire of Victoria was very clear about the need for censorship and self-censorship. It drew a strict line between public life and private life; within private life it drew a strict line between what might and what might not emerge into the public gaze. The erotic belonged to the cordoned-off part of private life, and representations of the erotic accordingly found no place in the Empire's self-presentation (or rather, since it is not in the nature of Eros to be repressed, emerged only in disguise). In *A Vision of the Past* there is no representation of the erotic undisguised, and certainly no trace of the pornographic. Yet ever since its invention photography has been intimately linked with pornography. Dirty pictures were part of the underlife of Victorian South Africa as they were of Victorian England; and if dirty pictures do not belong in social history, where do they belong?

There is another questionable exclusion: photographs illustrating the social life and customs of 'primitive' peoples (such as James Chapman's photographs of the Bushmen), as well as anthropometric photographs recording 'primitive' physical types. A strong argument can be made that such pictures, particularly the anthropometric ones, are in spirit closely allied to pornography, both subjecting the body to an aggressively prying gaze. Such ethnographic photographs occupy a peculiar position nowadays, on the point of being relegated from the category of empirical documentation to the category of the forbidden. Nevertheless, insofar as they proclaim themselves to be social history – the social history of people about to be steamrollered by history – leaving them out of a book like this deserves at least a justificatory paragraph.

Though primarily a picture book, *A Vision of the Past* contains brief essays – bland and uncontroversial – introducing each of its eight sections, as well as some introductory pages on the history of photography in South Africa, pages that tell us rather less than we might want to know about the technology of early photography and photographic reproduction. (Eadweard Muybridge's pioneering photographic analysis of animal locomotion is cited here as '*Animal Location* by . . . Edward Muybridge,' a mistake that does not breed confidence in the compilers' scholarship.) For technical information the reader still needs to go to A.D. Bensusan's *Silver Images: A History of Photography in South Africa*. But neither Bensusan nor the present compilers answer a question that presents itself more and more insistently as one pages through the book: why are the technicians from Cape Town and Hong Kong who made this expensive book unable to match the skill of craftsmen of ninety years ago at reproducing photographic material, particularly at the level of microscopic detail? A related question: Why is it that a photograph (reproduced on p. 223) of a street scene from the Cape Town of 1902, a photograph that would seem to have been taken with an exposure of 1/10 second or longer, has a subtlety of gradation of blacks that one no longer sees in today's photographic prints?

Despite such cavilling, *A Vision of the Past* contains scores of absorbing pictures in which one can lose oneself for hours on end. Many of them are poignant, less for what they represent than for what they promise and what failed to arrive – a snap (dated 1900), for instance, of ragged black children playing cricket (untutored, unsupervised) in the veld outside Aliwal North.

29   The 1995 Rugby World Cup

IF ONE'S VERDICT on the 1999 rugby World Cup is that the South African team was mildly unlucky to end up in third place, rather than second or even first, then the verdict on the 1995 Cup must be that South Africa was mildly lucky to end up first. Though solid in all departments, well drilled and determined, the 1995 team was not the most talented or inventive on show. The New Zealanders they beat were a stronger combination, who on the day of the final happened to make too many jittery mistakes.

But the World Cup is not just about rugby. It is the occasion for a month-long orgy of chauvinism and mime-show of war among nations. When South Africa hosted the tournament in 1995, it was unabashedly used as a political exercise in nation building. So it is not unsporting to look back critically on the packaging of the 1995 tournament, and specifically on the opening and closing ceremonies, where the 'philosophy' behind the World Cup bared itself particularly nakedly.

These ceremonies, recast, to suit the roving eye of the television cameras, away from old-style brass bands and marching phalanxes in the direction of extravaganza of the Miss Universe kind, betrayed how the designers of the spectacle – professionals hired by the operators who nowadays own the game – conceive of the new South Africa. The new South Africa they put on show at Newlands

351

and Ellis Park was very different from the South Africa exhibited by the old regime in the spectacles it organised. It was more feminine, or more sexualised: the grim-faced, men-only, militaristic muscle flexing had disappeared. At a deeper level, however, it remained disturbingly similar, so similar, in fact, that one might call the concept (to adopt the word the professionals must use among themselves) naïve, at the very least.

The master metaphor behind the two ceremonies was clearly Archbishop Desmond Tutu's 'Rainbow People', modified for the occasion into 'Rainbow Nation'. The rainbow metaphor does not originate with Tutu, of course: he brought it back from his travels in America, where rainbowness has a history going back at least to the 1930s. 'Rainbow' thus entered South African discourse in a self-aware fashion as an ideological term, a substitute for a long series of discredited synonyms: 'plural', '*veelvolkig*', and the like. It absolved itself of the taint of mere synonymy by the instrumental intention behind it: it was to be set to work to reverse the mindset of a population locked by its former masters into ethnic-political compartments. Specifically, it predicated the nation as a mental construct and nationhood as a collective state of mind. If a group of people can be encouraged to believe they are a nation and to act together like a nation, even if only in play, then they are a nation.

This conception of what nationhood consists in differs sharply from the conception that underlay apartheid, at least in its pristine years, and that still underlies such residual movements as Boere-Afrikanerdom and Zulu nationalism, which set as prerequisites a common history, common roots in a common territory, a common culture, and (most strikingly though also most vaguely) shared 'blood'.

The World Cup and the ballyhoo surrounding it were used by its South African backers as a vehicle for promoting a South African nationalism. The team selected by the South African Rugby Football Union, despite its predominant whiteness, was promoted as the embodiment of that nation. At a deeper level, rugby was used by the medium (television-sports or sports-television) to promote the idea that a nation and a national consciousness are to all intents and purposes the same thing, and therefore that sounds and images, if numerous and powerful enough, can create a nation.

What did the opening and closing ceremonies show? History remains a deeply contentious subject in South Africa. The struggle for the right to make up the story of the country is by no means over. Seeming to declare a truce on that front, the opening ceremony made an attempt to be history-less. It presented a dehistoricised vision of Tourist South Africa: contented tribesfolk and happy mineworkers, as in the old South Africa, but purified and sanctified, somehow, by the Rainbow.

When it got to the paler end of the spectrum, however, it found itself unable to proceed without becoming, intermittently, not only a pageant but an historical pageant as well. And so, to the procession of timeless Sotho in blankets and timeless Zulu in ostrich feathers it had to add what looked very much like happy eighteenth-century slaves and slave-owners in knee-breeches, bearing baskets of agricultural produce to the Rainbow feast. There were also, somewhere in the middle of the pageant, half a dozen lost-looking lads in khaki shirts and shorts whose presence seemed to be more symbolic than iconic (Voortrekkers? Baden-Powell Pioneers? mere generic whites?).

From the moment when the rainbow procession into the Newlands stadium slipped into the historical mode – a moment that was foreseeable, given the naïveté of the people who dreamed up the spectacle, to say nothing of the soteriological impulse behind Tutu's notion of a Rainbow People (a people who have passed through the fires of history and to that extent are elect or at least special) – it became difficult not to be aware of what was present in and what was absent from this new history.

Who, in 1995, were the principal absentees? The list began with Jan van Riebeeck himself and cut a swathe through all the colonial founding fathers, from Simon van der Stel to Piet Retief to Cecil John Rhodes. Absent too was the alternative line of fathers: Moshoeshoe, Gandhi, Luthuli, et al. No Famous Men at all, no Famous Women either, just People, of various tribes. Shangaan and Pedi but no Huguenots, no 1820 Settlers. Muslims and Indians but no Jews. More disturbingly, no San, no Khoi (and this on the continent, according to the theme song, 'where the world began'). Coon *kaskenades* but no *volkspele*. Gumboot-dancing but no *tiekiedraai*.

If the representation of the host country stepped a fine line between ethnic stereotyping and service of the Rainbow concept, the rest of the opening ceremony was an uninhibited riot of clichés: gaucho Argentinians, matelot Frenchmen, gondolier Italians, shamrock-green Irish leprechauns – the parts all played by bewildered children watched over by angel maidens in sexy, diaphanous white robes, children who had twenty seconds to shuffle about in the appropriate national dance before they were shunted off the platform to make way for the next nation.

When it came to the larger ex-colonies, rainbow nations in their own right, the image-makers faced a dilemma. What ethnic icons were appropriate to such countries as Canada and Australia? They settled, rather lamely, for separate but equal representation: in the opening ceremony the Canadians were clad in democratic blue jeans, the Australians in bushranger kit; in the closing ceremony the aboriginals had their day in the sun, beating drums, blowing didgeridoos.

Of course, the moment to wait for was the revelation of how the puzzle was to be solved of setting on the platform a single image of the Rainbow People. Were we going to have a cluster of happy black, white, Coloured and Indian faces as in the 'plural' South Africa of old ('One country, many nations')? And what were they going to wear? The solution that emerged had an air of desperation about it: cute black *pikkies* in mine overalls and helmets (*pikkie* from Portuguese *pequeño*, little; its English cousin has dropped out of polite usage).

For some, the opening and closing ceremonies were colourful extravaganzas, fun events which stirred the blood and brought tears to the eyes. For others, the predominating emotion was relief – relief that the ceremonies began and ended on time, that the sound system worked, that the choreography, if not exactly snappy, at least did not get into an irremediable muddle in front of the world's cameras, that only once (a bejewelled singer borne into the stadium in a litter on the shoulders of muscular old-Egyptian slaves) were the depths plumbed of Sun City tastelessness.

In some cases it was the World Cup anthem that lingered in memory long after the images of the pageant itself had vanished. The tune itself has a suspicious resemblance to the middle section of Gustav Holst's 'Jupiter' (since Holst's copyrights expired in 1984, arrangers were free to do with his music as they pleased). Already ponderously sentimental in Elgarian fashion, this tune now had saccharine harmonies superadded, and words of sonorous vacuity ('As we try to reach our destiny . . . to take our place in history and live with dignity'), sung by a large blonde woman doing an imitation of African American (not African) vocal timbre – a voice at the same time strident and aggressively sentimental, the voice in which the American music industry purveys its dreams of love and desire.

Part of the experience of being colonised is having images of yourself made up by outsiders stuffed down your throat. At the World Cup ceremonies, South African spectators learned, some for the first time, that they were Rainbow people, that, whether they liked it or not, they would be represented as such on the world's television screens. As to the terms in which they would be packaged, they would have no say on these. The words and music, the images and stereotypes in which the Rainbow concept was to be dressed, would be concocted not just by foreigners but by an industry dedicated to the manufacture and recycling of the exotic, to the construction of varieties of rainbowness across the globe. For present purposes, their country was to be offered as an exotic destination, different from other destinations certainly, but different only in a piquant, easily digested way, the way of sports tourism.

Notes and References

1 What Is a Classic? A Lecture

1 *What is a Classic?* (London: Faber, 1945). Hereafter cited as *WIC*.

2 'Le Poète de la latinité tout entière', quoted in Frank Kermode, *The Classic* (London: Faber, 1975), p. 16. Sainte-Beuve's lectures were published as *Etude sur Virgile* in 1857.

3 In a *Criterion* article of 1926 Eliot claims that Britain is part of 'a common culture of Western Europe'. The question is: 'Are there enough persons in Britain believing in that European culture, the Roman inheritance, believing in the place of Britain in that culture'. Two years later he assigns Britain a mediating role between Europe and the rest of the world: 'She is the only member of the European community that has established a genuine empire – that is to say, a world-wide empire as was the Roman empire – not only European but the connection between Europe and the rest of the world.' Quoted in Gareth Reeves, *T. S. Eliot: A Virgilian Poet* (London: Macmillan, 1989), pp. 111, 85.

4 Eliot left Harvard to study in Germany, then moved to Oxford when the First World War broke out, then married an Englishwoman, then tried to return to Harvard to defend his doctoral dissertation (but the ship on which he had a berth did not sail), then tried to get a job in the U.S. navy but failed, then – it seems – simply gave up trying, stayed in England, and eventually became a British subject. If the dice had fallen another way, it is not impossible to see him getting his PhD,

357

taking up the professorship that awaited him at Harvard and resuming his American life.

5 Eliot made no major public statement on his decision to leave the United States. However, in a 1928 letter to Herbert Read he did, somewhat plaintively, articulate his sense of rootlessness within the country of his birth: 'Some day I want to write an essay about the point of view of an American who wasn't an American, because he was born in the South and went to school in New England as a small boy with a nigger drawl, but who wasn't a southerner in the South because his people were northerners in a border state and looked down on all southerners and Virginians, and so who was never anything anywhere and who therefore felt himself to be more a Frenchman than an American and more an Englishman than a Frenchman and yet felt that the U.S.A. up to a hundred years ago was a family extension.' 'T.S. Eliot – A Memoir', in *T.S. Eliot: The Man and his Work*, ed. Allen Tate (New York: Delacorte, 1966), p. 15.

Three years later, in the *Criterion*, he saw the plight of the American intellectual as follows: 'The American intellectual of today has almost no chance of continuous development upon his own soil and in the environment which his ancestors, however humble, helped to form. He must be an expatriate: either to languish in a provincial university, or abroad, or, the most complete expatriation of all, in New York.' Quoted in William M. Chace, *The Political Identities of Ezra Pound and T. S. Eliot* (Stanford: Stanford University Press, 1973), p. 155. Eliot does concede, however, that this enforced deracination is more a feature of modern life than of specifically American circumstances.

6 'East Coker', in *Four Quartets* (London: Faber, 1944), pp. 22, 15, 20.

7 'Poetry is not a turning loose of emotion, but an escape from emotion; it is not the expression of personality, but an escape from personality.' 'Tradition and the Individual Talent' (1919), in *Selected Prose*, ed. John Hayward (Harmondsworth: Penguin, 1953), p. 30.

8 Reeves quotes the address of the Cumaean Sibyl to Aeneas (*Aeneid*, VI, 93–4): 'The cause of all this Trojan woe is again an alien bride [*coniunx hospita*], again a foreign marriage.' The alien brides who cause

woe to Troy are Menelaus's wife Helen, Phoenician Dido and Latin Lavinia. Reeves writes, 'Is not at least a portion of Eliot's woe his marriage to Vivien, an Englishwoman, a *coniunx hospita*?' (p. 47)

Eliot's reading of the meeting of Dido and Aeneas in the Underworld as, in the first place, 'civilised' is hard to understand. After Aeneas has addressed her, Dido

> fixed her eyes on the ground.
> Her features were not more stirred by his speech
> Than if they were made of hard flint or Marpesian marble.
> Then she flung herself off [*sese corripuit*] and fled back to the shadowy grove,
> Still hostile [*inimica*].

Aeneid, VI, 469–73, trans. L.R. Lind (Bloomington: Indiana University Press, 1963), p. 117.

9 In 'Virgil and the Christian World' (1951) Eliot distinguishes Virgil's 'conscious mind' from an aspect of his mind that remains discreetly unnamed but that may be responding to higher direction. *On Poetry and Poets* (London: Faber, 1957), p. 129. See also Reeves, *T. S. Eliot*, p. 102.

10 *Notes Toward a Definition of Culture*, completed in 1948, is in effect a response to Karl Mannheim, who in *Man and Society in an Age of Reconstruction* argued that the problems of the industrial Europe of the future could be solved only by a shift to conscious social planning, and more generally by the encouragement of new modes of thought. Direction would have to be given by an elite which had transcended class constraints.

Eliot opposed social engineering, future planning, and *dirigisme* in general. He foresaw that the cultivation of elites would foster class mobility and thereby transform society. It was better, he said, 'that the great majority of human beings should go on living in the place where they were born'. The self-consciousness Mannheim envisaged should remain a faculty of some form of aristocracy or presiding class. (Quoted in Chace, *Political Identities*, p. 197.)

Eliot's response to the moves toward European unity represented by the Hague conference of 1948 (which mooted the idea of a European Parliament) and the founding of the Council of Europe in 1949 is contained in a public letter of 1951, in which, distinguishing cultural questions from political decisions, he advocates a long-term effort to convince the people of Western Europe of their common culture and to conserve and cultivate regions, races, languages, each having a 'vocation' in relation to the others. See also Eliot's 'The Man of Letters and the Future of Europe' (1944), quoted in Roger Kojecky, *T.S. Eliot's Social Criticism* (London: Faber, 1971), p. 202.

11 Certain pieces did keep their place in specialised repertoires – some of the motets, for instance, remained in the repertory of the Thomaskirche in Leipzig, where Mozart heard 'Singet dem Herrn' in 1789.

12 Friedrich Blume, *Two Centuries of Bach*, trans. Stanley Godman (London: Oxford University Press, 1950), p. 12. I have amended Godman's translation slightly.

13 The historical sense of Bach's musician sons Wilhelm Friedemann, Carl Philipp Emanuel and Johann Christian was accurate too: not only did they do nothing after their father's death to promote his music or keep it alive, but they established themselves swiftly as leading exponents of the new music of reason and feeling.

   During his later years in Leipzig Bach was regarded as what Blume calls 'an intractable oddity, a sarcastic old fogey'. The authorities of the St Thomas Church in Leipzig, where he was Cantor, were all too visibly relieved when he died and they could hire a younger man more in tune with the times. Of his two most famous contemporaries, one (Telemann) expressed the verdict that Bach's sons, particularly Carl Philipp Emanuel, were his greatest gift to the world, while the other (Handel) took not the slightest notice of him. See Blume, *Two Centuries of Bach*, pp. 15–16, 23, 25–6.

14 The author was J.N. Forkel, director of music at the University of Göttingen. Quoted in ibid., p. 38.

15 Ibid., pp. 52–3, 56.

Notes and References

2 Daniel Defoe, *Robinson Crusoe*

1 *The Brevities*, ed. Burton R. Pollin (New York: Gordian Press, 1985), p. 547.

2 *History of English Literature*, vol. 2, trans. Henry van Laun (London: Colonial Press, 1900), p. 404.

3 Samuel Richardson, *Clarissa*

1 *Clarissa*, ed. Angus Ross (Harmondsworth: Penguin, 1985), p. 913. Ross's text is based on the first edition of 1747–8.

2 Marsilio Ficino, *El Libro dell'amore*, ed. Sandra Niccoli (Florence: Olschki Editore, 1987), p. 34.

3 Commentary on Paul's Epistle to the Ephesians, quoted in Mary Daly, *The Church and the Second Sex* (Boston: Beacon Press, 1968), p. 85.

4 Marina Warner, *Alone of All her Sex* (London: Picador, 1985), p. 47; Giulia Sissa, *Greek Virginity*, trans. Arthur Goldhammer (Cambridge, Mass.: Harvard University Press, 1990), p. 116.

5 Nancy Miller, *The Heroine's Text* (New York: Columbia University Press, 1980), p. 84.

6 'My will is unviolated. The evil . . . is merely personal . . . I have, through grace, triumphed.' (p. 1254)

7 Simone de Beauvoir, *The Second Sex*, trans. H.M. Parshley (Harmondsworth: Penguin, 1983), p. 184.

8 Terry Eagleton, *The Rape of Clarissa* (Minneapolis: University of Minnesota Press, 1982), p. 61.

5 Harry Mulisch, *The Discovery of Heaven*

1 Harry Mulisch, *The Discovery of Heaven* (New York: Viking, 1996), p. 729.

2 *Voer voor psychologen* (Amsterdam: De Bezige Bij, 1974), pp. 13–14.

3 *Een spookgeschiedenis / Eine Gespenstergeschichte / A Ghost Story* (Amsterdam: De Bezige Bij, 1993), pp. 53–4.

4 *The Stone Bridal Bed*, trans. Adrienne Dixon (New York: Abelard-Schuman, 1962), p. 96.

5 *De Zuilen van Hercules* (Amsterdam: De Bezige Bij, 1990), p. 43.

6   Cees Nooteboom, Novelist and Traveller

1   *In the Dutch Mountains*, trans. Adrienne Dixon (New York: Harcourt Brace, 1997), p. 121. Dixon mistranslates 'irrepressible desire' as 'irresponsible desire'.

2   *Philip and the Others* (1955; English translation, 1988) and *The Knight Has Died* (1963; English translation, 1990) have both been brought out by Louisiana State University Press, Nooteboom's main champion in the English-speaking world.

3   *De zucht naar het Westen* (Amsterdam: Arbeiderspers, 1985), p. 184.

4   *Roads to Santiago: Detours and Riddles in the Lands and History of Spain*, trans. Ina Rilke (New York: Harcourt Brace, 1997), p. 5.

5   See Daan Cartens (ed.), *Over Cees Nooteboom: beschouwingen en interviews* (The Hague: Bezige Bij, 1984), p. 23.

7   William Gass's Rilke

1   William H. Gass, *Reading Rilke: Reflections on the Problems of Translation* (New York: Knopf, 1999).

2   *The Essential Rilke*, ed. and trans. Galway Kinnell and Hannah Liebmann (New York: Ecco Press, 1999); *Duino Elegies: A Bilingual Edition*, trans. Edward Snow (San Francisco: North Point Press, 2000).

3   Quoted in Eudo C. Mason, *Rilke, Europe and the English-Speaking World* (Cambridge: Cambridge University Press, 1961), p. 11.

4   'The Poet in the Age of Prose', in Gerald Chapple and Hans H. Schulte (ed.), *The Turn of the Century* (Bonn: Bouvier Verlag, 1981), p. 11.

5   Letter of 13 November 1925. *Briefe*, vol. 2 (Wiesbaden: Insel Verlag, 1950), pp. 482–3. The translation is taken, in part, from Mason, *Rilke*, p. 163.

6   Letter of 11 February 1922, *Briefe*, vol. 2, p. 309.

7   Quoted in H.F. Peters, *Rainer Maria Rilke* (Seattle: University of Washington Press, 1960), p. 125.

8   Letters of 23 September 1911 and 9 October 1915, quoted in Mason, *Rilke*, p. 177.

9   *Rainer Maria Rilke: Selected Works*, 2 vols, trans. J.B. Leishman (New

York: New Directions, 1960); *Duino Elegies and Sonnets to Orpheus*, trans. André Poulin Jr. (Boston: Houghton Mifflin, 1977); *The Selected Poetry of Rainer Maria Rilke*, ed. and trans. Stephen Mitchell (New York: Random House, 1982).

8 Translating Kafka

1 Edwin Muir, *An Autobiography* (London: Hogarth Press, 1954), pp. 222, 227.

2 *Selected Letters*, ed. P.H. Butter (London: Hogarth Press, 1974), p. 67.

3 'Introduction', *The Castle*, trans. Edwin and Willa Muir (New York: Knopf, 1930), p. x.

4 Edwin and Willa Muir, 'Translating from the German', in *On Translation*, ed. Reuben Brower (New York: Oxford University Press, 1966), p. 93.

5 *The Trial*, trans. Edwin and Willa Muir (Harmondsworth: Penguin, 1953), p. 19.

6 Edwin Muir, 'Franz Kafka', in *Essays on Literature and Society* (Cambridge, Mass.: Harvard University Press, 1967), p. 123.

7 Stephen D. Dowden, *Kafka's Castle and the Critical Imagination* (Columbia, SC: Camden House, 1995), p. 8.

8 *The Castle*, trans. Mark Harman (New York: Schocken, 1998).

9 Dieter Jakobs, 'Das Kafka-Bild in England', *Oxford German Studies*, 5 (1970), p. 105.

10 *Testaments Betrayed*, trans. Linda Asher (London: Faber, 1995), p. 42.

11 Brod, 'Epilogue', *The Trial*, trans. Muir and Muir, p. 253.

12 Ibid., p. 252.

13 *Testaments Betrayed*, pp. 101–20.

14 'Digging the Pit of Babel', *New Literary History*, 27 (1996), pp. 291–311.

9 Robert Musil's *Diaries*

1 *Diaries, 1899–1941*, selected, translated and annotated by Philip Payne; preface by Philip Payne; edited and with an introduction by

Mark Mirsky (New York: Basic Books, 1998). The quotation is from p. 384.

2 *The Man without Qualities*, trans. Sophie Wilkins, with additional material ed. and trans. Burton Pike (New York: Knopf, 1995), vol. 2, p. 1761.

3 Werner Mittenzwei, *Exil in der Schweiz* (Leipzig: Reclam, 1978), pp. 19, 22–3.

4 Ignazio Silone, 'Begegnungen mit Musil', in Karl Dinklage (ed.), *Robert Musil: Studien zu seinem Werk* (Reinbek: Rowohlt, 1970), p. 355.

5 Quoted in Karl Dinklage, 'Musil's Definition des Mannes ohne Eigenschaften', in ibid., p. 114.

6 Quoted in David S. Luft, *Robert Musil and the Crisis of European Culture, 1880–1942* (Berkeley: University of California Press, 1980), p. 108.

7 Rolf Kieser, *Erzwungene Symbiose: Thomas Mann, Robert Musil, Georg Kaiser und Bertolt Brecht im Schweizer Exil* (Bern: Paul Haupt, 1984), pp. 89, 93.

8 Christian Rogowski, *Distinguished Outsider: Robert Musil and His Critics* (Columbia, SC: Camden House, 1994), pp. 20, 23.

9 Sophie Wilkins, 'Einige Notizen zum Fall der Übersetzerin der Knopf-Auflage des *MoE: The Man without Qualities*', in Annette Daigger and Gerti Milizer (ed.), *Die Übersetzung literarischer Texte am Beispiel Robert Musil* (Stuttgart: Akademischer Verlag, 1988), pp. 222, 225.

10 Josef Skvorecky

1 Quoted in *The Achievement of Josef Skvorecky*, ed. Sam Solecki (Toronto: University of Toronto Press, 1994), p. 155.

2 *The Bride of Texas*, trans. Kacá Poláčková Henley (New York: Knopf, 1996), p. 294.

3 Solecki (ed.), *Achievement*, p. 29.

4 *Headed for the Blues: A Memoir*, trans. Káca Poláčková Henley (New York: Ecco Press, 1996), p. 16.

11   Dostoevsky: The Miraculous Years

1 Joseph Frank, *Dostoevsky: The Miraculous Years, 1865–71* (Princeton: Princeton University Press, 1997).

2 *Fathers and Sons*, trans. Constance Garnett, translation revised Ralph E. Matlaw (New York: Norton, 1966), p. 39.

3 Edward Wasiolek (ed.), *The Notebooks for* The Idiot (Chicago: University of Chicago Press, 1967); Robin Feuer Miller, *Dostoevsky and* The Idiot (Cambridge: Harvard University Press, 1981).

4 There is fuller discussion of Bakhtin's thought, both judicious and generous, in Frank's own *Through the Russian Prism* (Princeton: Princeton University Press, 1990).

5 *Dostoevsky: The Seeds of Revolt, 1821–49* (Princeton: Princeton University Press, 1976), p. x; *Dostoevsky: The Years of Ordeal, 1850–9* (Princeton: Princeton University Press, 1983), p. xiii.

6 Reprinted in Joseph Frank, *The Widening Gyre* (New Brunswick: Rutgers University Press, 1963), pp. 3–62.

12   The Essays of Joseph Brodsky

1 *On Grief and Reason: Essays* (New York: Farrar, Straus, Giroux, 1995), p. 14.

2 *Ezra Pound, Letters 1907–41*, ed. D.D. Paige (New York: Harcourt Brace, 1950), p. 264.

3 *Less than One* (New York: Farrar, Straus, Giroux, 1986), p. 52.

4 *Brodsky Through the Eyes of his Contemporaries* (London: St Martin's Press, 1992).

5 *Joseph Brodsky and the Creation of Exile* (Princeton: Princeton University Press, 1994), p. 234.

13   J. L. Borges, *Collected Fictions*

1 Quoted in Jaime Alazraki, *Borges and the Kabbalah* (Cambridge: Cambridge University Press, 1988), p. 156.

2 (New York: Viking, 1998); hereafter referred to as *CF*.

3 The other two volumes are *Selected Non-Fictions*, ed. Eliot Weinberger and *Selected Poems*, ed. Alexander Coleman.

4 James Woodall, *The Man in the Mirror of the Book* (London: Hodder & Stoughton, 1996), p. 278.

5 Quoted in James E. Irby, 'Borges and the Idea of Utopia', in Harold Bloom (ed.), *Jorge Luis Borges* (New York: Chelsea House, 1986), p. 102.

6 'Nathaniel Hawthorne', in *Other Inquisitions, 1937–52* (New York: Simon & Schuster, 1968), p. 60.

7 1967 interview, quoted in Carter Wheelock, 'Borges' New Prose', in Bloom (ed.), *Borges*, p. 108.

8 Harold Bloom, 'Introduction', in ibid., pp. 2–3.

9 *Oeuvres complètes*, vol. 1, ed. Jean-Pierre Bernés (Paris: Gallimard, 1993), p. 272.

10 Quoted in Beatriz Sarlo, *Jorge Luis Borges*, ed. John King (London: Verso, 1993), p. 20.

11 Foreword to *In Praise of Darkness* (1969), *CF*, p. 333.

12 *Doctor Brodie's Report*, trans. Norman Thomas di Giovanni in collaboration with the author (New York: Dutton, 1972), p. 40; *CF*, p. 390.

13 Preface to *El Aleph* (London: Jonathan Cape, 1971).

14 A. S. Byatt

1 *Babel Tower* (New York: Knopf, 1995), p. 102.

2 *Still Life* (London: Hogarth Press, 1985), p. 323.

3 *Women Writers Talking*, ed. Janet Todd (New York: Holmes & Meier, 1983), pp. 187–8.

15 Caryl Phillips

1 *The Middle Passage* (London: André Deutsch, 1962), p. 68.

2 *Capitalism and Slavery* (London: André Deutsch, 1964), p. 7.

3 Jamaica Kincaid, *A Small Place* (New York: Farrar, Straus, Giroux, 1988), p. 31.

4 'Living and Writing in the Caribbean', *Kunapipi*, 11/2 (1989), p. 48.

5 *The European Tribe* (New York: Farrar, Straus, Giroux, 1987), p. 9.

6 *The Final Passage* (London: Faber, 1985), p. 199.

7 *Crossing the River* (New York: Knopf, 1994), p. 164.

8 Ibid., pp. 18, 64.

9 *The Higher Ground* (New York: Viking, 1989), pp. 103, 84.

10 *The European Tribe*, p. 126.

11 Quoted in ibid., p. 54.

12 Ibid., pp. 47, 49.

13 *The Nature of Blood* (New York: Knopf, 1997), p. 201.

14 Carol Davidson, interview with Caryl Phillips, *Ariel*, 25/4 (1994), p. 94.

16 Salman Rushdie, *The Moor's Last Sigh*

1 *Midnight's Children* (New York: Knopf, 1981), p. 370.

2 *The Moor's Last Sigh* (New York: Pantheon, 1995), p. 164.

17 Aharon Appelfeld, *The Iron Tracks*

1 *Beyond Despair*, trans. Jeffrey M. Green (New York: Fromm International, 1994), pp. ix, 35.

2 Quoted in Gila Ramras-Rauch, *Aharon Appelfeld* (Bloomington: Indiana University Press, 1994), p. 16.

3 *Beyond Despair*, p. 39.

4 Aharon Appelfeld, *The Iron Tracks*, trans. Jeffrey M. Green (New York: Schocken Books, 1998), pp. 13, 14.

5 See Appelfeld's 'A Personal Statement', in *Tradition and Trauma: Studies in the Fiction of S.J. Agnon*, ed. David Patterson and Glenda Abramson (Boulder: Westview Press, 1994), p. 212.

6 *Beyond Despair*, pp. 77–8.

7 See Gershon Shaked, 'Appelfeld and his Times', *Hebrew Studies*, 36 (1995), pp. 98–100.

8 *Beyond Despair*, p. 66.

18 Amos Oz

1 *Panther in the Basement*, trans. Nicholas de Lange (New York: Harcourt Brace, 1997), p. 35.

2 *Under This Blazing Light: Essays*, trans. Nicholas de Lange (Cambridge: Cambridge University Press, 1995), p. 159.

3 From an interview: 'I am sitting in a room full of books, writing even more books, which is probably exactly what my father hoped from me.' Some of the best pages of *Panther in the Basement* are given over to Proffy's explorations in his father's library. Interview with Eleanor Wachtel, *Queens Quarterly*, 98/2 (1991), p. 425.

4 In a 1982 interview with Eugene Goodheart, Oz adds more terms to the father's prescription: 'The new Israeli: simple, blond, cleansed of Jewish neurosis, tough, gentile-looking', *Partisan Review*, 49/3 (1982), p. 359.

5 *Under This Blazing Light*, p. 169.

6 Ibid., pp. 169, 170.

7 *The Hill of Evil Counsel: Three Stories*, trans. Nicholas de Lange (London: Fontana, 1980), p. 150.

19 Naguib Mahfouz, *The Harafish*

1 *Cultural Schizophrenia: Islamic Societies Confronting the West* (London: Saqui Books, 1992), pp. 64, 60.

2 See Roger Allen, 'Naguib Mahfouz and the Arabic Novel', in Michael Beard and Adnan Haydar (eds), *Naguib Mahfouz* (Syracuse: Syracuse University Press, 1993), p. 32; Salma Jayyusi, 'The Arab Laureate', in ibid., pp. 11–13.

3 'Naguib Mahfouz Remembers', in ibid., pp. 42–4.

4 Review in *New Republic*, 7 May 1990, pp. 33–4.

5 See Allen, 'Naguib Mahfouz and the Arabic Novel', p. 35.

6 Salih Altoma, 'Naguib Mahfouz', *International Fiction Review*, 17/2 (1990), pp. 128–9; C. Nijland, 'Nagib Mahfouz and Islam', *Welt des Islams*, 23–4 (1984), pp. 136–55; Menaham Milson, 'Najib Mahfouz and Jamal 'Abd al-Nasir', *Asian and African Studies*, 23 (1989), p. 6.

7 Altoma, 'Naguib Mahfouz', p. 131; Samia Mehrez, 'Respected Sir', in Beard and Haydar (eds) *Naguib Mahfouz*, pp. 65–8; Michael Beard, 'The Mahfouzian Sublime', in ibid., p. 100.

8 Mehrez, 'Respected Sir', pp. 67–8; Ghosh, *New Republic*, p. 36.

9 See Roger Allen, 'Najib Mahfouz', *World Literature Today*, 63/1 (1989), p. 7.

10 Altoma, 'Naguib Mahfouz', p. 131; Mehrez, 'Respected Sir', p. 76; Allen, 'Naguib Mahfouz and the Arabic Novel', p. 31; Anton Shammas, review in *New York Review of Books*, 2 February 1989, pp. 19–21.

11 See Adnan Maydar and Michael Beard, 'Mapping the World of Naguib Mahfouz', in Beard and Haydar (eds), *Naguib Mahfouz*, pp. 6–7.

12 Miriam Cooke, 'Men Constructed in the Mirror of Prostitution', in ibid., pp. 124–5.

13 See Beard and Haydar, 'Mapping the World of Naguib Mahfouz', in ibid., p. 5.

14 By Nijland, 'Naguib Mahfouz and Islam', p. 137.

15 Naguib Mahfouz, *The Harafish*, trans. Catherine Cobham (New York: Doubleday, 1994), p. 63.

16 Galen Strawson, review in *Times Literary Supplement*, 27 April 1990, pp. 435–6.

21 The Poems of Thomas Pringle

1 Ernest Pereira and Michael Chapman, eds., *African Poems of Thomas Pringle* (Durban: Killie Campbell Africana Library; Pietermaritzburg: University of Natal Press, 1989).

22 Daphne Rooke

1 Daphne Rooke, *Mittee* (London: Penguin, 1991), p. 59.

23 Gordimer and Turgenev

1 'A Writer's Freedom', in *The Essential Gesture: Writing, Politics and Places* (Johannesburg: Taurus; Cape Town: David Philip, 1988), pp. 87, 89.

2 Ibid., p. 89.

3 Ibid., p. 91.

4 'Relevance and Commitment', in *The Essential Gesture*, pp. 114, 115.

5 'Living in the Interregnum', in ibid., p. 224.

6 'The Essential Gesture' (1984), in ibid., p. 247.

7 Ibid., p. 247.

8 See Richard Freeborn, *Turgenev: The Novelist's Novelist* (Westport, Conn.: Greenwood Press, 1978), p. 15.

9 'Belinsky was just as much of an idealist as he was a social critic; he criticised in the name of an ideal . . . Belinsky devoted himself entirely to the service of this ideal; in all his sympathies and all his activity he belonged to the camp of the Westernists . . . The acceptance of the results of the Western way of life, the application of them to our own life . . . – that was the way in which we could, in his opinion, finally achieve something distinctively Russian, an idea which he cherished considerably more than is generally believed.' Quoted in ibid., p. 14.

10 In 'A Writer's Freedom' Gordimer does, however, give the puzzling impression that she reads Bazarov as standing for Turgenev himself: 'The radicals and liberals, among whom Turgenev himself belonged, lambasted him as a traitor because Bazarov was presented with all the faults and contradictions that Turgenev saw in his own type, in himself, so to speak.' (p. 90) The faults and contradictions of the anglophile dandy Pavel Petrovich Kirsanov are surely Turgenev's as much as are the faults of Bazarov.

11 In 'Living in the Interregnum' (1982), p. 229n, Gordimer paraphrases an unmemorable phrase by Chernyshevsky. Again one has the impression that invoking Chernyshevsky's name and reputation is more important to Gordimer than his actual words.

12 Turgenev: *Fathers and Sons* 'deprived me, for ever . . . of the good opinion of the Russian younger generation'. *Literary Reminiscences and Autobiographical Fragments*, trans. David Magarshak (London: Faber, 1959), pp. 168, 169.

13 'Fathers and Children: Turgenev and the Liberal Predicament', in Ivan Turgenev, *Fathers and Sons*, trans. Rosemary Edmonds (Harmondsworth: Penguin, 1975), pp. 19–20.

14 Berlin, 'Fathers and Children', p. 37; Joe Andrew, *Russian Writers and Society in the Second Half of the Nineteenth Century* (London: Macmillan, 1982), p. 33.

15 Freeborn, *Turgenev*, p. 134.

16 'All my story is directed against the gentry as the most important class', he wrote in a letter to K. K. Sluchevsky, 1862. *Letters*, ed. and trans. A.V. Knowles (London: Athlone Press, 1983), p. 105. Freeborn's gloss: 'He was acknowledging the moral superiority of the *raznochintsy* as a class.' (p. 100)

17 *Letters*, p. 106.

18 'My conscience was clear . . . My attitude towards the character I had created was honest . . . I have too great a respect for the vocation of an artist, a writer, to act against my conscience.' (*Literary Reminiscences*, p. 169) 'I started with no preconceived idea, no "tendency"; I wrote naïvely, as if myself astonished at what was emerging.' (Letter to Saltykov-Shchedrin, 1876, quoted in Berlin, 'Fathers and Children', p. 26.)

19 Quoted in Berlin, 'Fathers and Children', p. 35.

20 For discussion, see Andrew, *Russian Writers and Society*, pp. 8–9.

21 Freeborn, *Turgenev*, p. 46.

22 A Norwegian writer who met Turgenev in about 1874 records him as saying that the first image of Bazarov that came to him was of a dying man. Ibid., p. 69.

23 '*Fathers and Sons*: Fathers and Children', in John Garrard (ed.), *The Russian Novel from Pushkin to Pasternak* (New Haven: Yale University Press, 1983), pp. 77–8.

24 Berlin, 'Fathers and Children', pp. 51–2.

25 'I am . . . determined to find my place "in history" while yet referring as a writer to the values that are beyond history. I shall never give them up.' ('Living in the Interregnum', p. 233) Gordimer is taking up a challenge from Camus: 'Is it possible . . . to be in history while still referring to values which go beyond it?' (quoted ibid., p. 231). For a highly critical account of Gordimer's position here, see Dagmar Barnouw, 'Nadine Gordimer: Dark Times, Interior Worlds, and the Obscurities of Difference', *Contemporary Literature*, 35 (1994), pp. 252–80. 'Her work . . . can be read as a case history of the writer's powerful, indeed religious belief in the redemptive potential of high-cultural fictional discourse.' (p. 278)

26 It is 'in the nature' of the artist 'to want to transform the world'. In that sense he is 'always moving toward truth, true consciousness'. 'Relevance and Commitment', p. 118.

27 'The Essential Gesture', pp. 243, 241. Gordimer's source is Ernst Fischer, *The Necessity of Art* (Harmondsworth: Penguin, 1963), p. 47.

28 There may have been more intimate reasons as well for Gordimer's sense of kinship with Turgenev. There is a striking similarity between Turgenev's expressed attitude toward serfdom and Gordimer's toward racism. 'There are two absolutes in my life,' wrote Gordimer in 1982. 'One is that racism is evil – human damnation in the Old Testament sense, and no compromises, as well as sacrifices, should be too great in the fight against it.' ('Living in the Interregnum', p. 231) Compare Turgenev: 'I could not breathe the same air or remain close to what I hated so much . . . In my eyes this enemy took a definite form and bore a particular name: this enemy was – serfdom. Under this heading I gathered and concentrated everything against which I had decided to fight to the bitter end, with which I had sworn never to come to terms . . . This was my Hannibal's oath.' Quoted in Freeborn, *Turgenev*, p. 6.

29 In *Writing and Being* (Cambridge, Mass.: Harvard University Press, 1995) Gordimer revises her position on the category of nonfictional writing she calls testimony. Whereas in the 1970s she had criticised testimony for lacking a 'transforming imagi-native dimension', for dealing only with 'the surface reality of experience', for amounting often to no more than 'thinly disguised autobiography', she now (1995) says that her 'approach . . . is different'. She celebrates testimony as 'witness', as part of 'the struggle against forgetting' and therefore as part of the creation of a history. (pp. 22–3) Some pages later, however, she returns to the contrast between testimony and imaginative literature. In Homer, she points out, the poetry continues to 'carry the experience' long after the history on which it was based has vanished from awareness. Thus in Homer 'the Greek experience definitive for humankind lives on among us'. (p. 41) Again the question of a double standard looms.

24   The Autobiography of Doris Lessing

1   *Under my Skin: Volume One of My Autobiography* (New York: HarperCollins, 1994), pp. 29–30, 15.

2   *The Grass Is Singing* (New York: HarperCollins, 1997), p. 372.

3   Though the whole project is billed as an autobiography, in the text Lessing refers to the second volume as 'memoirs'. (p. 358)

25   The Memoirs of Breyten Breytenbach

1   *A Season in Paradise*, trans. Rike Vaughan (New York: Persea Books, 1980), p. 156.

2   *True Confessions of an Albino Terrorist* (New York: Farrar, Straus, Giroux, 1985), p. 280.

3   *Return to Paradise* (New York: Harcourt Brace, 1993), pp. 31, 201, 215, 214. The book appeared in Dutch before it appeared in English. The Dutch text is considerably longer. Passages cut include reminiscences of bohemian life in the Cape Town of the 1950s and of Breytenbach's travels in Africa.

4   *Dog Heart: A Memoir* (New York: Harcourt Brace, 1999), p. 180.

5   *The Memory of Birds in Times of Revolution* (London: Faber, 1996), p. 105.

26   South African Liberals: Alan Paton, Helen Suzman

1   *Towards the Mountain* (Cape Town: David Philip, 1980), p. 272.

2   *Cry, the Beloved Country* (New York: Scribner, 1948), p. 80.

3   'Alan Paton: The Honour of Meditation', *English in Africa*, 10/2 (1983), p. 4.

4   *Save the Beloved Country*, ed. Hans Strydom and David Jones (Melville: Hans Strydom, 1987; New York: Scribner's, 1989), pp. 255-6, hereafter referred to as *SBC*. The statement dates from 1953.

5   *In No Uncertain Terms: A South African Memoir* (New York: Knopf, 1993), p. 18.

27   Noël Mostert and the Eastern Cape Frontier

1   Noël Mostert, *Frontiers: The Epic of South Africa's Creation and the*

Tragedy of the Xhosa People (New York: Knopf, 1992), p. 358.

28   Photographs of South Africa
1 Mona de Beer and Brian Johnson Barker, *A Vision of the Past: South Africa in Photographs, 1843–1910* (Cape Town: Struik, 1992).